The IDEA MAGAZINE FOR TEACHERS®
MAILBOX®

2012–2013 YEARBOOK

The Education Center, LLC
Greensboro, North Carolina

The Mailbox® 2012–2013 Preschool Yearbook

Managing Editor, *The Mailbox* Magazine: Kimberly A. Brugger

Editorial Team: Becky S. Andrews, Diane Badden, Kimberley Bruck, Karen A. Brudnak, Pam Crane, Chris Curry, Brenda Fay, Phyllis Gaddy, Tazmen Fisher Hansen, Marsha Heim, Lori Z. Henry, Troy Lawrence, Tina Petersen, Gary Phillips (COVER ARTIST), Mark Rainey, Greg D. Rieves, Hope Rodgers-Medina, Rebecca Saunders, Donna K. Teal, Sharon M. Tresino, Zane Williard

ISBN 978-1-61276-414-6
ISSN 1088-5536

© 2013 The Education Center, LLC, PO Box 9753, Greensboro, NC 27429-0753

Printed in the United States of America.

The Mailbox® Yearbook
PO Box 6189
Harlan, IA 51593-1689

Look for *The Mailbox® 2013–2014 Preschool Yearbook* in the summer of 2014. The Education Center, LLC, is the publisher of *The Mailbox*®, *Teacher's Helper*®, and *Learning*® magazines, as well as other fine products. Look for these wherever quality teacher materials are sold, call 1-866-477-4273, or visit www.themailbox.com.

HPS249271

Contents

Departments

Features

Book Units

Center Units

Literacy Units

Math Units

Teacher Resource Units

Thematic Units

Index

Arts & Crafts for Little Hands

Arts & Crafts for Little Hands

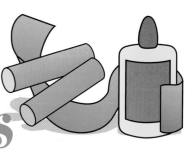

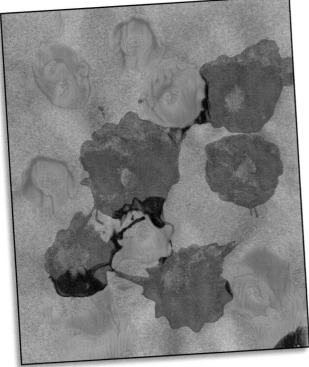

Process Art

Splat!

This mess-free hammer painting is terrific for hand-eye coordination! To make one, place dollops of paint on a sheet of construction paper and then slide the paper into an oversize resealable plastic bag. (Two-gallon bags are great for this project!) Seal the bag and then hit the dollops of paint with a play hammer until a desired effect is achieved. How cute!

Noel James
Greater Wenatchee Parent-Child Preschool
Wenatchee, WA

Process Art

Block Painting

To prepare, gather a variety of blocks and place each one near a shallow pan of paint. (Consider using interlocking blocks as well as plain wooden blocks.) Press a block in the paint and then on the paper as desired. Continue in the same way to make a lovely printed masterpiece!

Michelle Espelien
Community Christian Preschool
Poway, CA

Handsome Apple Tree!

This adorable apple tree will no doubt become a family keepsake! To make one of these projects, glue a tree trunk cutout to a sheet of paper. Then press your hand in a pan of green paint and make prints above the trunk so they resemble the top of a tree. Next, glue red pom-poms (or red circle cutouts) to the tree.

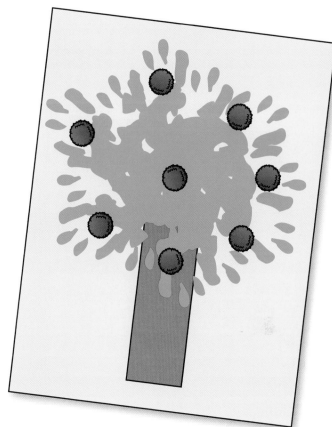

Process Art

Puffy Color Mixing

Learn about primary and secondary colors with this printmaking process art! Spread a layer of nonmentholated shaving cream on a baking sheet. Add drops of food coloring in two primary colors to the shaving cream. Then use a craft stick or other tool to slightly swirl the colors, noticing that a new color is produced. Next, place a sheet of paper over the shaving cream and smooth it with your hand. Remove the paper and scrape off the excess shaving cream. The result is a gorgeous print!

Cassie Knight
Argyle Christian Preschool and Kindergarten
Jacksonville, FL

Arts & Crafts for Little Hands

Fall in the City

To make this fantastic fall artwork, place a piece of Con-Tact covering on a tabletop, sticky-side up. Then press a construction paper frame onto it. Use a yellow or white crayon to draw windows on black rectangle cutouts and press the rectangles on the paper. Next, press leaves onto any part of the Con-Tact covering still showing. Finally, place another sheet of Con-Tact covering over the back of the project. How unique!

Sara Barbour
Apple Tree Christian Learning Center
Rockford, MI

Process Art

Spiders Painting

Attach a large plastic spider to a string. Hold the opposite end of the string and drag the spider in a shallow pan of paint. Then bounce and drag the spider over a sheet of paper. Continue with other paint colors to make a masterpiece!

Lori Dworsky
Wilmington, DE

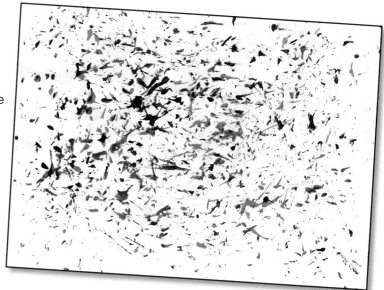

A Pair of Jacks

This Halloween project gives fine-motor skills a workout! To make one, prepare squeeze bottles of orange and black paint. Fold a sheet of 12" x 18" white construction paper in half; then unfold the paper. Squeeze orange paint to make a circle on one half of the paper and then squeeze some orange paint into the center of the circle as well. Squeeze black paint to make jack-o'-lantern features. Then fold the paper and smooth it with your hand. Open the paper and add green stem cutouts to your jack-o'-lanterns!

Darica Adams
Sutter Park School
Powell, OH

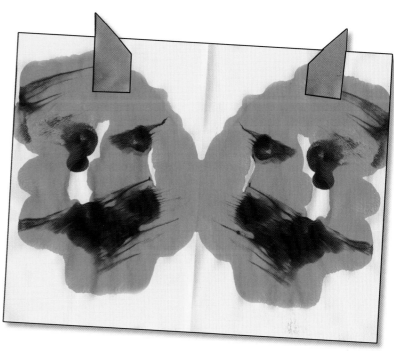

A Fine Feast

Cut a tablecloth shape from patterned scrapbooking paper. Then attach brown paper strips to the back of the tablecloth so they resemble table legs. Glue the resulting table to a sheet of construction paper. Cut out a variety of Thanksgiving foods from grocery store food flyers and glue them on the tabletop. Finally, glue a card labeled "Happy Thanksgiving Day!" above the table.

Sharon C. Smith
Penfield Village Nursery School
Penfield, NY

Watercolors With Markers!

Don't throw away those dried-out markers—they can be used for this fabulous artwork! Gather dried-out markers and a small cup of water. Uncap a marker and dip the tip in the water. Then draw on the paper with the moistened marker. The resulting artwork will resemble watercolors. Continue with other colors, adding desired details to your picture.

Janey Lashbrook
McDanield Early Learning Center
Bonner Springs, KS

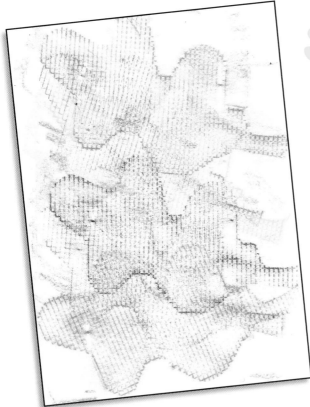

Process Art

Textured Leaves

Cut leaf shapes from plastic canvas (found in the needlework section of craft stores). Put rolls of heavy-duty tape on the backs of the leaves and attach them to a tabletop. Place a sheet of paper over the leaves and then rub the paper with a fall-colored unwrapped crayon. Move the paper slightly and repeat the process with a different crayon. Continue in the same way with different fall colors until you've made a pile of lovely leaf rubbings.

Laura Miller
Severy Elementary
Severy, KS

Arts & Crafts for Little Hands

Waterless Snow Globe

This snow globe will be the highlight of your winter decor! To make one, paint the front of a heavy-weight paper plate blue (or black for a night sky). Dip a toothbrush in white paint and flick it over the plate (snow-flakes). Glue cotton batting near the bottom of the plate; then use craft foam shapes and markers to complete the winter scene. Finally, attach to the plate a clear lid from a to-go container (or clear plastic wrap) as shown. Lovely!

Lisa Arcos, Streamwood Montessori, Streamwood, IL
Monica Zenyuh, Thomas J. Lahey Elementary, Greenlawn, NY

Process Art

Winter Wear Prints

This process art incorporates plenty of hands-on action! To prepare, spread two colors of paint on separate sides of a tray. Put a mitten on one hand and a glove on the other. (Hint: Wear a pair of latex-free gloves under the garments.) Press each hand in the paint and then on a sheet of construction paper. Repeat the process, over-lapping the prints and blending the colors. Then glue a cotton batting border around this wintry masterpiece.

Yvonne Watson, Lith, IL

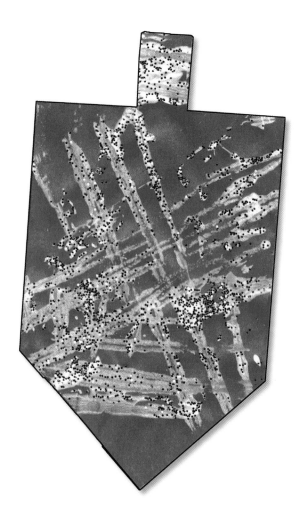

 Process Art

Dreidel Designs

To prepare, cut a dreidel shape from blue construction paper or tagboard. Wrap yarn around a thick, round candle. Roll the candle through a shallow pan of white paint and then across the dreidel, adding more paint to the candle as needed. Then sprinkle silver glitter on the wet paint.

 **Process Art**

Hygienic Snow Scene

Deodorant isn't just for hygiene anymore! To make a winter scene, rub stick deodorant across black construction paper to create the illusion of snow. Then use a round-end toothpick or a craft stick to draw in the faux snow. If you decide to change the details, simply rub deodorant over the design and start again. Nifty!

Cathy Calder
CC's Tater Tots
Roswell, NM

Christmas Candy

The appearance and scent of this Christmas craft could be tempting to the taste buds! Paint a white tagboard circle with a mixture of nonmentholated, unscented shaving cream; peppermint extract; and glue. Dip a craft stick in red or green paint scented with the extract and swirl it through the painted mixture. Allow a few days for the mixture to dry. Then attach a jumbo drinking straw to the craft and adorn it with a holiday ribbon.

Anne Marie Thomas
Augusta Prep Day School
Martinez, GA

New Year Gear

Ring in the New Year wearing fabulous headgear! Glue to a tagboard strip die-cut numbers that represent the upcoming year. Then decorate the strip with craft materials, such as sequins, stickers, metallic markers, and glitter glue. Adjust the band to fit your head and then staple the ends together.

Denise Kittle
Grace Preschool
Auburn, AL

Strawberry Hearts

Here's a real sweet heart for someone special on Valentine's Day! To prepare, slice a few strawberries in half. (Hint: The riper the strawberries, the brighter the prints!) Then gently press a strawberry half onto a white paper heart to make mini heart prints! To complete this lovely keepsake, glue the strawberry heart atop a paper doily and attach a pretty ribbon.

Carol Hargett
Kinderhaus Early Learning Center
Fairborn, OH

Radical Ramp

This process art idea helps the artist learn about motion and create abstract designs! Prop a flat material, like thick cardboard, at an angle to make a ramp; then tape a sheet of paper to the ramp. Place a container at the base of the ramp. To begin, dip a ball or marble in paint and let it roll down the ramp. Repeat the process with other round items and colors of paint, adjusting the angle of the ramp as you work. When the paint is dry, mount the artwork to a sheet of paper in a contrasting color.

Shelby Witmer
Neffsville Christian School
Lancaster, PA

The Mane Course

To make this adorable lion, glue jumbo wiggle eyes to a light brown tagboard circle. Glue a craft foam triangle to the circle so it resembles a nose; then use a marker to draw details similar to those shown. Place cooked angel hair pasta (spaghetti and other pasta types work as well) around the edge of the circle to make the lion's mane. The noodles will adhere to the paper without glue and will dry to resemble the lion's mane!

Carla O'Guin
Hillard Collins Elementary
Florence, KY

Process Art

Swaying Sand

This process art is so much fun to make! To prepare, attach a string to a small funnel. Peel the backing from a sheet of clear, self-adhesive Con-Tact covering; then place the covering in a box lid sticky-side up. Attach paper circles (planets) and star cutouts to the covering. Next, hold the funnel by the string while a helper pours colorful sand and glitter into the funnel. Then gently sway the funnel over the paper, allowing the contents to create lines on the Cont-Tact covering. Gorgeous!

Evelyn Harmon
Franklin Children's School
Franklin, MA

tip → To add an extra element of shine to the project, use self-adhesive foil paper in gold or silver instead of clear Con-Tact covering!

Arts & Crafts for Little Hands

Process Art

Painted Pan Press

Muffin pans are the inspiration for this process art! Flip a muffin pan upside down and paint the cup bottoms using several colors of paint. Then turn the pan right-side up and press it onto a sheet of paper. Clean the paint off the pan with a wipe or wet paper towel and repeat the process if desired.

Janet Boyce
Cokato, MN

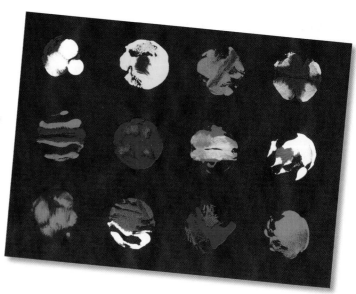

Suncatcher Cup

All you need to make this suncatcher is a clear disposable cup, tissue paper squares in rainbow colors, and glue! To make one, brush glue on the outside of the cup and press tissue paper on the glue. Repeat the process until the cup is covered with tissue; then brush slightly diluted glue over the surface of the cup. When the glue is dry, display the suncatcher on a windowsill or attach a ribbon and hang it in a window!

Deborah Ryan
Milwaukie, OR

Butterfly Napkin

To make a butterfly, gather a paper napkin, as shown, to create a pair of wings. Secure the middle with clear tape; then attach a body made from satin gift ribbon (or other craft materials). To complete the butterfly, add a pair of antennae and decorate the wings with squares of glitter paper. Simple, yet so elegant!

Deborah Ryan
Milwaukie, OR

Jiggling Jelly Beans

This process art activity gives small and large muscles a workout! Lightly tape a jelly bean cutout inside a lidded box. Use a spoon to dip several large jelly bean candies in paint and then place them atop the cutout. Secure the lid in place and then vigorously jiggle the box to manipulate the jelly beans. Remove the candies from the box; then repeat the process with other jelly beans and colors of paint until a desired effect is achieved. After the activity, throw away the jelly beans in a safe location.

Eileen Wambach
Funshine Nursery School
Red Hook, NY

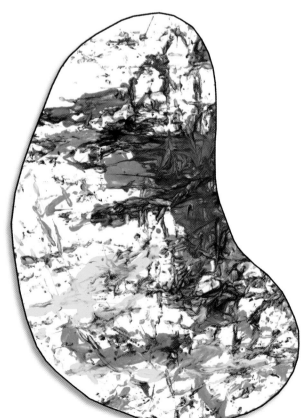

Bunny Tails

This project fine-tunes the artist's pincer grasp and results in a meadow of bunny tails! To prepare, gather pom-poms in different sizes and clip a clothespin to each one. Secure the clothespins with tape so they won't open and release the pom-poms. Dip the pom-pom from a resulting paint tool in white paint and then press it on green construction paper. After making several bunny tails, glue green crinkle shreds around the prints.

Melannie Stevenson
San Juan Capistrano, CA

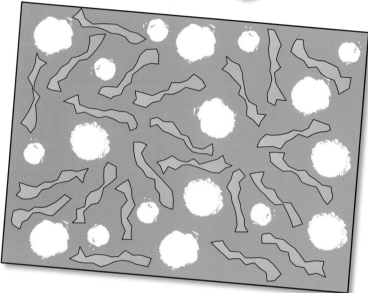

Recycling Helps the Earth!

Spotlight recycling and Earth Day with this environmentally friendly idea! Lightly tape to a tray a large newspaper circle (earth). Then dip a wad of crumpled newspaper in green paint and press it on the earth so it represents land. Repeat the process with another wad of newspaper and blue paint so it represents water. Continue until the earth is covered with land and water. When the paint is dry, write the words "Recycling Helps the Earth!" on the project.

adapted from an idea by Karla Broad
Our Savior Preschool
Naples, FL

Process Art

Near or Far

The prints in this project appear close and far! Dip the bottom of a flat-bottom disposable cup in white paint and then press it onto black paper. Repeat the process several times. Then dip the eraser of an unsharpened pencil in the paint and press it on the paper. Repeat the process until a desired effect is achieved.

Janet Boyce
Cokato, MN

Jellyfish Fun!

To make a jellyfish, use colorful washable markers to make marks on a coffee filter; then spritz the filter with water. When the filter is dry, glue it to an inverted, clear plastic cup; then glue a paper plate to the project as shown. To make the tentacles, tape iridescent ribbon to the rim of the cup.

Janet Boyce

A Fun Option!

Attach a length of elastic cord to the project. Then hold the cord and bounce the jellyfish gently to make it jiggle!

Busy Beaver

For this adorable craft, make a simple body cutout from brown faux fur and a paper tail cutout. Brush black paint on a piece of plastic canvas and then place the tail on the paint and rub it lightly with your fingertips. Remove the tail and let it dry. Glue the body and tail to a sheet of blue construction paper (water); then glue eyes, a nose, and toothpicks to the project.

Betty Selchert
Alcester-Hudson Elementary
Alcester, SD

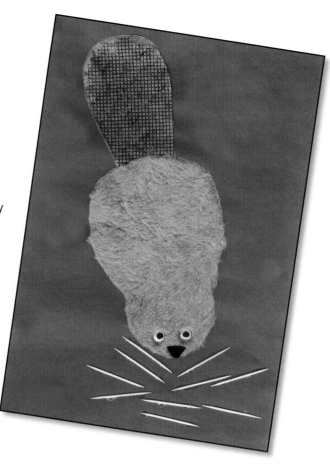

Process Art

Red, White, and Blue

This project results in a multipurpose masterpiece. Dip a star-shaped cookie cutter in blue paint and press it on a sheet of red construction paper several times, adding more paint to the cookie cutter as needed. Then dip a toothbrush in white paint and splatter the paint onto the paper. Finally, sprinkle glitter over the wet paint. Now that's one perfectly patriotic project that can be transformed into a flag, a windsock, or a holiday placemat!

Keely Saunders
Bonney Lake Early Childhood Education
Assistance Program
Bonney Lake, WA

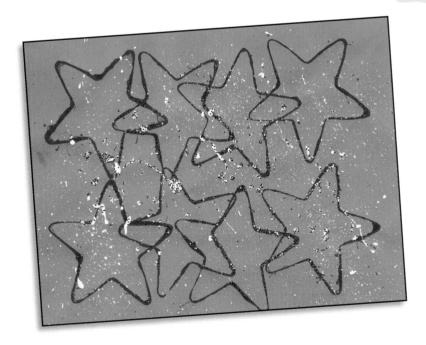

BUSY HANDS

Fine-Motor Explorations for the Season

MARKER CAP PRINTS

Draw three large trees on a length of bulletin board paper and attach the paper to a table. Provide marker caps and shallow containers of green, yellow, and red paint. Use the marker caps to make a few prints (apples) of each color on separate trees. Then have students add more apples to the trees!

Tricia Brown, Bowling Green, KY

FACE PUZZLES

Print out a large picture of each youngster's face and laminate it for durability. Then cut each picture in half. A child attempts to match all the picture halves. Or she can have fun pairing mismatched halves!

Tricia Brown

FRIENDLY COLLAGE

Gather magazines that show pictures of people who appear happy and friendly. Discuss with youngsters what it means to be friends. Explain that friends treat you kindly and are happy to see you. Then help students tear photos from magazines that show people being friendly and encourage them to glue the photos to a piece of poster board. Display the resulting poster.

COLANDER POKE

Provide a plastic colander and colorful pipe cleaners. Little ones visit the area and poke the pipe cleaners into the openings of the colander. What a simple way to keep hands busy at the beginning of the school year!

APPLE PIE!

Put five large red pom-poms (apples) and a plastic shovel at a center along with a pie pan. A child places the pom-poms in the shovel and then says "Apple pie!" as she uses the shovel to toss the apples into the tin. The child evaluates her performance. If the child is able, she counts the apples that made it into the pie tin. Then she plays the game again!

See page 34 for a
reproducible activity
that targets fine-motor skills.

Busy Hands

Fine-Motor Explorations for the Season

ideas contributed by Roxanne LaBell Dearman
North Carolina Early Intervention Program for Children Who Are Deaf or Hard of Hearing
Charlotte, NC

HARVEST SOUP

Provide plastic or real vegetables, a soft brush, a soup pot, empty spice bottles, a ladle, and plastic bowls. A child brushes the veggies to get them nice and clean. Then she puts them in the soup pot, pretends to add spices, and ladles the soup into bowls.

BABY TURKEYS IN THE STRAW

Place straw (or paper shreds) in a box so it resembles a turkey nest. Put brown pom-poms (poults) in plastic eggs and place them in the nest. Encourage students to visit the center and pretend the poults are hatching by breaking open the eggs. Then encourage little ones to have the poults play in the straw.

Supper for Spider

Draw a spiderweb on a piece of bulletin board paper and place shallow pans of paint and an assortment of plastic bugs nearby. Encourage youngsters to press the bugs in the paint and then make prints on the web. When the web is full, display it with a large plastic spider.

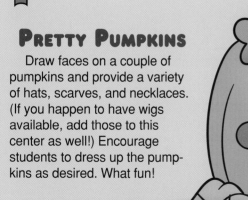

No Bobbing Required!

Place apples in your water table. Instead of bobbing for these apples, have students remove them from the water with tongs!

Tricia Kylene Brown
Bowling Green, KY

Pretty Pumpkins

Draw faces on a couple of pumpkins and provide a variety of hats, scarves, and necklaces. (If you happen to have wigs available, add those to this center as well!) Encourage students to dress up the pumpkins as desired. What fun!

See page 35 for a **reproducible activity** that targets fine-motor skills.

Fine-Motor Explorations for the Season

ideas contributed by Janet Boyce, Cokato, MN

SILVER ICICLES

Place sheets of aluminum foil, sections of bulletin board border, and tape at a table. A student visits the table and tears strips of foil so they resemble icicles. Then she tapes the icicles to a section of border. For a chilly, wintry display, hang the borders around windows and door frames!

CANDY CANE GARLAND

Suspend a length of rope tinsel between two chairs or table legs. Provide plastic or individually wrapped candy canes. A child hangs the candy canes along the garland. How festive!

POLAR PAL

Have youngsters stretch cotton balls and glue them to an oversize polar bear head cutout. After the bear is covered with "fur," add a large black pom-pom (nose) and two jumbo wiggle eyes.

ICE FISHING

Float ice cubes in your water table. Provide a pair of tongs and place a small bucket nearby. A youngster uses the tongs to "catch" the ice cubes and drops them in the bucket. Then he dumps the ice back in the water. (Be sure to keep extra ice on hand to replace melted cubes.)

HANUKKAH CANDLES

Provide a wooden block (menorah) and nine jumbo crayons (candles). A child positions each candle on the menorah. Then she takes one candle (*shammash*) and uses it to "light" the other candles. When she's finished playing, she "blows" out all the candles.

 See page 36 for a **reproducible activity** that targets fine-motor skills.

Busy Hands

Fine-Motor Explorations for the Season

ideas contributed by Janet Boyce, Cokato, MN

MEADOW LAMBS

Attach a piece of green bulletin board paper (meadow) to a tabletop. Provide cotton balls, a black stamp pad, a marker, and glue. A child glues a cotton ball (lamb's body) to the paper, adds a black thumbprint head, and then uses the marker to draw legs. Youngsters continue until the meadow is filled with soft, woolly lambs.

PLUCKING NUGGETS

Fill a widemouthed plastic jar with green-tinted rice and small yellow pom-poms (gold nuggets). Provide long tweezers and a black plastic pot (or pot cutout). A youngster pretends to be a leprechaun eager to fill his pot with gold. To retrieve the hidden gold, he uses the tweezers to pluck the nuggets from the rice and place them in the pot.

SUNNY SHAMROCK FIELD

Attach yellow bulletin board paper to a wall or tabletop. Provide corks, green stamp pads, and green markers. A student uses a cork and stamp pad to stamp three prints close together so they resemble a shamrock; then she adds a marker-drawn stem. Students continue until the paper looks like a sunny field of shamrocks.

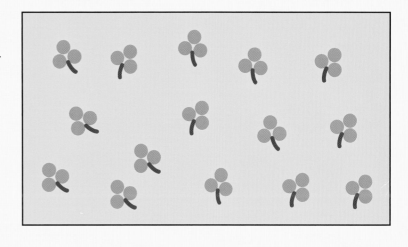

MINTY FRESH

Place at a table white play dough scented with peppermint extract, a large pink tagboard semicircle (smile), and scissors. A child rolls play dough into a ropelike shape. Then he snips the dough to make "teeth" and arranges them on the smile.

HUGS AND KISSES

Set out a gift bag containing *X* and *O* letter cards, each with a jumbo paper clip attached. Provide a magnetic wand and a heart cutout. A youngster uses the wand to remove a card from the bag. Then she identifies the letter and writes it on the heart. She continues until the heart is covered with hugs and kisses.

 See page 37 for a **reproducible** that targets fine-motor skills.

Fine-Motor Explorations for the Season

ideas contributed by Janet Boyce, Cokato, MN

WIGGLE WORMS

Provide brown play dough (mud), unsharpened chunky pencils, and pipe cleaners (worms). A youngster manipulates a handful of mud and then pushes a pencil through it to make several tunnels. Then he threads a worm in and out of the holes, pretending it's tunneling through the mud.

tip → For extra sensory fun, knead fresh coffee grounds or oatmeal into the play dough!

POCKET CHART PLANTING

Suspend a small pocket chart (garden) and place a strip of brown paper (soil) in each row. Provide craft foam seeds and a pair of tweezers. A child uses the tweezers to pick up each seed and "plant" it in the garden.

BILLOWY CLOUDS

Attach a length of light blue bulletin board paper (sky) to a tabletop; then draw several cloud outlines in the sky. Provide cotton balls, plastic spring-style clothespins, and a container of glue. Little ones visit the table, use a clothespin to pick up and dip a cotton ball in the glue, and then place the cotton ball inside an outline. Youngsters continue until each outline is turned into a billowy cloud.

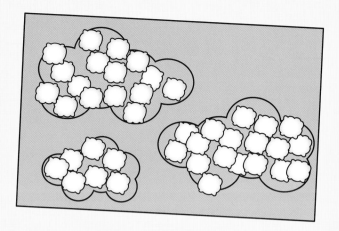

SPRING!

Set out a container of pipe cleaners in different sizes and a few cylindrical objects, such as a pencil, a fat crayon, and a candle. A child winds a pipe cleaner around one of the items and then removes it, noticing it resembles a spring! He continues with other pipe cleaners and previously curled pipe cleaners, straightening them and curling them again.

FAMISHED FROG

Hot-glue two jumbo wiggle-eyes to a small green glove to make a frog puppet. Scatter black pom-poms (flies) on the floor and place a log cutout nearby. A child wears the frog and uses it to "catch" each fly. Each time she catches one, she says, "Ribbit, ribbit!" and then drops the fly on the log. She continues until the frog catches all the flies.

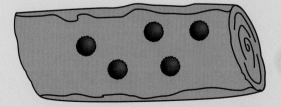

See page 38 for a **reproducible activity** that targets fine-motor skills.

Busy Hands

Fine-Motor Explorations for the Season

SERVING UP LEMONADE!

Provide a tub of large yellow pom-poms (lemons), a plastic pitcher, plastic cups, measuring cups, and tongs. Encourage youngsters to use the items to take part in lemonade-themed pretend play that exercises fine-motor skills!

OCEAN DIORAMA

Cover the inside of a large, flapless box with blue cellophane. Provide sea life stickers and self-adhesive craft foam shapes. Students visit the area and use the stickers and shapes to decorate the cellophane. To complete the diorama, poke several holes in the top; then use fishing line and craft sticks to suspend toy sea critters as shown. To move the critters, a child simply manipulates the fishing line!

Joanne DeMarco
Creative World School Management
Land O' Lakes, FL

SQUIRT, TOSS, ROLL

Here's a splendid outdoor project! Place in a baby pool a large sheet of light blue paper trimmed as shown. Provide a squeeze bottle of white paint and a small beach ball. Youngsters squirt paint onto the paper, toss the ball into the pool, and then manipulate the pool to roll the ball through the paint. If desired, display the painted paper as shown, with a boat cutout and a trimmed photo of each child.

Tricia Kylene Brown
Bowling Green, KY

SANDY IMPRESSIONS

Fill your sensory table with moist sand. Provide several sturdy seashells in a pail as well as a magnifying glass. A child visits the table and chooses a shell. She presses the shell in the sand and then removes it and uses the magnifying glass to study the impression. She continues with other seashells as desired.

Tricia Kylene Brown

COVERED WITH SPRINKLES

Place an oversize ice cream cone and a container of colorful pom-poms (sprinkles) on the floor. A child stands several feet from the cone and tosses sprinkles, attempting to get them on the scoop.

See page 40 for a **reproducible activity** that targets fine-motor skills.

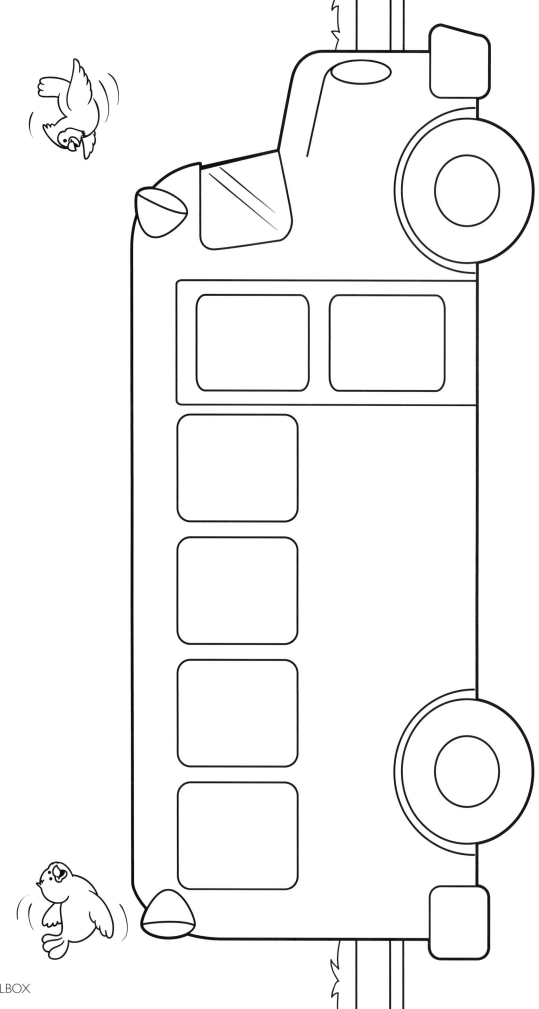

"Thumb-body" Went to School!

Note to the teacher: Have each child make a thumbprint (head) in each window. Use a fine-tip marker to add a smiley face to each print. Then prompt the child to color the page as desired. **(For a school keepsake,** have the child add thumbprints as described to a yellow copy of this page and then attach a first-day-of-school photo to the bus.)

Gobble Gobble Grub

Note to the teacher: Have each child color a copy of this page. Have her make green and yellow prints with a pencil eraser (peas and corn kernels) on the plate. Also encourage her to glue crumpled white tissue paper squares (mashed potatoes) to the plate.

Let's Build a Fort!

Note to the teacher: Give each child a copy of this page. Encourage her to trace the rectangle and then glue white paper rectangles inside the tracing to make a snow fort. When she's finished, have her spread glue on the fort and then sprinkle clear iridescent glitter on the glue.

"Bee" Mine!

Note to the teacher: Give each child a copy of this page. Have her trace the lines. Then encourage her to make yellow fingerprints on the page. Help her add details to the fingerprints to transform them into bees.

Follow the Carrot Trail

Note to the teacher: Have each child trace the bunny; then have her tear white facial tissue and glue it to the bunny's head and body. Encourage her to glue on a white pom-pom tail and then color the rest of the page as desired.

Piles of Potatoes

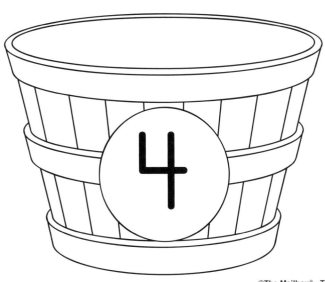

Note to the teacher: Give a child a copy of this page. Have her identify each number and then make a corresponding set of brown fingerprints (potatoes) in the basket above the number. For extra fun, use a black fine-tip marker to draw a face on each potato.

Melting!

Note to the teacher: Have each child brush glue mixed with glitter onto the glass. Then have her tear cotton balls and glue them to the scoop. To complete the treat, have her drizzle glue on the cotton balls and then sprinkle confetti on the glue.

CIRCLE TIME

Circle Time

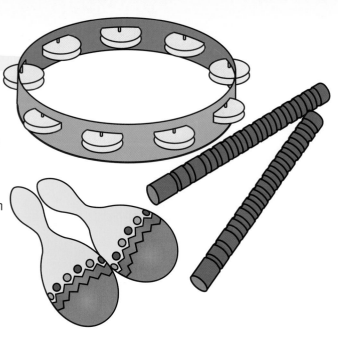

A Preschool Symphony

To prepare, place chairs in a circle, being sure there is one less chair than there are students participating. Put a rhythm instrument on each chair. As you play a recording of lively music, have students walk around the inside of the circle. Stop the music and direct each youngster to pick up an instrument and sit in the chair. Give the student without a chair a wooden dowel (conductor's baton) and invite him to lead the group in playing the instruments. Encourage him to vary the tempo of the music as he leads the group. Play several rounds of this fun musical game!

Sandy Blumstein
Paley Early Learning Center
Philadelphia, PA

Proud to Be Me

Youngsters identify things that make them unique with this toe-tapping activity. Encourage a child to name something she likes about herself. Then lead the group in singing the song shown. Repeat the activity several times with different youngsters.

(sung to the tune of "If You're Happy and You Know It")

If you see a [girl] with [freckles],
Shout yippee! (Yippee!)
If you see a [girl] with [freckles],
Shout yippee! (Yippee!)
It is nice for us to be
Here in preschool, you'll agree.
If you see a [girl] with [freckles],
Shout yippee! (Yippee!)

Kate Franzmann
Barneveld, WI

We All Move

Quickly assess youngsters' gross-motor skills with this entertaining activity. Lead students in performing the traditional song "Ring Around the Rosie." Then have youngsters perform the song again, singing the version below. Continue in the same way with other actions. (See the suggestions below.)

Ring around the rosie,
A pocketful of posies,
Ashes, ashes,
We all [touch our toes]!

Continue with the following: *flap our arms, touch our noses, hop five times, run in place, jump up and down, pat our heads, stomp our feet, stretch up high, wiggle our hips*

Shelby Angst
Lebanon, MO

Animals on the Loose!

Oh no! The animals have escaped from the zoo! Personalize a zoo animal cutout (patterns on page 58) for each child. Place a length of bulletin board paper (zoo) on the floor and scatter the animals around it. As you lead the group in saying the chant shown, have a youngster find the animal labeled with his name, show it to his classmates, and place it in the zoo. Continue until all the animals are safely returned to the zoo.

The animals are out!
Look at them run!
Let's round them up,
One by one!

Connie Massingill
Dawn Til Dusk Daycare
Zionsville, IN

Circle Time

Do We Need It?

Gather school-related objects along with a few distracter objects and place them in a bag. (Be sure there is an object for each child.) Then place the objects and a backpack in your circle-time area. Have a child choose an object from the bag and identify it. Then lead the group in determining if the object is needed for school. If it is, have the group discuss its use before having the child place it in the backpack. If not, have the child set it aside. To conclude the activity, challenge the group to remember the objects that were placed in the backpack.

There are more princes than princesses!

Prince and Princess Sort

This simple sort is a lot of fun for your little ones! Designate an area in your classroom as the castle for princes and another area as the castle for princesses. Invite youngsters to sort themselves into two groups by sitting in the appropriate castles. Have students help count the princes and then count the princesses. Then guide little ones in comparing the numbers, using words such as *more*, *fewer*, and *equal*. Ask, "Would princes or princesses need a bigger castle?" Encourage youngsters to explain their answers.

Karen Guess
St. Richard's School
Indianapolis, IN

Pumpkin Stick Voting

Read aloud two pumpkin-themed books, such as *The Runaway Pumpkin* by Kevin Lewis and *Pumpkin Heads!* by Wendell Minor. Have each child draw, personalize, and cut out a small pumpkin and attach it to a craft stick. Display the books and place a blob of green play dough (pumpkin patch) in front of each one. Have each child vote for his favorite story by pushing his pumpkin into the corresponding pumpkin patch. Then discuss the results of the vote with the students, having them explain why they voted as they did.

Sara Juszkiewicz
Buffalo, NY

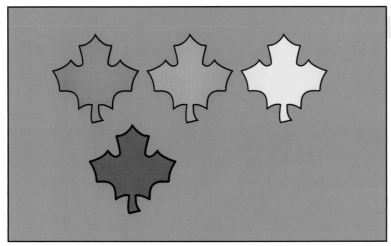

Time to Rake!

Help youngsters understand the concept of zero with this adorable and timely rhyme! Cut five simple felt leaves and attach them to your flannelboard. Lead youngsters in reciting the poem shown. During the third line, prompt students to shake and wiggle; during the fourth line, drop one leaf to the floor. Continue in the same way for four more verses until all the leaves have fallen.

Way up high in the maple tree,
[Five] little leaves smiled at me.
I gave that tree a great big shake.
Down came a leaf—
I need a rake!

Robin Johnson
Cromwell-Wright Public School
Cromwell, MN

Circle Time

Save the Letters!

Draw a spiderweb on a length of bulletin board paper and place it on your floor. (As an alternative, use a large fake spiderweb.) Place die-cut letters on the web. Tell students that they need to save the letters caught in the spider's web. Then have a few students tiptoe quietly to the web and remove a letter. Help each child identify his letter and set it aside. Play several rounds of this activity until all the letters have been saved!

Rhyme and Move

Reinforce rhyming words with this simple anytime movement activity. Stand on one side of the classroom and have students stand on the opposite side. Name two words. If the words rhyme, students take a step toward you. If they don't rhyme, students stay where they are. Continue until the youngsters reach you. Consider repeating the activity with other movement options, such as crawling or walking backward.

Tall, ball!

Personalized Ornaments

Little ones identify classmates' names with this tree-decorating idea! For each child, label a tagboard ornament with his name. Place the ornaments in a holiday-related gift bag. Mount a poster board evergreen tree in the area. To begin, pull an ornament from the bag and say, "Whose name, whose name do you see? Then we'll add it to the tree!" Have students identify the name. Then have that child attach the ornament to the tree with Sticky-Tac or rolled tape. Continue in the same way until each child has helped decorate the tree.

Keely Saunders
Bonney Lake ECEAP
Bonney Lake, WA

Tick, tick!

Where's the Timer?

This activity develops listening skills and concentration and sharpens youngsters' sense of hearing. Obtain a timer with an audible ticking sound. Have little ones close their eyes while you hide the timer. Then prompt students to open their eyes, encouraging them to locate the timer using their sense of hearing. The child who finds the timer calls out, "Tick, tick!" and reveals its location. Play several rounds of this engaging game!

Heather Palmatier, Penfield Presbyterian Day Care Center, Penfield, NY

Circle Time

Mixed-Up Tools

Put in a paper sack items a cookie baker would use, such as a plastic mixing bowl, a spatula, a recipe card, a cookie cutter, and a baking sheet. Add a few other items, like a hammer, a tape measure, and glue. To begin, say, "A cookie baker uses special tools. If he uses this one, will he follow the rules?" Then display an item from the sack. When it's something a cookie baker would use, little ones pretend to mix cookie dough. When it's not, they stay still.

Kim Harker
Discovery Express Preschool
Mendon, CT

Gift Box Surprise

Youngsters identify beginning sounds with this gift of an idea! Cover a box with a removable lid with seasonal gift wrap. Tuck inside the box a few "gift items" that begin with different sounds. Tip the lid and invite a child to take a gift from the box. Have her identify the item and its beginning sound. Then encourage the group to name other things that begin with that sound. Set the item aside and continue until the box is empty.

Deborah Luke
Fairmount Nursery School
Syracuse, NY

 tip
As an alternative, put craft foam letters in the box and have students name things that begin with each letter sound!

Rock-and-Roll Rhymes

Youngsters get plenty of rhyming practice and show off their dance moves with this fun idea. Play a recording of music and encourage youngsters to move to the beat. After a few moments, clap your hands to get youngsters' attention and then announce two words. If the words rhyme, students freeze in place. If they do not, little ones continue dancing. Repeat the activity for several rounds or until youngsters get too tired to dance!

Katie Zuehlke
Bendit Elementary
Annandale, MN

Car...
star.

Snag a Snowball

Students practice number recognition with this engaging activity! Have the group stand in two teams facing each other. Give each child crumpled white paper (snowball) labeled with a number from 1 to 10. On your signal, have each child throw her snowball at the opposing team. Then have each student retrieve a snowball and smooth out the paper. Call out a number and ask students with that number to hold it in the air. Continue with the remaining numbers; then have youngsters reshape their snowballs and repeat the process. If desired, repeat the activity on a different day using snowballs labeled with letters.

Jennie Jensen
North Cedar Elementary
Lowden, IA

Circle Time

Energetic Leprechauns

Your little leprechauns will be eager to play this fun copycat game! Invite a child (leprechaun) to stand and face the group; then hand him a pot-of-gold cutout (pattern on page 59). Lead the group in chanting the first couplet shown and the leprechaun in responding with the second couplet. At the end of the last line, prompt the leprechaun to perform a desired action and the group to follow along. Then have the leprechaun hand the pot of gold to a classmate and repeat the activity! ***Gross motor***

Leprechaun, leprechaun, small and bold,
May I have your pot of gold?

I'm not sure yet, fiddle-dee-dee.
Do this trick, and we will see!

Donna Olp
St. Gregory the Great Preschool
South Euclid, OH

Pat Your Rose!

Turn a traditional game of Simon Says into a giggle-inducing rhyming activity! Give a direction that includes a word that rhymes with a body part, emphasizing that word. For example, say, "Put your finger on your rose *(nose)*," "Rub your mummy *(tummy)*," or "Pat your tack *(back)*." Prompt youngsters to follow the directions by touching the body part that rhymes with the emphasized word. How fun! ***Rhyming***

Jennifer Gemar
Tripp-Delmont Elementary
Tripp, SD

I see a triangle looking at me!

Wake Up, Groundhog!

Students practice shape or number identification skills with this fun idea! To prepare, program cards with symbols to reinforce a desired skill. Then give each child a brown construction paper groundhog (pattern on page 59). Instruct youngsters to pretend their groundhogs are asleep. Then display a card and say, "Wake up groundhogs! What do you see?" prompting little ones to hold up their groundhogs and say, "I see a [symbol] looking at me!" After confirming a correct symbol, have the groundhogs go back to sleep. Repeat the process until the bag is empty. *Identifying shapes, identifying numbers*

Donna Olp
St. Gregory the Great Preschool
South Euclid, OH

Mending a Broken Heart

Students learn kindness and compassion with this activity. Puzzle-cut a large poster board heart into several pieces. Label each piece with a scenario that describes someone with a broken heart. For example, label a piece "A child has a broken heart because her dog ran away." Put the puzzle pieces facedown in a pile. To begin, explain that having a broken heart means feeling really sad. Then take a puzzle piece and read the scenario aloud. Ask, "What would you do to help this person mend her broken heart?" After young-sters share their thoughts, place the piece faceup on the floor. Continue until all the pieces are in place and the broken heart is mended. *Speaking; character education: caring, compassion*

Donna Olp

Circle Time

Scout It Out

Identifying letters

Help students practice letter identification and learn about bees! Label several beehive mats (page 231) with different letters and post them around the room. Explain that when a beehive gets overcrowded, the queen bee and many worker bees leave as a swarm and several scouts look for a new hive. After finding one, the scouts return and do a special dance to let the other bees know. Next, have your little bees leave the circle (hive) and "swarm" to another area. Then reveal to a few students (scouts) a letter that matches one on a hive. Ask them to find the designated hive, return and do a little dance, and then lead the swarm to the hive. Then ask students to identify the letter and return to their original hive. Repeat with the remaining letters.

Tricia Kylene Brown, Bowling Green, KY

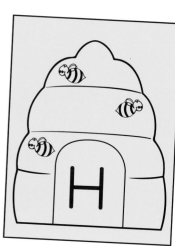

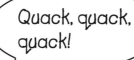

Quack, quack, quack!

What Do They Say?

Counting

Place a large pond-shaped cutout (or a blue blanket) on the floor. Invite five youngsters (ducklings) to waddle around the edge of the pond as you lead the rest of the group in singing the song shown, prompting the ducklings to respond to the third line by "flapping their wings" and completing the song. Then repeat the activity with five new students. **To extend the activity**, insert other pond animal names, sounds, and movements, like *froglets, ribbit* (hop); *fishies, splash* (swim); *turtles, snap* (crawl); and *snakelets, hiss* (slither).

(sung to the tune of "Five Little Ducks")

Five little [ducklings], count with me,
One, two, three, four, five, I see.
Five little [ducklings], what do they say?
[Quack, quack, quack,]—we're on our way!

Ada Goren, Winston-Salem, NC

I'm a beautiful sunflower!

Growing Tall

Investigating living things; speaking

Little ones develop gross-motor stability with this garden-themed activity! Review with youngsters how plants need soil, water, and sunlight to grow. Then dim the lights and have each child crouch and pretend to be a flower seed. Pretend to scoop soil over each student. Next, walk around the garden, pretending to water each seed. (For extra fun, use a spray bottle on the mist setting and lightly mist over youngsters' heads.) Then turn up the lights to simulate the sun coming out. Prompt each child to slowly rise to her tiptoes as if growing into a beautiful flower; then invite her to tell what type or color of flower she is.

Deborah Garmon, Groton, CT

Left or Right?

Differentiating left from right

Youngsters practice left and right with this fun game! Label two cards "left" and "right" and put them in a bag. Also gather three or four refillable plastic eggs. Conceal a green pom-pom in each egg (rotten eggs). Hand out the eggs, making sure there are several children between each egg. Then pull a card from the bag, identify the word, and have students pass the eggs in that direction as you say the chant shown. Prompt youngsters to stop when the chant ends; then return the card to the bag and repeat the process several times. After a final round, have the students open the eggs. When you see the green pom-poms, hold your nose and say, "Oh no—rotten eggs!" Repeat the activity several times. You're sure to hear lots of giggles!

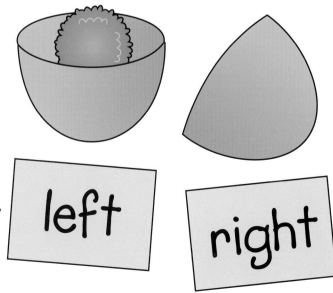

left

right

Pass the eggs, but hold them tight.
Let's see if they'll go left or right!

Amber Smith, Red Barn Learning Center: Hillside Academy, Duvall, WA

Circle Time

It Makes Scents

Sense of smell, speaking

This oral language activity is designed to trigger the olfactory sense! Gather several disposable cups. Place in each cup an aromatic substance, such as a food item, soap, or cotton balls soaked with baking extracts or cologne. To play, invite a volunteer to sit blindfolded facing the group. Hand him a cup to sniff as you lead the class in saying the chant shown. At the end of the chant, prompt the child to guess the scent, describe it, or tell something it makes him think about. After he guesses or shares his thoughts, remove the blindfold and reveal the scent. Continue in the same way with other cups and students.

Sniff, sniff, sniff, and tell
About the scent that you smell!

tip → A sleep mask makes a fun and simple blindfold!

Anne Forline
Cold Springs School
Gloucester, NJ

Color and Graph

Graphing

Make copies of two or three spring-related coloring pages. Then have a child choose his favorite page to color. Next, label a floor graph with the different coloring page options. Then have each child place his coloring page in the correct column of the graph. Have students compare the columns, using the words *more*, *fewer,* and *equal*.

Steffanie Edinbyrd
William Lipscomb
Dallas, TX

Dance, Twist, and Shimmy!

Get little ones moving with this giggle-inducing partner dance! To begin, help each child find a partner and then have the pair stand back-to-back. Sing the song shown, prompting youngsters to perform the actions. Then have students pair up with different partners and repeat the activity. *Gross motor, listening skills*

(sung to the tune of "Pop! Goes the Weasel")

Back-to-back, we clap to the beat.
Then side-to-side, we twist.
Front-to-front, we all do the shimmy.
Then we stomp our feet!

Erica Haver
Herkimer BOCES
Herkimer, NY

Simply Similar

Boost youngsters' visual discrimination skills with a unique twist on I Spy. Scan youngsters for visual similarities, such as clothing patterns and colors; shoe style and fasteners; hair and eye color; and wearable accessories like hair bows, jewelry, and glasses. Then invite students with a similar attribute to stand and face the group. Ask, "What is similar about these classmates?" When a child spots a similarity, he calls out, "I spy a similarity!" and then shares it with the group. If there is more than one similarity, prompt students to continue looking. When there are no more similarities to be revealed, play another round of this eye-opening game! *Visual discrimination, participating in a game*

They are wearing red shirts!

Risa Little
First Reformed Church Preschool
Landis, NC

Circle Time

Watermelon Patch

This fun activity reinforces letter and number skills! Label green construction paper watermelons with letters and numbers as shown. Spread the watermelons facedown on the floor (watermelon patch) and set out two containers programmed as shown. To begin, have a child "pick" a watermelon from the patch and show the symbol to the group. Ask, "Is the symbol on this watermelon a letter or a number?" After confirming a correct answer, have youngsters identify the symbol. Then prompt the child to place the watermelon in the appropriate container. Continue with other students until all the watermelons have been sorted. *Discriminating letters and numbers, letter and number identification, sorting*

Amy Brinton
Garden Heights Preschool
Madison, WI

What Does It Say?

Encourage little ones to generate letter-sound association words with this simple ditty! Display a letter *B* card and ask the group to identify the letter and its sound. Next, ask students to name several words that begin with the /b/ sound. Then lead youngsters in singing the song shown, inserting the student-generated words at the end. Repeat the activity several times, using a different letter card each time. *Letter identification, letter-sound association*

(sung to the tune of "Mary Had a Little Lamb")

The letter [*B*] says [/b/, /b/, /b/],
[/b/, /b/, /b/], [/b/, /b/, /b/].
The letter [*B*] says [/b/, /b/, /b/].
[Ball, bat, balloon].

Kris Bartel
Mercer Elementary
Cincinnati, OH

Boy, ball, and bee!

Swim, Little Fish!

Little ones will be swimming in color-recognition skills with this action-packed activity! Cut out a class supply of fish (patterns on page 60) in several different colors. Arrange the class in two lines with students in each line facing each other. (Make sure the lines are several feet apart.) Hand out the fish, giving each pair of youngsters who are facing each other the same color. To play, say the chant shown, inserting a color word where indicated. At the end of the chant, each youngster with that color of fish "swims" to the other side, switching places with the classmate opposite her. Continue with each remaining color; then redistribute the fish and play another round. **Color recognition, participating in a game**

Swim across the deep, dark sea.
Swim [red] fish as quick as can be!

Kathleen Zimmer
Adirondack Enrichment Preschool
Glens Falls, NY

Ant Antics

For this picnic-related math activity, obtain a large toy ant (or wear a black glove to simulate an ant). Spread a blanket on the floor and place several play or real food items atop the blanket. To begin, lead youngsters in counting the food items to determine the total number. Then help the ant crawl onto the blanket and carry away a desired number of items. When the ant is finished hauling away the food, ask little ones to tell how many items are left. After confirming a correct answer, lead youngsters in saying the subtraction sentence; then repeat the activity. **Counting, subtraction with objects**

Danielle Lockwood
Colchester, CT

Zoo Animal Patterns

Use with "Animals on the Loose!" on page 43.

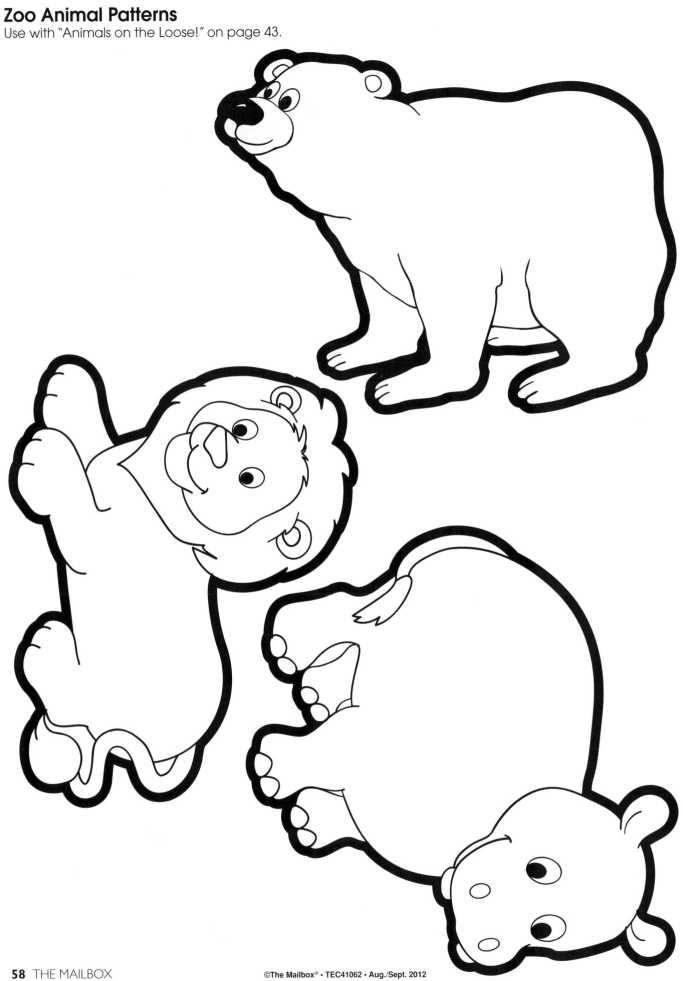

Pot of Gold Pattern
Use with "Energetic Leprechauns"
on page 50.

TEC41065

Groundhog Pattern
Use with "Wake Up, Groundhog!" on page 51.

TEC41065

Fish Patterns

Use with "Swim, Little Fish!" on page 57.

TEC41067

TEC41067

CLASSROOM DISPLAYS

CLASSROOM DISPLAYS

"Whooo" Are My Helpers?

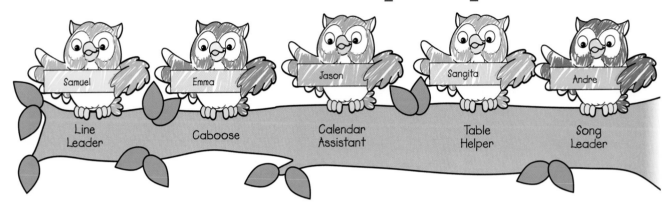

Samuel — Line Leader
Emma — Caboose
Jason — Calendar Assistant
Sangita — Table Helper
Andre — Song Leader

Make a simple branch cutout from bulletin board paper and attach it to a wall. Write job titles on the branch and title the display as shown. Then have each child color a cutout copy of the owl on page 70. Write each youngster's name on his owl. To assign each job, attach a different owl above each job title. Adorable!

Amy Jandebeur, Frogs to Fairy Dust, Yukon, OK

"CDs" Great Kids We Have!

Laura, Seth, Bruce, Anna, David, Mia, Sophia, Todd

To make this adorable and easy-to-prepare display, take a photo of each child. Then have him attach his photo to a CD. Use a permanent marker to write each child's name on his CD. Then display the CDs with the title shown and a sassy border. (The title is sure to make classroom visitors smile!)

Denise Manly
Ottawa County Early Childhood Center
Oak Harbor, OH

Here's an adorable birthday display your little ones will love! Have each child snip fringe around large leaf cutouts. Display the leaves, a trunk cutout, and coconut cutouts personalized with youngsters' names and birthdays. Next, give each child a die-cut of the first letter in her name and have her attach it to the trunk. Finally, title the display.

Jocelyn Vernet
Greene County PreK Center
Snow Hill, NC

Chicka Chicka Birthdays!

A Good Mathematician...

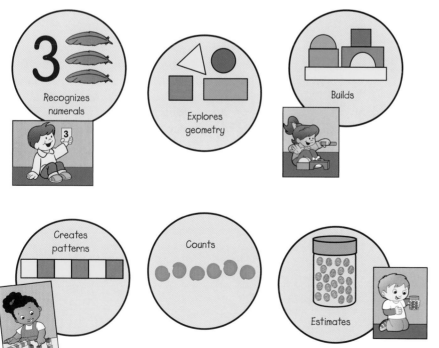

Recognizes numerals

Explores geometry

Builds

Creates patterns

Counts

Estimates

Spotlight preschool math skills with a display that is perfect for parent perusal! Write a variety of math skills and add simple drawings on separate construction paper circles demonstrating each skill. Attach them to a wall with the title shown. Take photos of youngsters working on the skills throughout the year and attach them to the board. That's informative, simple, and eye-catching!

Amanda M. Bradley
Volma Overton Elementary
Austin, TX

CLASSROOM DISPLAYS

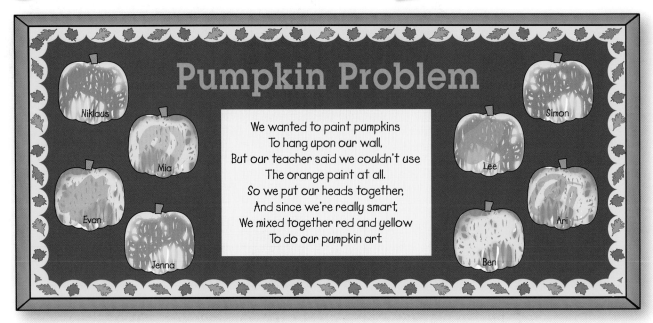

Pumpkin Problem

We wanted to paint pumpkins
To hang upon our wall,
But our teacher said we couldn't use
The orange paint at all.
So we put our heads together,
And since we're really smart,
We mixed together red and yellow
To do our pumpkin art.

Give a pumpkin shape to each child. Then explain to youngsters with much dramatic flair that you want them to paint pumpkins today, but you are out of orange paint. Tell them they will have to use red and yellow paint instead. Put a dollop of each paint color on each child's pumpkin and have her fingerpaint. Then exclaim with delight when—much to everyone's surprise—the red and yellow paints create orange! If desired, repeat the process with blue and yellow to make green stems for the pumpkins. Display the pumpkins with this adorable poem.

Dorthy Livengood, Lancaster, PA

Youngsters use their imaginations to disguise turkeys! Give each child a copy of the turkey pattern on page 71. Have her decide on something the turkey can pretend to be in order to hide on Thanksgiving Day. Then have her use craft items to disguise the turkey. Display the turkeys with labels as shown.

During a health-related unit, have each child paint a freeform shape (germ). Encourage her to add eye cutouts to her germ. Then have her use a bingo dauber to add spots. Next, encourage her to dictate what she knows about germs. Write her words on a card and then display the germs and cards with the title shown.

Nichole Sunde
The Little School @ Kids Cottage
Dover, DE

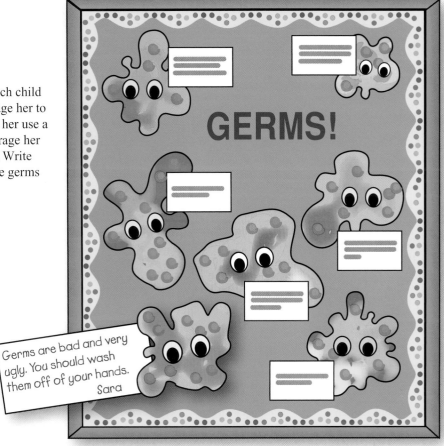

Germs are bad and very ugly. You should wash them off of your hands.
Sara

Have youngsters make simple handprint farm animals, such as horses, cows, and chickens. (The chicken is made by painting only the palm and thumb of a hand!) Then mount the animals on a board decorated with a barn cutout and add the adorable title shown! What a fun display for a farm-themed unit.

Marcia Longo, Hancock North Central Elementary, Pass Christian, MS

CLASSROOM DISPLAYS

Mittens, Mittens Everywhere! Look and You Will Find a Pair!

To make this wintry I Spy board, invite each child to drizzle paint on a mitten cutout. Help him press a second mitten atop the painted one and then peel the cutouts apart. Encourage him to glue a cotton ball cuff onto each mitten. Then randomly display the mittens on a board and attach the pairs with lengths of yarn.

Rose Cox, Elkhart and St. Joseph Counties Head Start Consortium—York Elementary, Bristol, IN

If I were Santa's elf, I would...

make toys

make cookies

learn how to ice-skate

play with the other elves

work

wrap presents

feed the reindeer

Take a photo of each child wearing a Santa hat. Enlarge the photos and then print them and attach them to a wall. Next, have each youngster dictate to complete the prompt shown. Write her response on a speech bubble and attach it to her photo. Have each child decorate a construction paper square and then attach a bow to the square. Display the resulting presents as shown. If desired, border the display with festive tinsel rope!

Marti Ventolo
Enon United Methodist Preschool
Enon, OH

For this unique Valentine's Day display, have each child paint a pink star cutout (patterns on page 72) with slightly diluted glue. Have her attach a headshot photo of herself to the star and sprinkle glitter on the wet glue. Then help her attach lengths of ribbon to the craft so it resembles a shooting star. Display the projects with a moon cutout decorated as shown.

Rosellen Roberts, Adams Brown Head Start, Georgetown, OH

Encourage a love of reading with this home-school connection display! Invite each child to paint a white tagboard circle with a mixture of purple paint and grape-flavored drink mix. Send each circle home with a note asking for a family member to record the title of a book they read with the child. Mount the circles so they resemble bunches of grapes and add details and the title shown.

inspired by an idea by Jodi-Linda Remington
Busy Day Child Care
Okemos, MI

CLASSROOM DISPLAYS

Don't Wake the Bear!

Read aloud *We're Going on a Bear Hunt* by Michael Rosen. Then create this woodland display! Attach a paper cave and a sleeping bear cutout to a board or wall as shown. Then help students use craft materials and markers to add forest-like details. Invite each child to post a trimmed photo of himself somewhere in the scene. Then ask him to tell how he would get past the bear without waking it. Record his response on a speech bubble and attach it near his photo.

Blooming With Kindness!

Kindness helps this garden bloom! Invite students to fringe-cut green paper so it resembles grass. Then help them attach the grass, paper stems, and leaves to a board titled as shown. Each time a child exhibits a kind behavior, record what she did on a die-cut flower and have her attach it to a stem. When everyone has a flower that has "bloomed," reward students for their kind behavior!

Lorie Vanwerven
Blossom Childcare & Learning Center
Bellingham, WA

Oh, Say Can You See?

For this adorable display, trim a photo of each child facing away from you and looking up in the air. To create colorful fireworks, have youngsters squeeze lines of glue onto black bulletin board paper and then shake glitter on the glue. Display the paper with the photos and the details shown.

Jeanie Odegaard and Rosie McCarthy
Northfield Montessori
Northfield, MN

Label each section of a supersize beach ball cutout with a different color. Then have students color the sections. Also have youngsters use brown crayons to make dots on brown bulletin board paper so it resembles sand. Ask each child to tell about her summer plans and use a black permanent marker to record her words on the beach ball. Then display the ball and the beach along with beach-related details and the title shown.

Mandi Ellis
Minnieland Private Day School
Gainesville, VA

Sensational Summer Plans!

orange purple blue pink green

Owl Pattern
Use with "'Whoooo' Are My Helpers?" on page 62.

TEC41062

Turkey Pattern
Use with "Turkeys in Disguise!" on page 64 and
"Turkey Tail Feathers" on page 96.

TEC41063

TEC41065

TEC41065

INSTANT SEASONAL ACTIVITIES

Instant Seasonal Activities

A Pumpkin's Life

Encourage little ones to act out the life cycle of a pumpkin! Encourage them to curl up like little seeds, sprout and wiggle like growing vines, move their arms like blooming blossoms, form little balls like small pumpkins, and then get big and round like full-grown pumpkins. What an excellent no-prep gross-motor activity!

Adapted from an idea by Marielle Lopez
Makalapa Elementary
Honolulu, HI

Fall Colors

Explain to students that people think of certain colors when they think of fall. Have students brainstorm fall colors; write the colors on your board. Then choose a color and have students name other objects that are that color. For example, red is a fall color, and strawberries, fire engines, and apples are also red!

Ring Around the Pumpkins

Gather youngsters in a circle around a few pumpkins and lead them in performing this twist on "Ring Around the Rosie"!

Ring around the pumpkins,	*Hold hands and circle to the right.*
A pocket full of candy,	*Circle to the left.*
Trick-or-treat!	*Drop hands and shake hips.*
Trick-or-treat!	*Shake hips.*
We all say, "Boo!"	*Cup hands over mouth.*

Chris Pipenger
Valley Forge Elementary
Huber Heights, OH

What Do You See?

Attach a squirrel cutout to a sheet of chart paper. Say, "Brown squirrel, brown squirrel, what do you [see]?" Have students name things the squirrel might see in the fall; write the words on the chart paper. Continue with other senses.

Spider Sing!

Place a few spider cards in a deck of letter, number, or shape cards. Have the class name the symbols on the cards. When you come to a spider card, prompt youngsters to sing "The Itsy-Bitsy Spider." Continue the activity, encouraging students to sing the song faster for each subsequent spider card encountered. Youngsters will get lots of skill practice, and you'll hear lots of giggles!

Jennifer Gemar
Tripp-Delmont Elementary
Tripp, SD

Instant Seasonal Activities

A Blizzard of Learning

Gather a variety of colorful shape cards. Show a card to a youngster and ask her to identify the shape or color. Then encourage her to draw a simple snowflake on the board. Continue until there are ten snowflakes. Then say, "It's a blizzard!" and have students stand, wave their arms, and make noises like whooshing wind. Play several rounds of this activity.

Marshmallow Count

Gather four students and 16 cotton balls (marshmallows). Tell the students that you want to make sure that everyone gets the same number of marshmallows in their hot chocolate. Help students work together to make sure everyone gets the same number. Repeat the activity with different numbers of marshmallows.

Icicle Race

Place linking cubes at a center and provide a sand timer. Two youngsters visit the center and flip the timer. Then they each quickly make towers with white cubes to make icicles. When the sand runs out, they hold their icicles next to each other and determine which one is longer and which one is shorter.

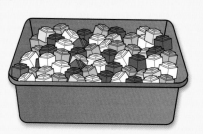
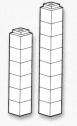

Pass the Snowman

Make a small play dough snowman. Gather youngsters in a circle. Then have students pass the snowman as quickly as possible as you lead them in singing the song. At the end of the song, have the child with the snowman remove a bit of the play dough. Continue playing until the snowman has disappeared!

(sung to the tune of "Clementine")

Pass the snowman, pass the snowman,
Pass the snowman all around.
We had better pass it quickly,
Or it will melt to the ground.

Penguin, Penguin

Get a penguin cutout. Say, "Penguin, penguin, play the game. Penguin, penguin, say your name." Then give the penguin to a child and encourage her to say her name. Recite the chant again, prompting the child to give the penguin to another child, who then says his name. Play continues in the same way.

Cari Charron
Quesnel Childcare Resource and Referral
Quesnel, British Columbia, Canada

Instant Seasonal Activities

V-A-L-E-N-T-I-N-E
Reinforcing letter names
Program a wipe-off board as shown. Place a poster board heart on the floor. Lead students in saying, "Nine special letters are all we need to spell *valentine*, yes indeed!" Then have a child toss a pom-pom toward the heart. If the pom-pom lands on the heart, write the letter *v* in the first space. If not, leave the space blank. Repeat with other students until the word is complete. *Ada Goren, Winston-Salem, NC*

valentine
v a l e n _ _ _ _

Cupid's Arrow
Playing a group game
Have a child (Cupid) sit in a chair with his back to the group. Put a tagboard arrow under the chair. Signal a classmate to quietly take the arrow to his seat and say, "I have Cupid's arrow!" Then have Cupid guess the classmate. When the classmate is revealed, continue with a different Cupid. *Ada Goren*

I have Cupid's arrow!

G Is for *Gold*!
Beginning sounds
Draw a pot on the board (or a sheet of chart paper). Have students say, "Gold," and listen for the /g/ sound. Next, say a random word. If the word begins with /g/, like *gold*, have a child draw a piece of gold above the pot. Continue with several words.

Lion or Lamb?
Speaking to share an opinion
Invite youngsters to tell what they know about lions and lambs. Then ask, "If you could be a lion or a lamb for just one day, which animal would you rather be?" Encourage each child to answer the question and explain her thoughts. Then invite little ones to act out their chosen animals. *Karen Guess, St. Richard's School, Indianapolis, IN*

Blow-by-Blow
Oral-motor skills
Place two cotton balls at one end of a table. Give each of two children a straw. Then prompt the students to blow the cotton balls to the opposite end of the table using the straws. Repeat with other pairs of students. *Connie D. Massingill, Dawn 'til Dusk Preschool, Zionsville, IN*

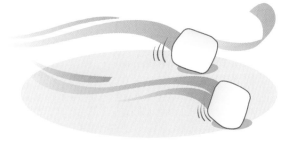

Instant Seasonal Activities

Noisy Pond

Divide the class into several groups and assign each group a different pond animal. Gather a letter card for the first letter of each animal's name. To play, hold up a card, prompting the students in the corresponding group to mimic their animal. Lower the card, signaling them to stop. Repeat the process, alternating the cards or holding up more than one at a time.
Tricia Kylene Brown,
Bowling Green, KY

Shoo, Fly!

Scatter a handful of black pom-poms (flies) on the floor. Ask a skill-related question, such as "What is the opposite of *hot*?" When a correct response is given, prompt the group to shout, "Shoo, fly!" Then have the child remove one of the flies. Continue until all the flies are gone.
Tricia Kylene Brown

Hop, Hop, Hop!

Seat students in a circle and hand a child a frog cutout. Count a number sequence aloud, pausing and prompting the child to say the next number. Then have him walk around the circle, counting and making the frog hop on the same number of children as in the sequence. The final child who is hopped on takes the next turn. *Tricia Kylene Brown*

Dunking Ducks

Have youngsters kneel in a circle and pretend to be ducks at a pond. Then announce a word. If the word begins with /d/, like *duck*, the ducks quack and dunk their heads in the water. If the word begins with a different sound, the ducks stay quiet. *Tricia Kylene Brown*

Handy Transformation

Have students follow along as you perform this butterfly metamorphosis. Make a fist (egg). Next, wiggle your index finger from your other hand (caterpillar) through the egg; then hold your hand flat like a leaf for the caterpillar to "nibble." Conceal the caterpillar between your fists (chrysalis); then unfold your hands with thumbs together and flap your fingers like butterfly wings! *Tricia Kylene Brown*

Seasonal Activities

At the Beach
Critical thinking
Display several beach-themed objects and place a beach towel nearby. Secretly place an object under the towel. Then invite youngsters to study the towel and guess the hidden object. Continue with the other objects. *Deborah Ryan, Milwaukie, OR*

Pick a Pair
Beginning sounds
Help students brainstorm a list of words related to summer. Be sure to include words that begin with the same sounds, such as *picnic* and *pool* or *beach* and *boat*. Next, name pairs of words from the list and have youngsters say, "Sounds the same" if the words begin with the same sound. If the words begin differently, youngsters say, "Sounds different." *Ruth Zabelin, Kleberg Elementary, Kingsville, TX*

Under the Sea
Drawing shapes
Draw a blue wavy line on a whiteboard. Name a shape and then invite a volunteer to draw the shape on the board. After checking for accuracy, add details to the shape so it resembles a sea critter. Allow several youngsters to have an opportunity to draw.

Lip-Smacking Lemonade
Counting
Incorporate counting into a simple no-prep pantomime activity! Have students pretend to pick ten lemons from a tree and then cut and squeeze each lemon. Then have them pretend to add the juice to a pitcher, along with two cups of sugar and eight cups of water. Encourage them to pantomime stirring the mixture as they count to 20. Then have students pretend to pour the mixture into ten different cups! What fun!

Light Up the Sky
Review
Post a piece of black bulletin board paper. Ask a skill-related question and invite a volunteer to answer it. When he gives the correct answer, lead the group in saying, "Boom! Bang! Pow!" as you use a white crayon to draw a very simple firework on the paper. Continue with different questions.

More fun! Once there are several fireworks on the paper, place it at a center with red and blue glitter paint pens. Encourage youngsters to visit the center and add glittery details to the fireworks!

KIDS IN THE KITCHEN

Kids in the Kitchen

Your little ones are sure to enjoy being herbivores just like some of the dinosaurs that lived long ago.

Delicious Dinosaurs

Ingredients for one:
section of prebaked pizza crust
whipped cream cheese spread
finely chopped vegetables

Jarah Hagerty
Indianapolis, IN

Utensils and supplies:
paper plate
dinosaur-shaped cookie cutters
plastic knife

Teacher preparation:
Arrange the ingredients and supplies near a colored copy of the step-by-step recipe cards (see page 81).

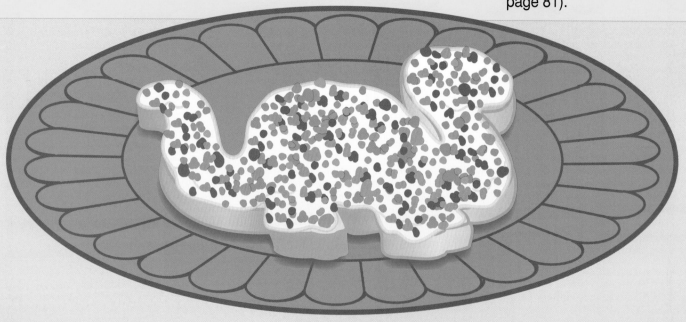

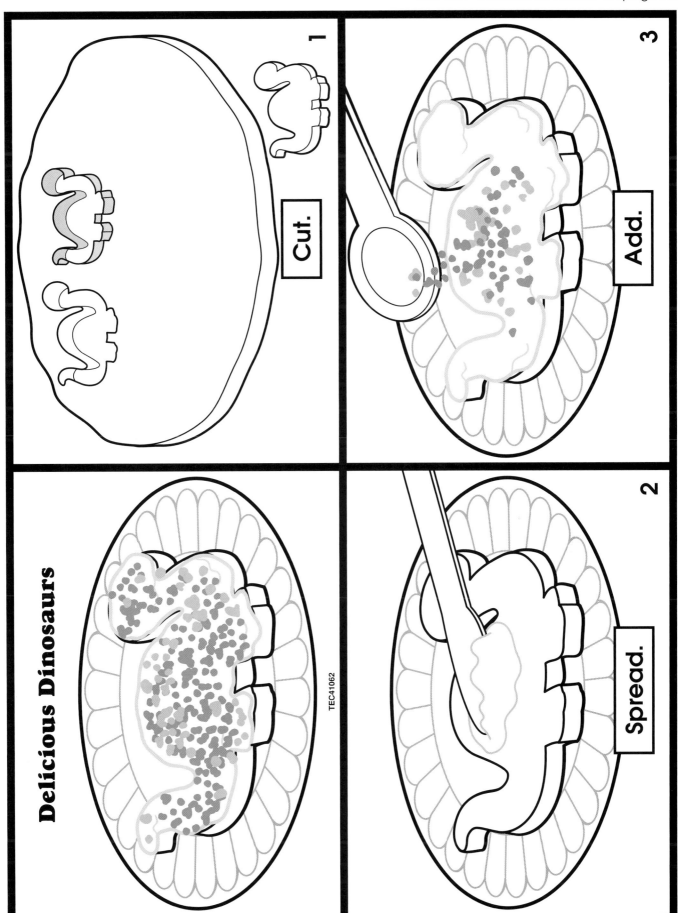

Delicious Dinosaurs

TEC41062

1 — Cut.

2 — Spread.

3 — Add.

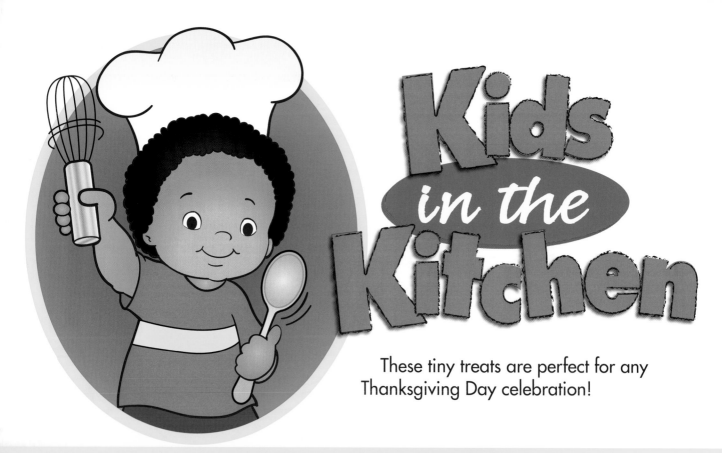

Kids in the Kitchen

These tiny treats are perfect for any Thanksgiving Day celebration!

Mini Cornucopias

Ingredients for one:
Bugles corn snacks
frosting
M&M's Minis

Bobbi Stutts
Woodhaven Baptist CDC
Rock Hill, SC

Utensils and supplies:
paper plate
resealable plastic bag
scissors

Teacher preparation:
Place the frosting in the resealable plastic bag and trim off one corner of the bag. Arrange the ingredients and supplies near a colored copy of the step-by-step recipe cards (see page 83).

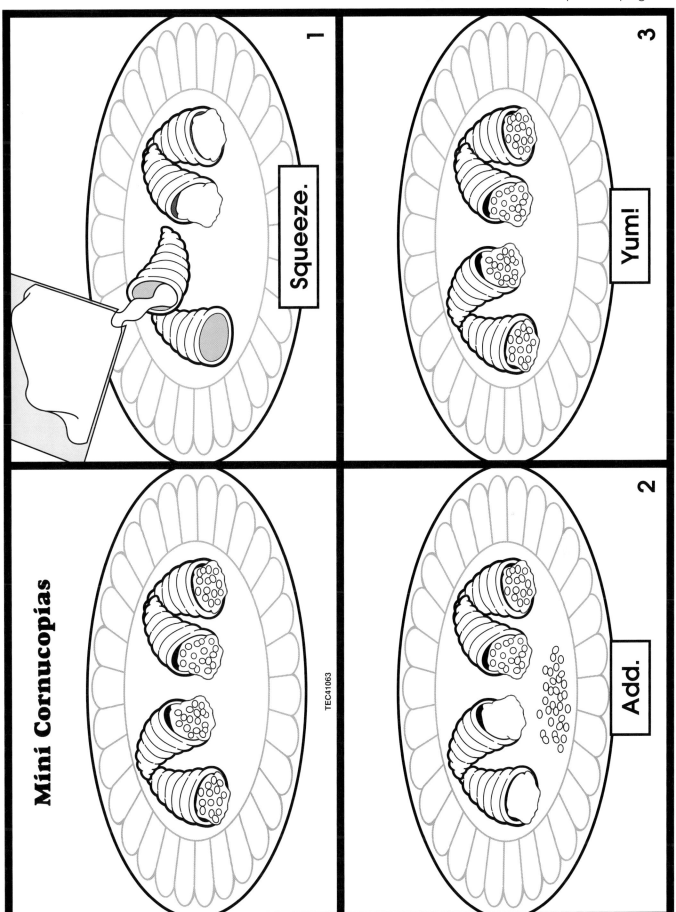

1 Squeeze.

3 Yum!

Mini Cornucopias

TEC41063

2 Add.

Kids in the Kitchen

Celebrate Kwanzaa with this yummy snack that features the colors red, green, and black!

Kwanzaa Fruit Pizza

Ingredients for one:
chocolate graham cracker
whipped cream cheese
strawberries (finely chopped)
kiwifruit (finely chopped)

Utensils and supplies:
paper plate
plastic knife
2 plastic spoons

Teacher preparation:
Arrange the ingredients and supplies near a colored copy of the step-by-step recipe cards (see page 85).

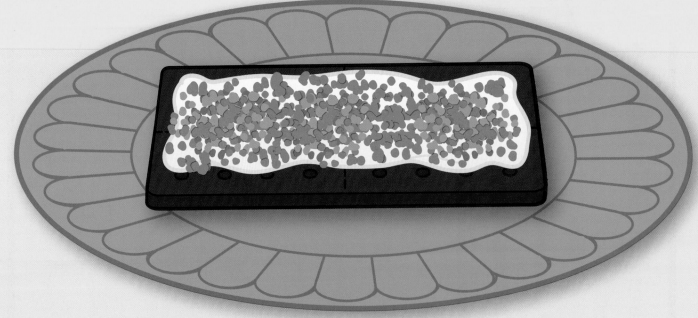

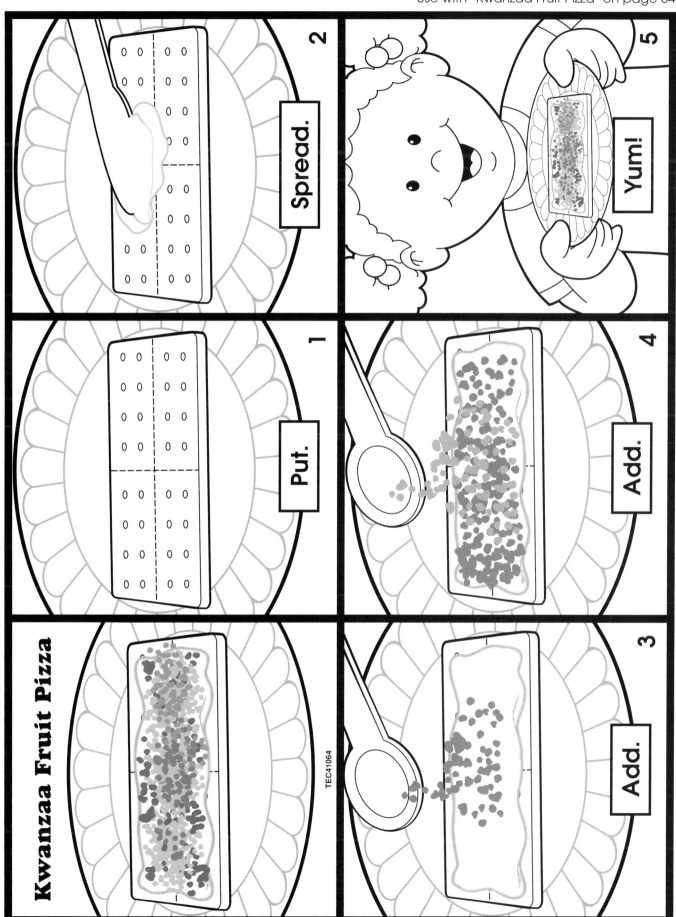

Kwanzaa Fruit Pizza

Put. 1

Spread. 2

Add. 3

Add. 4

Yum! 5

TEC41064

Kids in the Kitchen

This yummy treat is the perfect snack for a St. Patrick's Day celebration.

Leprechaun's Gold

Ingredients for one:
E. L. Fudge sandwich cookie
   (leprechaun)
puffed corn cereal (gold)

Lindsey Bachman
YMCA Early Learning Center
Duluth, MN

Utensils and supplies:
5-ounce paper cup
plastic spoon

Teacher Preparation:
   Arrange the ingredients and supplies near a colored copy of the step-by-step recipe cards (see page 87).

1 Add.

3 Fill.

Leprechaun's Gold

TEC41065

2 Put.

Kids in the Kitchen

This "egg-stra" special snack is a healthy option for little ones!

Excellent Egg Salad

Ingredients for one:
hard-boiled egg (peeled)
light mayonnaise
mustard in a squeeze bottle
crackers

Jenny Stauffer
Bethel Preschool and Daycare
Carlisle, PA

Utensils and supplies:
resealable plastic bag
plastic spoon
napkin

 tip → For extra fine-motor fun, have little ones crack and peel the eggs!

Teacher Preparation:
Arrange the ingredients and supplies near a color copy of the step-by-step recipe cards (see page 89).

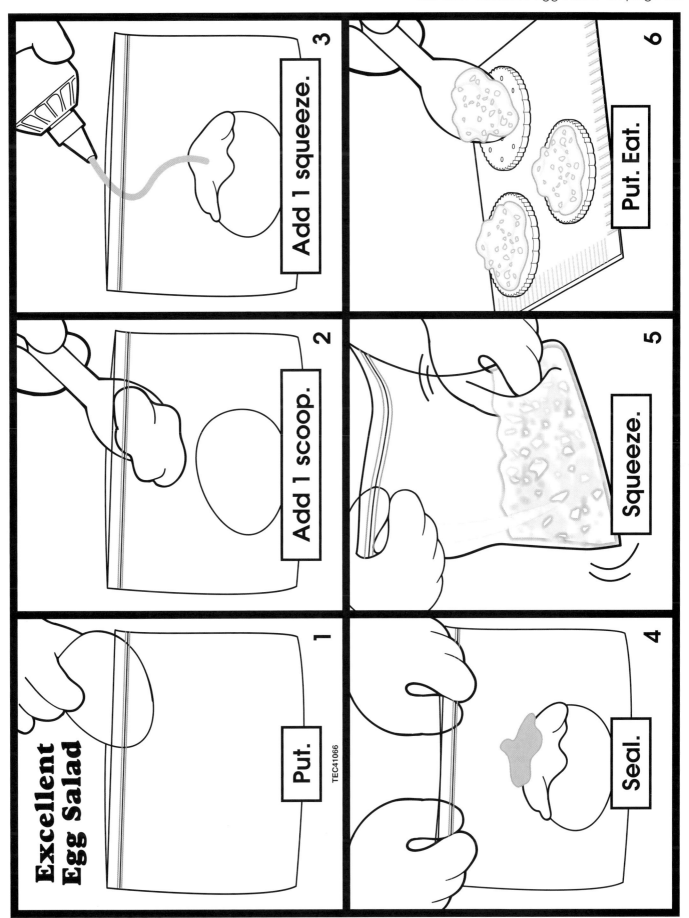

Excellent Egg Salad

Put.

TEC41066

Add 1 scoop.

Add 1 squeeze.

Seal.

Squeeze.

Put. Eat.

Kids in the Kitchen

This healthy snack is the perfect conclusion to a unit on ocean animals.

Jolly Jellyfish

Ingredients for one:
English muffin half
light strawberry cream cheese
reduced fat string cheese

Barbara Kronberger
Bollman Bridge Elementary
Jessup, MD

Utensils and supplies:
paper plate
plastic knife

Teacher preparation:
Arrange the ingredients and supplies near a colored copy of the step-by-step recipe cards (see page 91).

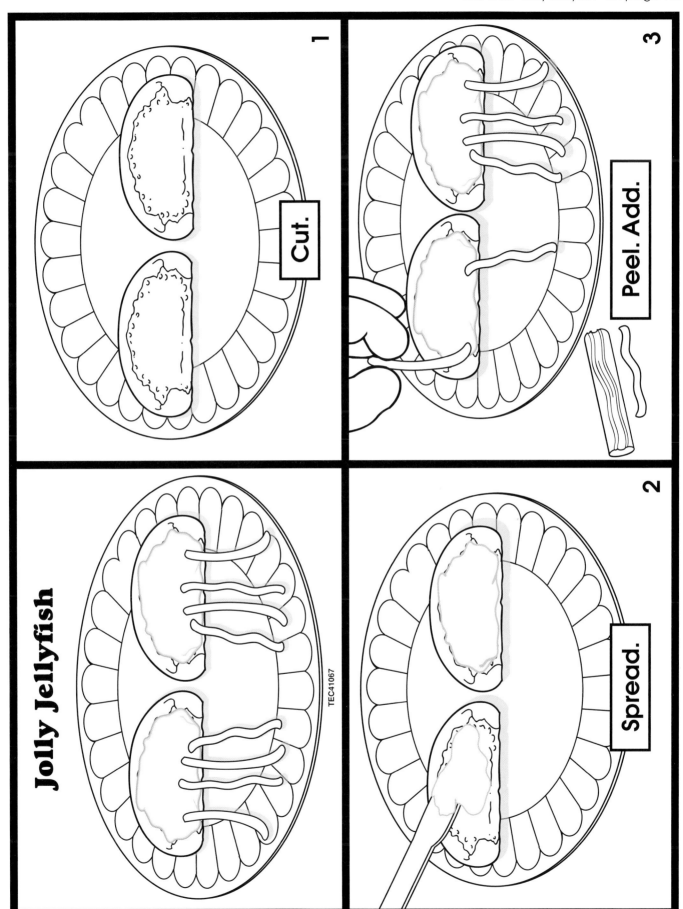

Jolly Jellyfish

1 | Cut.

2 | Spread.

3 | Peel. Add.

TEC41067

Dear Parent/Guardian,
    We are making a snack titled "Jolly Jellyfish." We would be grateful if you could help by providing the following ingredient(s):

_____

_____

_____

We need the ingredient(s) listed above by _____.
                                                        date
    Please let me know whether you are able to send the ingredient(s).

                        Thank you,

                        _____
                                        teacher

☐ Yes, I am able to send the ingredient(s).
☐ No, I am unable to send the ingredient(s) this time.

                        _____
                                parent/guardian signature

©The Mailbox®

Dear Parent/Guardian,
    We are making a snack titled "Jolly Jellyfish." We would be grateful if you could help by providing the following ingredient(s):

_____

_____

_____

We need the ingredient(s) listed above by _____.
                                                        date
    Please let me know whether you are able to send the ingredient(s).

                        Thank you,

                        _____
                                        teacher

☐ Yes, I am able to send the ingredient(s).
☐ No, I am unable to send the ingredient(s) this time.

                        _____
                                parent/guardian signature

©The Mailbox®

LEARNING CENTERS

Learning Centers

Bag Shake
Sensory Center

Pour cornmeal into a large heavy-duty resealable plastic bag. Then place a variety of random manipulatives—such as linking cubes, small toy bugs or dinosaurs, magnetic letters, and bear counters—in the bag. Close the bag and reinforce the seal with tape. A child manipulates the bag to find the objects.

Janet Boyce
Cokato, MN

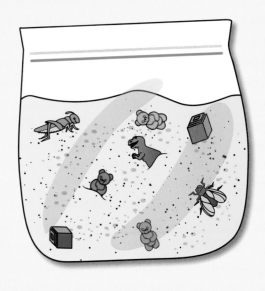

Magnet Fun
Literacy Center

Make an oversize letter card for the first letter in each child's name. Provide a baking sheet and a collection of random magnets. A child attaches his card to the baking sheet. Then he places magnets on the letter. Finally, he runs his hand over the magnets and says the letter's name.

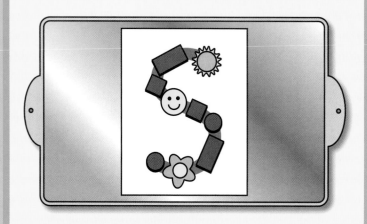

Stuffed!
Fine-Motor Area

Gather a variety of pom-poms and stuff them in empty plastic water bottles. Then place the bottles at a center. A youngster takes a bottle and works to remove the pom-poms, using his fingers or tools such as tweezers or unsharpened pencils. This little activity gives a great fine-motor workout and keeps tiny fingers busy!

Mary Margaret Cline
Apostles Learning Center
Atlanta, GA

This is also an excellent idea for keeping your non-nappers busy while other youngsters are resting!

This Is Me!
Writing Center

To prepare for this center, write the rhyme shown on a sheet of paper and then make a copy for each child. Print a photo of each youngster and place it in the center. Arrange for an adult helper. A child colors a page as desired and then glues her photo in the middle of the page. The adult writes the child's name below her picture. When all the pages are finished, bind them together to create a class book!

Kristen Hanson
Early Head Start Child Care
Mayville, ND

I am special, yes sirree!
I am very special. This is me!

Karley

Fun With Cards
Math Center

Encourage parents to donate old playing cards to the classroom. Place the cards in a container and place it in a center. Encourage youngsters to sort, match, pattern, or manipulate the cards any way they desire.

Margie Dacheff
Miss Margie's Home Child Care
Spring Grove, IL

Toss and Catch
Gross-Motor Area

Trim the top off of a clean gallon milk jug and then apply tape to any sharp edges. Provide milk jug lids or other manipulatives. One child holds the jug by the handle and attempts to catch the lids tossed by a classmate. What a fun way to practice hand-eye coordination!

Carole Watkins
Timothy Ball Elementary
Crown Point, IN

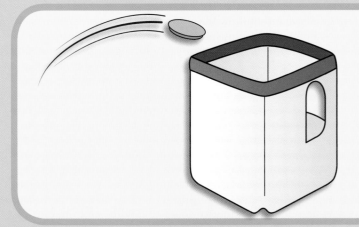

Learning Centers

Turkey Tail Feathers
Math Center

Youngsters practice counting, identifying numbers, and one-to-one correspondence with this Thanksgiving-themed idea! Cut out several copies of the turkey on page 71. Trim off the tail feathers and write a different number on each turkey. Attach the turkeys to paper plates and place them in a center along with spring-style clothespins (tail feathers). A youngster attaches the appropriate number of tail feathers to a turkey. Then he touches each tail feather, saying "Gobble!" each time he does so. He continues with each turkey.

Angela Nolan
Lafayette Academy Preschool
Floyds Knobs, IN

Gobble!

Yarn Stick
Literacy Center

Use a crayon to write letters on sheets of sandpaper. Provide lengths of yarn. A child traces a letter with her finger and then attaches thick, fuzzy yarn to the sandpaper to cover the letter. The yarn will stick! **For a more challenging version,** do not write letters on the sandpaper. Instead have the little ones use a letter card as a guide to place the yarn on the sandpaper in the correct arrangement.

Sharon Jenkins
Fairland Christian Preschool
Fairland, IN

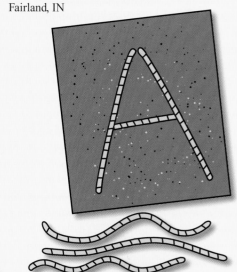

Surprise Eyes!
Play Dough Center

This simple center is perfect for Halloween! Hide jumbo wiggle eyes in green play dough. Encourage little ones to dig and search through the play dough to find the eyes. If desired, place tools such as chopsticks in the center to help with the search!

Suzanne Moore
Tucson, AZ

Learning Centers

Hungry Bat!
Game Center

This twist on the traditional fishing game is perfect for fall! Cut out a copy of the bat pattern (see page 106) and several copies of the cards on page 106. Attach a magnet to the bat and then attach the bat to a dowel rod (or yardstick) fishing pole as shown. Put a jumbo paper clip on each card and then scatter the cards facedown on the floor. A child manipulates the pole to make the bat catch a card. Then he looks at the card and decides if the item pictured is something a bat should eat. He continues with the remaining cards.

Rachel Stegall
Novi Community Preschool
Northville, MI

Slippery Noodles
Sensory Center

To prepare for this center, toss cooked noodles with a little bit of vegetable oil and then place the noodles in a tub. Youngsters touch and swirl the noodles for a fun sensory experience!

Suzanne Moore
Tucson, AZ

Vegetable Oil

Squirt!
Fine-Motor Center

Get a toy house (or cut windows and doorways in a cardboard box) and place it in your empty water table. Stuff red and orange tissue paper into the windows and doorways and provide mini squirt bottles filled with water. A child squirts the flames to put out the fire! To add extra play opportunities, provide toy people figures and a toy fire engine!

Erin Brown
Neighborhood Preschool
Middletown, CT

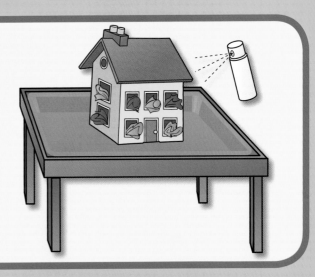

Learning Centers

Coupon Mania!
Dramatic–Play Area

Stock your dramatic-play area with "holiday merchandise," such as toys and gift items. Also provide slips of paper, crayons, play money, gift bags, and boxes. Little ones use the paper slips to create coupons. (You may consider putting some coupons at the center for inspiration!) Little ones use the props to engage in pretend holiday shopping. For added fun and fine-motor exercise, set up a gift wrap station as well!

Ellen Grimm
Good Shepherd Preschool
Montague, MI

Wrecking Ball
Block Center

This fun center helps develop eye-hand coordination! Put a tennis ball in the toe of a knee-high stocking and tie the opening closed. Place the resulting wrecking ball in your block center. A youngster uses blocks to build a structure. Then he holds the wrecking ball near the structure and swings it like a pendulum trying to knock down the blocks. He continues swinging the ball until the structure is demolished.

Cat Van Horn
Troy R-111 Early Childhood Education Center
Troy, MO

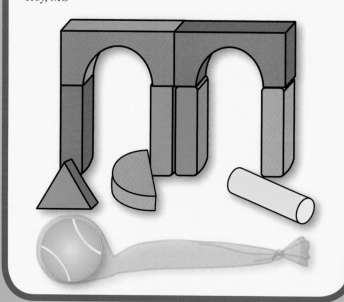

Snowy Footprints
Math Center

Trace each child's shoe onto white craft foam. Then cut out each footprint and use a permanent marker to label it with the child's name. Place these snowy footprints in a tub and put the tub at a center. A child manipulates the footprints as desired. Perhaps he'll match sizes, order them by size, or sort them into piles by boy or girl.

Roxanne LaBell Dearman
Early Intervention Program for Children Who Are Deaf or Hard of Hearing
Charlotte, NC

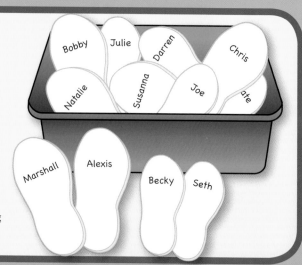

Merry Matchups
Puzzle Center

Gather used holiday cards with distinct pictures or patterns. Remove the front panel from each card and puzzle-cut the panel into two or more pieces. Mix the pieces together. A student takes a puzzle piece and studies the design. Then he finds the remaining piece, or pieces, and assembles the puzzle. He continues in the same way to assemble the remaining card puzzles.

Donna Ream
Ms. Donna's Daycare
Plainfield, IL

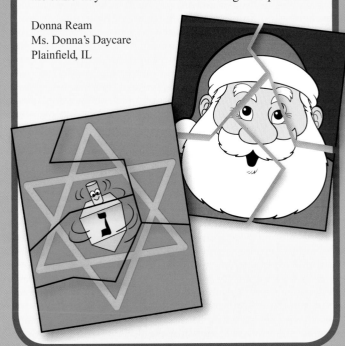

Alphabet Lacer
Literacy

Punch holes around the edge of a tagboard circle. Label the holes with letters in alphabetical order; then attach a length of yarn to the hole labeled *A*. A youngster laces the yarn through each hole following the correct letter sequence. As he works, he names each letter.

Jolynn Mertz
Merry-Go-Round Preschool
Bismark, ND

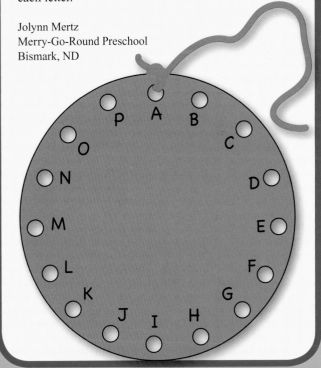

Hot Chocolate and Marshmallows
Fine-Motor Center

Provide plastic or foam cups, scraps of brown paper, and cotton balls. A child visits the center and makes cups of hot chocolate for herself and her friends! To make one, she crumples brown paper and stuffs it in a cup. Then she adds cotton ball marshmallows.

Barb Dover
Giggly Wiggly Preschool
Issaquah, WA

Learning Centers

Clean Mud
Sensory Center

In your sensory table or a large plastic tub, grate a bar of soap and shred two to three rolls of toilet paper; then add warm water and mix. Provide items like a mixing spoon, scoopers, and disposable cups. A student uses his senses of smell and touch, along with the props, to investigate the gooey mixture. *Exploring the senses*

Sarah Dean
University of Idaho Early Childhood Center
Moscow, ID

St. Patrick's Day Kite
Art Center

Station an adult at this center and provide a black pot cutout for each child, crepe paper streamers in rainbow colors, and glitter. To make a kite, a child brushes glue along the rim of the pot and sprinkles glitter on the glue. Next, he glues lengths of crepe paper streamers to the pot as shown. Finally, he uses masking tape to attach a length of yarn to the pot. To fly his kite, he goes outside on a breezy day, holds the yarn, and runs, letting the streamers trail behind him. *Fine-motor and gross-motor skills*

Deborah Jarett
The Friendship School
Waterford, CT

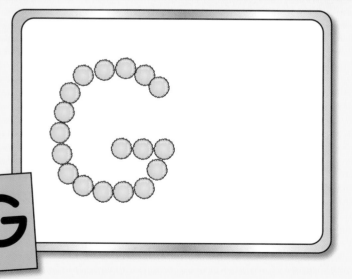

Gold Letters
Literacy Center

Hot-glue yellow pom-poms (gold) to individual magnets (or pieces of magnet tape). Place the gold, along with desired letter cards, near a magnetic board. A child takes a card, traces the letter with her finger, and uses the gold to form the letter on the board. Then she removes the letter and repeats the process with the remaining cards. *Forming letters*

Donna Ream
Ms. Donna's Daycare
Plainfield, IL

Learning Centers

Chopstick Transfer
Fine-Motor Area

Place at a table a wok (or large bowl) partially filled with medium-size pom-poms (food). Provide several paper plates and a pair of chopsticks for each plate. A child uses the chopsticks as desired to transfer food from the wok to a plate. After putting several items on his plate, he pretends to eat the food using the chopsticks. When he's finished, he returns the pom-poms to the wok.
Fine-motor skills

Gayle Selsback and Sue Millard
Playhouse Preschool
Maple Grove, MN

To make chopsticks more kid-friendly, secure the ends with a rubber band and then wedge a small, rolled-up strip of paper between the chopsticks.

Sparkle and Shine
Math Center

Here's a simple center that's just perfect for the season! Gather a variety of items in valentine colors, such as glittery, sparkly scrapbook paper; glittered felt; and sparkly pom-poms. Cut the paper and felt into squares. Place the items at a center along with strips of white construction paper. A child arranges items on the paper to make a pattern. Then he glues the items in place. When the glue dries, fold the project in half, bend the loose ends, and tape the ends together to make a heart! ***Making a pattern***

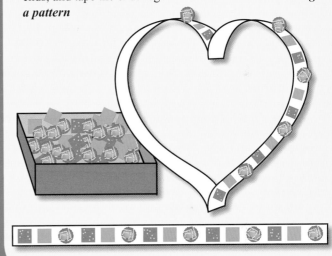

Delectable Rainbow
Nutrition Center

Attach a colorful rainbow cutout to a tabletop. Provide grocery circulars, scissors, and glue. Students visit the center and look through the circulars for healthy foods that correspond to the colors of the rainbow. When a child finds an item (and an adult helper agrees that it is a healthy food), he tears or cuts out the picture and glues it to the appropriate color arc. When he's finished, he washes his hands and goes to a nearby station to nibble a healthy snack!
Developing healthy habits

Julie Christensen
Parker, CO

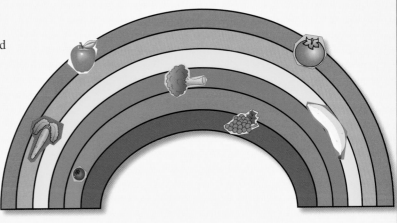

Learning Centers

Colorful Creations
Fine-Motor Center

To make this three-dimensional art, provide cotton balls (clouds) and strips of construction paper in rainbow colors. A child makes a tab on the end of a strip, with help as needed, and then glues the tabs to the paper to make arches. She repeats the process with other strips as desired. Then she glues clouds around the strips. Next, she dictates for you to write on her project information about rainbows and how they make her feel.

Roxanne LaBell Dearman
NC Early Intervention Program for Children Who Are Deaf or
    Hard of Hearing
Charlotte, NC

Rainbows have lots of colors. All the colors make me happy. Samantha

Sand Pipes
Sand Table

Add pieces of PVC pipe, scoops, and funnels to the sand table. Youngsters stand the PVC pipes in the sand and then use the funnel to fill them. What fun! *Fine-motor skills, capacity*

Linda Heavrin
Benton, IL

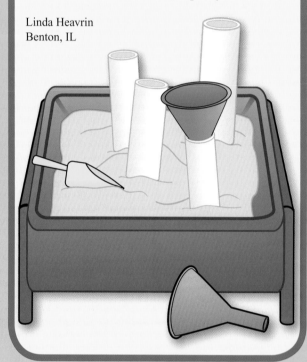

Moldable Metamorphosis
Play Dough Center

Set out play dough, laminated leaf cutouts, and a butterfly cookie cutter. Also provide a picture reference showing the life cycle of a butterfly. A child uses play dough to mold the various stages of a butterfly's life cycle and places them on a leaf. *Butterfly life cycle*

adapted from an idea by Caitlin Meadows
West Virginia University Early Learning Center
Morgantown, WV

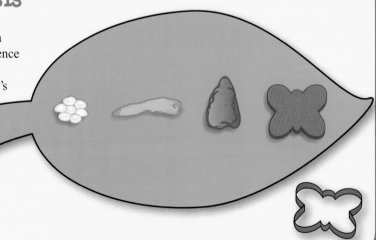

Build a Road!
Block Center

Ask for a donation of wooden paint sticks at a local home improvement store and place the sticks along with toy vehicles in your block center. Youngsters use the sticks and blocks to build roads and bridges. Then they play with the vehicles on their newly built roadways! *Spatial skills*

Danielle M. Rieth, World Academy, Washua, NH

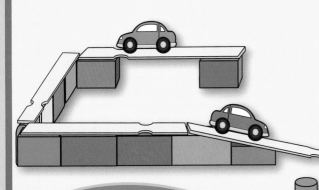

Feeling crafty? Paint one side of each stick brown and the other side black. Then use paint pens to create a railroad track on each brown side and to add a dashed line (road) on each black side. Youngsters will love using these reversible roads and railways!

Oodles of Yolks!
Math Center

Normal eggs may have one or two yolks, but the eggs in this center have quite a few! Label plastic eggs with different numbers and place them in a resealable plastic bag. Provide yellow mini pom-poms (yolks) and a basket. A child selects an egg and identifies the number. Then she counts out that number of yolks and puts them in the egg. She places the egg in the basket and continues. *Identifying numbers, counting*

Lynn Wagoner
Greensboro, NC

It's a Frog's Life
Science Center

Cut out a copy of the cards on page 107 and program a pond-shaped cutout as shown. Place the frog life cycle card faceup in the top box and scatter the remaining cards facedown near the pond. A child flips a card and places it in the appropriate box according to the life cycle card. He continues until all the cards are sequenced. Then he uses the picture cards to tell the life cycle of a frog, saying "Ribbit, ribbit!" when he's done. *Frog life cycle*

Deborah Garmon
Groton, CT

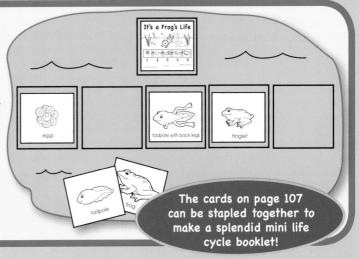

The cards on page 107 can be stapled together to make a splendid mini life cycle booklet!

Learning Centers

Rock Pile
Literacy Center

Use a permanent marker to label a collection of clean rocks with letters, writing *R* on most. Place the rocks in a pile, letter-side down. Two youngsters visit the center. One child takes a rock and identifies the letter. If the letter is an *R*, he places it in front of him. If it's a different letter, he sets the rock aside. Play continues, in turn, until there are no rocks left in the pile. ***Recognizing letters***

Karin Bulkow
Washington School for Comprehensive Literacy
Sheboygan, WI

Checkered Measurement
Math Center

Set out a basket or cooler filled with picnic-related items, such as plastic cutlery, a cup, a paper plate, a napkin, play food, and plastic ants. Also provide a measuring strip cut from a checkered tablecloth. A student takes an item from the basket and places it alongside the measuring strip. Then she counts to see approximately how many squares long the item is. She continues in the same way with each remaining item. ***Nonstandard measurement***

Janet Boyce
Cokato, MN

Coconut Castles
Play Dough Center

Follow the recipe to make play dough with a sandy texture and a scent reminiscent of the beach! Also provide plastic ice cube trays and knives. A child presses chunks of dough into an ice cube tray, sniffing the scent as he works. He uses a plastic knife to remove the sandy blocks and then uses them to build a coconut-scented sand castle. For added fun, provide toy figures and seashells! ***Exploring the senses, fine-motor skills***

Karen Smith, Little Tid-Bits, Fresno, CA

Sand Dough Recipe

2 c. play sand
1 c. cornstarch
2½ tsp. cream of tartar
1½ c. water
coconut extract

Mix the ingredients in a medium-size saucepan and cook on low heat until a ball forms. Remove the dough and let it cool before kneading.

Learning Centers

Swiss Cheese!
Fine-Motor Area

With this activity, little ones develop and strengthen their pincer grasps! Give each child a copy of page 108, a pencil, and crayons. Also set out a foam block and a golf tee. A child uses the pencil to trace the cheese; then she colors the cheese and the mouse. When she's finished, she places the page atop the foam block and pokes holes in the cheese with the golf tee. *Fine-motor skills*

adapted from an idea by Allison Annand
Hollis Primary School
Hollis, NH

Snacktime for Mouse

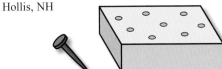

Jar Full of Fireflies
Art Center

Set out a supply of jar-shaped cutouts along with a black ink pad and marker, a squeeze bottle of glue, gold glitter, and aluminum foil. A child presses his fingertip on the ink pad and then the jar to make a firefly body; then he uses the marker to draw body parts on the print. To create a bioluminescent effect, he squeezes glue near the tip of the body and then sprinkles glitter on the glue. He makes several more fireflies and then glues a foil strip to the top of the jar. *Expressing oneself through art*

adapted from an idea by Donna Ream
Ms. Donna's Daycare
Plainfield, IL

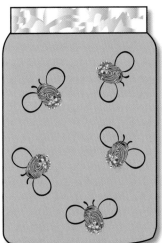

Journey Into Space
Sensory Center

Fill your sensory table or a large plastic tub with black-tinted rice; then sprinkle in a handful of white rice (stars). Add colorful balls (planets) along with space-related toy vehicles and figures. A child uses the materials to engage in outer space play. *Exploring the senses*

Darla Gordon
Orchard Valley Learning Center
Centennial, CO

Bat Pattern and Food Cards

Use with "Hungry Bat!" on page 97.

TEC41063

TEC41063

TEC41063

TEC41063

TEC41063

TEC41063

TEC41063

It's a Frog's Life

eggs

tadpole

tadpole with back legs

froglet

frog

Snacktime for Mouse

©The Mailbox® • TEC41067 • June/July 2013

Note to the teacher: Use with "Swiss Cheese!" on page 105.

MANAGEMENT TIPS & TIMESAVERS

Management Tips & Timesavers

Center Management

Personalize a bear cutout for each child and then label honeypot cutouts with center names (see page 114 for patterns.) Laminate the cutouts. Attach several Velcro fasteners to each honeypot (equal to the number of children you would like at each center). Then attach corresponding Velcro fasteners to the bears. When a child visits a center, he attaches his bear to the honeypot. *Sue Fleischmann, Sussex, WI*

Blocks

Olivia

Useful Information

Do you have lists or schedules that are needed for the entire year? Cut them out and glue them to the inside cover of your plan book. This will be helpful both for you and for substitute teachers! *Janice Sutherland, Louisiana Schnell Elementary, Placerville, CA*

Blooming Flower

Is it time to go home? Youngsters will know with this visual! Post an outline drawing of a flower in your classroom, making sure that there is a petal outline for every 30 minutes in the school day. Make matching petal cutouts. Every 30 minutes, have a child attach a petal. When the flower is complete, it's time to go home! *Jennifer Leiker, St. Andrew Catholic School, Independence, KS*

Listen or Talk?

Enlist Mr. Potato Head's help with classroom management! Remove all the features from the toy. When it is time for youngsters to look and listen, attach the ears and eyes to Mr. Potato Head and display it in a prominent location. When it's time for little ones to talk, remove the ears and eyes and attach the lips. What fun! *Litsa Jackson, Covington Integrated Arts Academy, Covington, TN*

A Calendar Rhyme

Counting is a natural part of calendar time! To help youngsters stay together when counting, recite the rhyme shown! Then lead little ones in counting the days in the current month. *Christina Kasler, A Home Away From Home Childcare, Vacaville, CA*

Let's count the days in [August]—
Not too fast,
Not too slow.
Ready? Let's go!

One, two, three, four, five...

Management Tips & Timesavers

Time to Transition

To transition to a new activity, label vinyl placemats with different letters and place them on your floor in a circle. Play music and have students walk around the mats. Then stop the music and have each child stand on a mat. Call on two (or more) youngsters and help them name their letters. Then have them give you their mats and transition to the next activity. Continue with the remaining students in the same way. *Ann Gutierrez, Ms. Ann's Kinder Care, Three Rivers, TX*

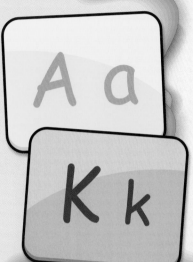

Clean and Dance

Encourage students to clean up quickly. If students clean up following center time within the designated time period, allow them to show off their dancing moves! Play an upbeat song while students dance. What a fun and simple reward! *Laurie Gordon, Triumphant Lutheran Preschool, Garden Ridge, TX*

Seasonal Stencils

When cutting out laminated seasonal shapes, save the remaining paper to use as stencils. Simply put a little piece of tape over the spot where you cut into the paper. You now have fabulous stencils to use for seasonal sponge painting. *Amy Freeman, Kiddie Kampus, Queen Creek, AZ*

Scissor Tip

Help each child hold her scissors appropriately. Then stamp or draw a small smiley face near the fleshy pad at the base of her thumb. Prompt her to look at her hand a few times during the activity. If her hand has rotated and she can no longer see the smiley face, help her correct her grip. *Charlene Rogers, Child Development Centre, Charlottetown, Prince Edward Island, Canada*

Meet Me There!

When it's time for students to gather in the group-time area, sing the song shown, inserting the name of an upcoming activity. *Donna Olp, St. Gregory the Great Preschool, South Euclid, OH*

(sung to the tune of "The Muffin Man")

Meet me at the teacher's chair,
The teacher's chair, the teacher's chair.
Meet me at the teacher's chair,
And we'll [read a book].

Management Tips & Timesavers

Helping Hands

Encourage parents to donate items with this helping hands display! The week before you have a special project planned, write each item you need and the date it is needed by on separate hand cutouts. Then display the hands and a sign like the one shown. A parent takes a hand and sends in the requested item. *Cassidy Fountain, Mt. Washington, KY*

Can You Give Us a Hand?

Glitter Wipes

To make glitter cleanup quick and easy, keep a box of dryer sheets on hand. Whenever you need to tidy up a glittery table, simply wipe a dryer sheet across it. The glitter will stick to the dryer sheet! *Jessica Price, Wee Care Preschool, Galion, OH*

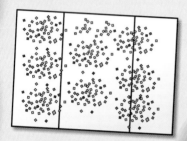

Snowy Helpers

Rejuvenate your classroom job display for winter! Write each classroom job on a separate white paper circle (snowman body) and display it. Personalize a snowman head and scarf cutout as shown. Attach Velcro fasteners to the bodies and the heads. To assign jobs, attach a head above each body! *Carole Schultz, Cedar Springs Weekday School, Knoxville, TN*

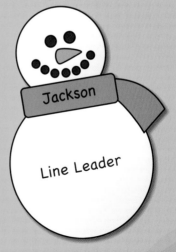

Jackson

Line Leader

Student Spies

Settle youngsters into a new activity quickly with this version of I Spy. To start, choose a child who is ready for the activity and then say, "I spy [Ava]. Who do you spy?" The named child spies another child who is ready. Continue until each child has been spied. *Dianne Giggey, Episcopal Day School, Pensacola, FL*

Lunchtime Rhyme

Remind youngsters of lunchtime (or snacktime) expectations by saying this poem each day. *Teresa Petty, Thompson Early Childhood Center, Jacksonville, NC*

We eat our lunch (snack) with style.
We sit, we eat, we talk a while.
When we're done, we know what to do.
We throw our trash away and recycle too.
We use our manners every day.
Please and thank-you are what we say.
We're at the table in our seats.
Now it's time for us to eat!

Management Tips & Timesavers

Skilled Transitions

Use Velcro fasteners to attach shape cards to the sides of a cube-shaped box. In turn, each child rolls the cube, names the shape, and then moves to the next activity. Change the cards often to review other skills, such as letters, numbers, rhyming, or counting. *Marie Rawley, Wiscasset Head Start and Early Learning Center, Wiscasset, ME*

Naptime Routine

When each child is on his mat for naptime, ask him if he would like his blanket fluffed. If he does (and no doubt he will), raise and lower the blanket three times, counting in a chosen language as you do so. What a soothing routine and a fun way to learn to count in different languages! *Annika Lunceford, Little One's Day Out, Columbia, MO*

Stoplight Behavior

Make a behavior display like the one shown and personalize a clothespin for each child. Explain what each circle represents. Green means "Go on being great!" Yellow means "Slow down and think about what you are doing." Red means "Stop and think about your choices." Place all the clothespins on green and move them as needed. *Misty Miller, Misty's Dayschool, Pflugerville, TX*

Go!

Slow!

Stop!

Leave a Message

To reduce unnecessary interruptions, place a toy phone in the listening center. When a child needs to tell you something but you are busy, she can use the phone to leave you a message. Listen as she leaves the message to determine if it is a matter that needs your attention. *Evon Rose Todd, Mid Cities Head Start, Euless, TX*

Boo-Boo Bags

To make a reusable cold pack, add corn syrup and food coloring to a resealable plastic bag. Seal the bag and place it in a freezer. When a child has a boo-boo, give him a bag to place on it. The bag can be manipulated to cover any body part. *Eileen Gingras, The Children's School at Deerfield Academy, Deerfield, MA*

Bear and Honeypot Patterns
Use with "Center Management" on page 110.

TEC41062

TEC41062

TEC41062

OUR READERS WRITE...

Our Readers WRITE...
(and EMAIL and BLOG and TWEET and POST)

A Memorable Collection

Here is a keepsake that parents are sure to treasure! I have each child make handprints on a large rectangular shirt box (or cake box). Then I add a heart labeled with the child's name and school year. I add a photo of the child on the left side of the heart. Throughout the year I invite her to put special art projects in her box. Near the end of the school year, I add a recently taken photo on the right side of the heart. I have each child present her box to her parents at an end-of-the-year celebration. *Katie Symonds, St. Ambrose School, Anderson, IN*

Allie
2012-2013

IF YOU TAKE A PARENT TO SCHOOL...

During our open house, I have the parents participate in a morning meeting, and I read aloud *If You Take a Mouse to School* by Laura Numeroff. After the read-aloud, I have parents complete a sentence starter like the one shown and illustrate their words as desired. I bind the pages between two covers and read the book aloud to my preschoolers. This is always a popular book in my reading center! *Beth Sharpe, The Malvern School of Medford, Medford, NJ*

If You Take a Parent to School

If you take a dad to school, he will <u>play dress-up and wear the silliest things!</u>

Morning Greetings

Need another job for your classroom job chart? Try the class greeter! The greeter's job is to welcome each child and teacher to the room with a good morning and a high five. This is one of my students' favorite jobs! *Melissa Bates, Lyle School, Kewanee, IL*

The MAILBOX BLOG

NUMBER OF THE DAY

Each morning, I have a child roll a pair of jumbo dice. We count the number of dots, and then I have a volunteer post a matching number card above a tree cutout. I ask the child to attach a matching number of apple cutouts to the tree. To keep interest high, I change the display each month. Youngsters put features on a jack-o'-lantern, feathers on a turkey, and ornaments on a holiday tree! *Carrie Gorden, North Elementary, Taylorville, IL*

Take a Peek

To introduce new classroom themes, I cover a clean potato chip can with gift wrap and, on the bottom, place an object or sticker that relates to our upcoming theme. I have my students sit in a circle. Then I encourage each child to peek inside the can before passing it to the next child. Finally, I prompt youngsters to speculate about the theme. This is an exciting way to kick off each new classroom theme! *Shelley Hoster, Jack and Jill Early Learning Center, Norcross, GA*

The MAILBOX BLOG

"The Mailbox makes a difference in the lives of so many people every day!*—Laura Mihalenko via The Mailbox Blog*

Flashy Answers

After reading a story aloud, I give each child a small flashlight and dim the lights. Then I ask several yes-or-no questions about the story. If the answer to a question is yes, each child turns on her flashlight and points the beam toward the ceiling. If the answer is no, she does nothing. *Sue Fleischmann, Sussex, WI*

"The Mailbox helps to keep my class running."*—Nancy G. Askew via Facebook*

Rule Review

I take photos of students following classroom rules or taking part in daily classroom procedures. Using a word processing program, I create book pages like the one shown. After reading the book aloud several times to reinforce rules and procedures, I store it in my reading center. My kids love it! **Amanda Kelly, Sonoran Heights Elementary, Surprise, AZ**

Julissa is raising her hand to ask a question. Turn the page to see what Gideon and Alexander are doing.

Our Readers WRITE...
(and EMAIL and BLOG and TWEET and POST)

The Princess and the Place Setting

To help students remember how to set the table, I gather a place setting and placemat. Then I tell them this story. Once upon a time in a castle far away (place the plate on a placemat), there lived a princess (place the spoon). In a forest outside the castle (place the napkin), there lived a dragon (place the fork). A prince with a sword (place the knife) kept the princess safe. The princess liked to go to the tower (place the cup) to look out over the kingdom. *Sandi Herron, High Point Christian School, Madison, WI*

Snip, Snip!

I've made this cutting center extra special for little ones! I find a cardboard box large enough for a child to sit in comfortably. Then I place in the box magazine pages, paper strips, die-cuts, large scraps of paper, and craft foam. I provide several pairs of scissors. A child climbs in the box and uses the provided materials to practice cutting. The small paper and foam pieces stay in the box so there is no cleanup! *Kathy Symanietz, Family Child Care, Park Rapids, MN*

f "I don't know what I'd do without *The Mailbox*® magazines! I love the easy, practical, and relevant activities in each magazine. My students always love the activities, and the magazine saves me a ton of time!"—*Danielle Hudson via Facebook*

The MAILBOX® BLOG

Turkey Talk
From...The Mailbox Blog

This fun Thanksgiving Day–themed skit is always a hit with my little ones. I set out a stuffed toy turkey and a basket of vegetables, including an ear of corn. I have two youngsters carry the basket and come across the hungry turkey. One child tries to feed the turkey a vegetable, such as a carrot. The other youngster moves the turkey's head to say no and then says, "Turkeys don't like carrots." The first child tries to feed the turkey other vegetables until he finally offers the corn. Then the second child makes the turkey's head nod, and she says, "Turkeys like corn!" I repeat the skit with different youngsters. Diana Oldham, Colt Early Childhood Center, Lansing, MI

GHOST GOODIES

Prior to the day we are making the Halloween snack, I bake a pumpkin cake in a 9" x 13" pan. To assemble the snack, I give each child a piece of cake. He puts a dollop of whipped topping (ghost) on his piece. Then he adds two miniature chocolate chip eyes to the ghost. *R. M. Tullis, Our Lady of Perpetual Help School, Germantown, TN*

For a pumpkin cake that is quick and easy to make, mix a 15 oz. can of pumpkin with a spice cake mix. Pour the mixture into a 9" x 13" greased cake pan. Bake at 350° for 25–30 minutes.

What's the Secret Passletter?

For each child, I make letter cards and put them on a metal ring. I ask parents to keep the cards near the door they use when leaving the house. Each time they leave, I suggest that they show a card to the child and ask him to name the secret passletter. My kids (and parents) love this game! *Kristie Adams, Sonshine Academy, Colleyville, TX*

Theme Review

For each theme, I prepare a jumbo cutout related to the theme, such as a large fall leaf or pumpkin. Then, on the last day of the unit, I invite each child to tell me something she knows or has learned, and I write it on the cutout. I post the cutout in the hallway for visitors to read! *Joanne Townsend, Hess Educational Complex, Mays Landing, NJ*

f I love using *The Mailbox®* ideas and activities as a curriculum supplement. Many of the activities are great for creating portable centers. I put the activities in resealable plastic bags, baskets, or recycled shoeboxes so students can complete the activities anywhere!—*Charisse Audra Collier via Facebook*

Pumpkin Picking

Since I am unable to take my youngsters to the pumpkin patch, I bring the pumpkin patch to them! I have families donate small pumpkins, and I put the pumpkins in my sensory table. I have my students sit in a circle and pass a pumpkin cutout as I play a musical recording. I stop the music and invite the child with the cutout to go and "pick" a pumpkin. I continue until each child has a pumpkin to take home. *Diana Oldham, Colt Early Childhood Center, Lansing, MI*

Our Readers WRITE...
(and EMAIL and BLOG and TWEET and POST)

Unwrap the Fun

I keep little ones focused during the holidays with this engaging idea! For each child, I wrap up the materials for a snack, craft, game, or other seasonal activity. Over several days, I invite a child to open a gift and display the contents for his classmates. Then we use the materials to complete the activity. *Luann Wilson, Jim Thorpe Elementary, Henderson, NV*

The MAILBOX BLOG

"I have used *The Mailbox* for 28 years! I love everything about the magazine and can't wait to read it once it arrives...Keep up the good work!"
—*Rhonda Mann via The Mailbox® Blog*

A Gingerbread Tale

A few weeks before this activity, I send a note to parents requesting that they contact relatives near and far and ask each of them to send a letter and/or a photo to our class about the gingerbread man's escapades in their towns. After I read aloud the story *The Gingerbread Man*, we make and bake a gingerbread man that then "escapes" from our oven. (I ask another teacher to remove it from the oven.) As the letters arrive, I share them with the students and we mark on a map all the states that the gingerbread man visits. To end the activity, I surprise youngsters with a plate full of gingerbread men for a snack. *Sue Lein, St. Jude the Apostle School, Wauwatosa, WI*

BLOCK GALLERY

I take pictures of my students building in the block center. Then I print the pictures and attach them to a wall in the center. My youngsters love to see themselves pictured on the wall, and they enjoy reviewing the creations they've made. Many also use the pictures as inspiration for their own block creations! It's become a very popular display in my room. *Linda Heavrin, Benton, IL*

"I like how practical the ideas are for the grade-level skills and how easy the reproducibles are for the activities and learning centers."—*Jeanine Bulber via Facebook*

PAINT CARTONS

Don't waste small amounts of leftover paint—try this! I pour each color of leftover paint into a separate section of an empty, sterilized egg carton. I let the paints dry until they are hard. Then my students use them like watercolors. **Lynn Hanney, A Child's Haven, Valrico, FL**

Winter Break Sharing

I plan show-and-tell for the day after winter break. I invite each child to bring in a favorite gift she received during the holidays. She shows the gift to her classmates and explains why it is a favorite. (If you have students whose families do not give gifts, have each child bring in an item that represents a favorite activity he participated in during the break.) *Patricia Kessler, Ridley Park Presbyterian Church Nursery School, Ridley Park, PA*

Praiseworthy Email

My best tip for working with parents is to send them a quick email about something specific their child said or did in class. The biggest hit is to send a photo of their child working on something. *Jill Exe, Harold Kaveolook School, Kaktovik, AK, via The Mailbox® Blog*

The MAILBOX® BLOG

"I love *The Mailbox* magazines. I have kept them over the years and have quite a collection! The magazines are jam-packed full of great stuff!—*Mary McGowan via The Mailbox® Blog*

A Blast From the Past

Give your music area a fun retro feel with vinyl records. I purchase all sizes of records at thrift stores and secondhand stores for next to nothing. I put some of the records on the wall of my music area, and I hang others from the ceiling. The records not only make great decorations, but they can also be used to reinforce the concept of small, medium, and large. **Nancy Foss, Wee Care Preschool, Galion, OH**

Which Way?

Help little ones differentiate between their left and right with this quick tip. I gather a class supply of shaped rubber bracelets. When we sing a song or do an activity that requires youngsters to know their left from their right, I put a bracelet on each child's right wrist. Youngsters can quickly identify their left and right by looking at their wrists! **Rose Kane, Dundee Children's Center, Dundee, NY**

Our Readers WRITE...

(and EMAIL and BLOG and TWEET and POST)

Funny Faces

I always keep my camera close at hand. When I see a child making a funny face or a face that shows excitement, amazement, or joy, I snap a picture. Then I print the photos and share them with my youngsters. I encourage them to discuss what they were doing and how they felt. Then I add the photos to a poster board display. Parents and visitors always enjoy checking out these fun and engaging photos! *Stephanie Angle, The Learning Center, Hagerstown, MD*

FILLED WITH KINDNESS

To promote kindness, I read the book *Have You Filled a Bucket Today?: A Guide to Daily Happiness for Kids* by Carol McCloud. Then I display a bucket labeled as shown. My youngsters let me know when they have done something kind or someone has done something kind for them. I write the kind deed on a slip of paper and invite the child to drop it in the bucket. Our goal is to fill the bucket by the end of the year. *Sharon Bianchetti, Dutch Neck Presbyterian Church Co-Op Nursery School, Princeton Junction, NJ*

Puzzle Mats

Our youngest preschoolers and those with motor difficulties have a tough time putting together puzzles. To make it easier, I put each puzzle together, scan it, and then print a color copy. I laminate the resulting mats and store each one with its corresponding puzzle. A child places the mat on a work surface and then puts the puzzle together on top of the mat. *Julie Burgel, Clark County Early Learning Center's Montessori Preschool, Winchester, KY*

All Aboard!

I encourage youngsters to be quiet in the hallways while reinforcing letter sounds. When my little ones line up, I say, "All aboard the [B] train." Then students whisper "/b/, /b/, /b/" as we walk down the hall. After a few minutes, I switch letters to practice a different sound!—*Jacqueline Harbison, Holy Savior Academy, South Plainfield, NJ*

Our Readers WRITE...

(and EMAIL and BLOG and TWEET and POST)

STUCK ON LEARNING

I created a magnet center from an oil drip pan! Simply go to a discount or an auto parts store and purchase an oil drip pan. They are approximately 2' x 4' long and can be attached to the backs of shelving units or can simply lean against a wall. Provide a variety of magnets, and your center is ready!
Brenda Taylor, Clements/Parsons Elementary, Copperas Cove, TX

A Sweet Topping

Cream cheese and frosting can be difficult for young preschoolers to spread. When a sweet recipe calls for one of these, I substitute whipped topping. It spreads easily and is just as yummy! *Chantal Bass, Little Scouts, Lake Forest, IL*

Project Memories

Whenever my youngsters are involved in a special project, I take several photos. Then I create a display that contains student work, the photos I have taken, and a summary of the project that includes the state standards that were met along with students' observations and comments. *Christine A. Jones, Teachable Moments Family Day Care, Juliustown, NJ*

A Heartfelt Keepsake

I purchase inexpensive wooden hearts at a craft store. Then I have each child paint a heart. When the paint is dry, I have her make fingerprints around the inside edge. Then I glue the child's photo to the heart. To complete the project, I add a small eye hook. Then I tie a bow around the hook and attach a ribbon loop for hanging.
Nancy J. Hilbert, Sonbeam Preschool, McKeesport, PA

The MAILBOX® BLOG

Make a Change

When a student demonstrates inappropriate behavior, I invite the students who it affects to tell him how his actions made them feel. Then I give the child a chance to try again using acceptable behavior. This approach helps struggling youngsters learn how their actions affect others. —*Linda Utley, Little Pals Preschool, Herriman, UT*

Our Readers WRITE...

(and EMAIL and BLOG and TWEET and POST)

Simple Socks

Windsocks can be a time-consuming craft. For an easier option, I have my students make theirs with paper lunch bags! A youngster simply trims the bottom from a bag and decorates it. Then I invite her to glue crepe paper streamers along the bottom of her windsock. To complete the project, I staple a paper handle to the top. *Mandi Ellis, Minnieland Private Day School, Gainsville, VA*

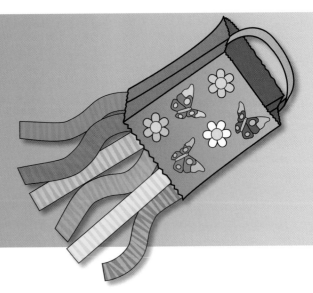

Visit the Park

During my spring theme, I decorate my dramatic-play area so it resembles our local park. I add a picnic basket filled with picnic supplies to the area. Youngsters play and make connections to experiences they've had in the real park. *Ruth Zabelin, Kleberg Elementary, Kingsville, TX*

Fun for April Fools' Day

This April Fools' Day prank is sure to elicit giggles from your little ones. Throughout the year, I save a few napkins from each holiday. Then, on April Fools' Day, I serve snacks on these napkins. I always hear lots of giggles during this snacktime! *Karen Eiben, The Learning House Preschool, La Salle, IL*

A NEW USE

Earth Day is a perfect time to show students how to reuse items. I save plastic takeout containers with lids, like the one shown. When youngsters are doing projects with several pieces, I give each child a container or lid. He places his pieces in the container or lid to keep them from getting lost or mixed with his neighbor's pieces. *Brenda Lehman, Westminster Preschool, West Chester, PA*

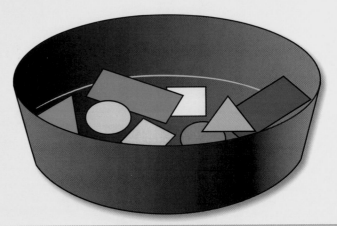

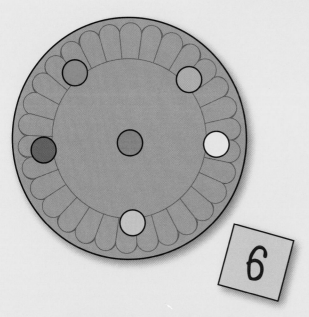

CANDY COOKIES

Sticky dots have many uses, but my students like to pretend that they are M&M's candies. I set out small paper plates, colorful sticky dots (candies), and a facedown stack of number cards. A child colors a plate so it resembles a cookie. Then she takes a card, reads the number and places a matching number of candies on her cookie. **Ruth Zabelin, Kleberg Elementary, Kingsville, TX**

Basic Needs

Here is a tip that I find helpful when working with ESL students. Before the child joins your class, find a resource, such as picture cards, that will give him a way to communicate his most basic needs, such as going to the bathroom, getting a drink of water, or feeling sick. *Darlene Taig, Willow Creek Preschool, Westland, MI*

On top of the box:
Moms are very busy from the day into the night.
You always take good care of me
And teach me wrong from right.
So here's a first aid kit for you.
It's filled with helpful things
To help you each and every day,
No matter what it brings.

Inside the box:
A tissue to dry your tears,
A Hug and a Kiss like the ones you give me,
A tiny eraser to rub out my little mistakes,
A bingo chip because you can count on me,
A tea bag so you can take a break,
My tiny hand for you to hold—
I love you mom and always will, even when I am very old.

First Aid For Mom

This Mother's Day treat is one that will be remembered for years to come. I help each child decorate a box. Then he glues a copy of the poem on the top of the box and a copy of the list on the inside lid. Finally, he places the following items in the box: a tissue, a Hershey's Kiss and a Hug, a small eraser, a bingo chip, a tea bag, and a hand cutout. **Joni Macaulay, Edwards-Knox Central School, Russell, NY**

PHONE A FRIEND

When a child has difficulty answering a question, I give him the option of "phoning" a friend! The child pretends to dial a phone and names a friend. Then the friends have a conversation about the answer to the question. *Katie King, Kinderhouse Preschool, Sarasota, FL*

Personable Pointers!

To hold my youngsters' attention during circle time, I give our pointers a bit of personality! I've attached various well-known characters, such as Barney and Yoda, to individual pointers. Then, when I point to something that needs identifying, I say, for example, "What is Yoda pointing to?" My youngsters love it! *Carole Watkins, Timothy Ball Elementary, Crown Point, IN*

A Beautiful Board

To add a little pizzazz to an ocean-themed bulletin board, I attach plastic wrap over the board! It gives the board a fun water-themed feel, as if my youngsters' fish and octopus crafts are in a large aquarium! —*Darlene Taig, Willow Creek Preschool, Westland, MI*

A Day With Our Dads

To celebrate Father's Day, I ask each child's father to sign up for a time to visit our classroom on a day near Father's Day. To ensure that no child is left out, grandfathers, uncles, or older brothers can fill in for a dad if necessary. During each dad's time, he can choose to do a lesson with the class, read a favorite book, or join in the activities the class is doing. At the end of his scheduled time, his child presents him with a small gift. *Kimberly Pausa, European School of Trieste, Trieste, Italy*

Patriotic Painting

Prior to this Fourth of July project, I study the American flag with my students, having them note the different parts of the design. Then I have each child paint a large river rock white. When the paint dries, I encourage her to paint the top left corner of her rock blue. Then I direct her to paint red stripes on the remainder of the rock. Finally, I have her add small white dots (stars) to the blue section. *Tina Borek, Gateway Christian, Albuquerque, NM*

PROBLEM SOLVED!

Problem Solved!

Your Solutions to Classroom Challenges

I have a pretty polished rock that I refer to as my peace stone. When a youngster is crying and distressed, I allow him to hold the stone and turn it over and over in his hands until he feels better. It really is quite soothing!

Donna Olp, St. Gregory the Great Preschool, South Euclid, OH

When a youngster's crying becomes a daily occurrence, I give the little one a small clock to carry around. I gently explain that when the clock hands reach a certain number, it is time to cry. Youngsters love the security of carrying something tangible, and they forget all about crying!

Ronna Adkins, First Baptist Church Day School, Pikeville, KY

Research has shown that teachers' positive interaction styles with children help children build emotionally secure relationships with adults.

M. M. Ostrosky and E. Y. Jung, Center on the Social and Emotional Foundations for Early Learning

I have parents send in family pictures, and I put them in a photo album. I place the album in a corner of the classroom along with a sign labeled "Cozy Corner." I also place pillows and a couple of snuggly stuffed toys in the area. When little ones are feeling blue, I have them visit the Cozy Corner for a few minutes to hold the stuffed toys and look at the pictures.

Amy Cannon, The Goddard School, Cranberry Township, PA

To calm little ones who are crying, I turn over a sand timer and lead students in quietly singing this song.

(sung to the tune of "London Bridge")

Sand is falling, sand is falling.
Tears are done, tears are done.
Sand is falling, sand is falling.
Tears are done.

Doria Owen, William Paca Old Post Road Elementary, Abingdon, MD

It's your turn! Share your ideas.
themailbox.com/submitideas

How do you monitor *student* progress?

 I have a binder in which each child has a section. I keep tiny sticky notes and a pen in my pocket at all times. When I see a student struggling or excelling in a particular area, I jot down a note. Then at the end of the day, I stick all the notes to the appropriate sections of the binder.

Amanda Tejkowski, Barkley Elementary, Ft. Campbell, KY

Anecdotal notes empower teachers by recognizing their judgment as essential to accurate records. Ann S. Epstein, Lawrence J. Schweinhart, Andrea DeBruin-Parecki, and Kenneth B. Robin, Preschool Assessment: A Guide to Developing a Balanced Approach

 To monitor youngsters' progress, I label index cards with different skills that need to be assessed and then I put the cards on a metal ring. I give identical rings to each adult working in the classroom. When an adult sees one of the skills being addressed by a specific child, she jots down a note on the card. I use these cards for focusing future observations and for parent-teacher conferences.

Carole Watkins, Crown Point, IN

 I keep a few sheets of blank adhesive mailing labels handy! I can jot down a few notes about a youngster's performance and then simply remove the label and attach it to that child's portfolio. Simple!

Beth Sharpe, The Malvern School of Medford, Medford, NJ

 To monitor progress of fine-motor skills, I make a packet of coloring pages for each child, labeling one page for each month in the school year. I do the same with cutting patterns. At the end of each month, I have each youngster color a page and cut out a pattern. I store their finished work and it's very easy to see student progress!

Rene Green, East Side Preschool, Effingham, IL

It's your turn! Share your ideas.
themailbox.com/submitideas

Problem Solved!

How do you *get youngsters dressed* quickly for winter weather?

Your Solutions to Classroom Challenges

A favorite **musical recording**, like "Frosty the Snowman," motivates my class to dress quickly for outdoor play! I have each child gather her winter garments. Then I play the recording and challenge youngsters to get dressed before the song ends.

Jennifer Gemar, Tripp-Delmont School, Tripp, SD

I have each parent send in a **canvas tote bag**. Students hang one strap on a coat hook and let the other strap hang free. Then they place mittens, hats, and scarves in the totes. The totes stay open, allowing children easy access.

Diane Harrison, St. Bernard's School, Watertown, WI

A lot of people like snow. I find it to be an unnecessary freezing of water.

—Carl Reiner

I encourage my students to zip their own coats with a story called **"The Hungry Monkey."** The hungry monkey (zipper pull) puts a whole banana (zipper pin) in his mouth and then climbs the tree (zips the coat) to finish eating so no one will take it away. My youngsters love to tell the story and practice zipping!

Alexis Gruehn, Classroom of Discovery, Sterling, VA; Mindi Morton, Mindi's Oak Tree Preschool, North San Juan, CA

I take pictures of a child putting on winter outerwear. Then I **post the photos** in sequential order. I help youngsters review the dressing sequence and then sing this song to keep them on track while dressing.

Claudine Fredy, Iola-Scandinavia Elementary, Iola, WI; Nancy Dawson, New Horizons Preschool, Anchorage, AK

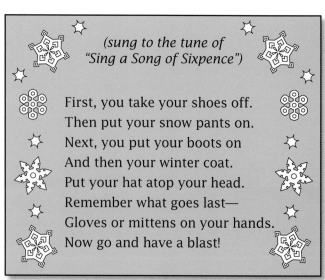

(sung to the tune of "Sing a Song of Sixpence")

First, you take your shoes off.
Then put your snow pants on.
Next, you put your boots on
And then your winter coat.
Put your hat atop your head.
Remember what goes last—
Gloves or mittens on your hands.
Now go and have a blast!

It's your turn! Share your ideas.
themailbox.com/submitideas

Problem Solved!

How do you organize your *lesson plans and props?*

Your Solutions to Classroom Challenges

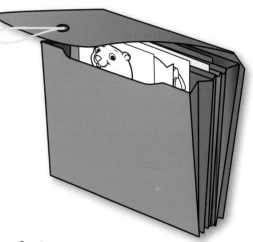

Three-prong folders are perfect for organizing my lesson plans. I write a theme name on the outside of a folder and add sheet protectors for storing curriculum ideas, patterns, and reproducibles. The folders are thin and easy to store, and the pockets are perfect for keeping art samples and a theme-related issue of *The Mailbox* magazine!

Christina Kasler, A Home Away From Home Childcare, Vacaville, CA

Accordion folders are great for storing lesson plans and small props like stick puppets, pointers, pattern pieces, and weather symbols. I prepare daily lessons and tuck each one into its own section labeled for that day. This system is convenient; takes up little space; and, if I'm out unexpectedly, coworkers and substitutes can easily find what they need!

Deborah Gill, Bright Beginnings, Limerick, PA

To organize my lesson plans, I use **color index cards**. I list art ideas on one color, math ideas on another, and so on. I bind the cards together on a metal ring for easy transport or place each card in an appropriate area for easy reference. Either way, it's easy!

Melanie Marie Hays, Crossgates Methodist Children's Center, Brandon, MS

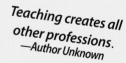

Teaching creates all other professions.
—Author Unknown

I use **monthly and holiday file folders** to organize my lesson plans, patterns, coloring pages, song cards, and more. Then I store the folders in a file crate for easy access. To keep a current lesson plan handy throughout the day, I simply attach it to a clipboard.

Heather Goodwin, SpringHouse Learning Station, Eighty-Four, PA
Kara Continenza, St. Mark's Building Blocks Preschool, Youngstown, OH

It's your turn! Share your ideas.
themailbox.com/submitideas

Problem Solved!

Your Solutions to Classroom Challenges

 How do you celebrate the *end of the school year* with your students?

A few weeks before our graduation ceremony, I ask each child to share memories and the things he likes about a few of his classmates. Then I make a **slide show,** to be shown during the graduation ceremony, using photos of each child and the comments her classmates made about her.

Sally Mowers, Pinckney Elementary, Pinckney, MI

An **ice cream social** is a fun and yummy way to celebrate the end of the school year. I send a note to each child's family inviting them to the social. I provide the ice cream, disposable bowls, and plastic spoons. Then I ask each family to bring an ice cream topping, such as chocolate syrup, sprinkles, cut-up fruit, or mini chocolate chips.

Jennifer Schear, Wright Elementary, Cedar Rapids, IA

I've learned that people will forget what you said, people will forget what you did, but people will never forget how you made them feel .

—*Maya Angelou*

Our end-of-the-year celebration is a **Beach and Boardwalk Day**. Students wear their favorite beach attire. They paint seashells, make sand art creations, and get temporary tattoos. The giggles continue as they play boardwalk-themed games to win tickets that can be redeemed for prizes. To conclude the celebration, we sit on our beach towels while we eat pizza and ice pops.

Laura Allison, Christ the Teacher Catholic School, Newark, DE

I give each child a blank white **notecard** and an envelope. On the front of the notecard, I have her draw a picture to show one of her favorite memories from the school year. Then I help her address her envelope to herself. During the summer, I write a note to each child on her card and mail it to her.

Roxanne LaBell Dearman, NC Early Intervention Program for Children Who Are Deaf or Hard of Hearing, Charlotte, NC

It's your turn! Share your ideas.
themailbox.com/submitideas

Science Explorations

Science Explorations

Terrific Textures

Little ones explore unique textures with this easy-to-prepare investigation!

idea contributed by Amanda Martz
McKenzie's Christian Learning Garden
Montoursville, PA

Materials:

shallow tub	water
oatmeal	mixing spoon
flour	

STEP 1

Pour oatmeal in the tub and have youngsters touch and manipulate the oatmeal. Ask them to describe how it looks and feels. If desired, prompt them with words such as *crumbly*, *soft*, or *fluffy*. Next, pour some flour in the tub.

STEP 2

Have students gently stir the flour and oatmeal together with their hands. Encourage them to describe how the texture is different from just plain oatmeal. Ask, "Do you like to touch the plain oatmeal or the oatmeal with the flour more? Why?"

STEP 3

Next, ask students to predict what will happen if you pour some water into the mixture. After students share their thoughts, pour a small amount of water in the tub and mix the ingredients. Prompt students to touch the mixture and describe how it has changed. The mixture feels gooey and sticky.

STEP 4

Keep adding water, encouraging students to describe how the increased water makes the mixture less sticky and more slimy. What a fun texture exploration!

What Next?

Have students compare this mixture to the cake batter mixture on page 195. Which mixture is more pleasing to touch? Why?

Science Explorations

Making Craters

This easy-to-prepare science investigation makes a big impact with little scientists!

Materials:
plastic container with high sides
flour
round rocks in three different sizes

STEP 1

Put flour in the container and have each child touch the flour and describe it. Shake the container gently to smooth out the surface of the flour. Encourage little ones to notice how smooth it is.

STEP 2

Pick up the smallest rock and have students touch and describe it. Then ask, "What do you think will happen if we drop the rock into the flour?" After youngsters share their thoughts, have a child drop the rock into the flour. Carefully remove the rock and have students notice the impact crater left behind. Prompt little ones to explain what happened.

STEP 3

Hold up the medium-size rock and lead students to notice that it's larger than the original rock. Ask youngsters to predict how this impact crater will be different. Continue as before, having a child drop the rock in the flour. Then encourage students to compare the two craters.

STEP 4

Repeat the process with the largest rock and compare all three craters.

What Next?

- Show youngsters a picture of the moon and have them notice the craters. Ask, "How do you think the moon got all its craters?"
- Repeat the experiment using only one rock, but dropping it from different heights.

Science Explorations

Amazing Magnetism!

Little ones discover firsthand how an invisible force called magnetism attracts objects containing certain types of metals.

idea contributed by Lee Ann McGee
Brockton Community Partnership Early Childhood Preschool Program
Brockton, MA

Materials:
strong magnet
magnetic materials (large safety pin, jumbo paper clip, nail, washer)
nonmagnetic materials (eraser, cork, plastic spoon, dime)
2 trays (one labeled "magnetic" and one "nonmagnetic")

STEP 1

Show the magnet. Ask, "Does anyone know what this object is?" After concluding that it's a magnet, ask youngsters to tell what they know about magnets. After children share their thoughts, explain that a magnet is an object that has an invisible force called magnetism that draws certain objects to it.

STEP 2

Display the nail and the cork. Ask, "What do you think will happen if the magnet touches the nail?" Repeat the question concerning the cork. Encourage youngsters to share their thoughts and explain their reasoning. Then invite a child to test both items with the magnet to see what happens. Have him place each item on the appropriate tray; then repeat the process with the remaining items and other students.

STEP 3

Ask, "Do you think magnets are important?" After youngsters have an opportunity to share, explain that many things we use every day—such as computers, DVD players, and speakers—have magnets in them to help make them work. Magnets are also useful for holding pictures and artwork on refrigerator doors!

What Next?

Give each child a magnet and have him walk around the classroom touching the magnet to various surfaces. Did he find anything that is attracted to the magnet?

Science Explorations

Animals and Oil

With this investigation, youngsters explore the negative effects of an oil spill on animals.

*idea contributed by Judy Charles
Kidtown USA, Schaumburg, IL*

Materials:

2 tubs of water
plastic sea animal toys
vegetable oil

black pepper
dish soap
scrub brush

STEP 1

Put the animals in a tub of water. Have students notice how clean the water is. Ask youngsters how they think the animals feel playing in the nice clean water.

STEP 2

Next, have each child take an animal out of the water and feel it. Encourage her to describe its texture. Prompt students to place their animals back in the water. Then put a generous amount of oil and black pepper in the water. (The pepper makes it easier for youngsters to see the oil.) Direct students to describe the water.

STEP 3

Encourage each child to touch one of the animals, describing how it feels. Ask, "What do you think the oil will do to the animals?" Discuss how the oil can hurt their skin or feathers and make them sick. Ask, "What could be done to clean the animals?" Have students discuss various options for removing the oil from the animals.

STEP 4

Provide the other tub of water, the soap, and the scrub brush. Have students scrub the animals with soap and clean water until the oily residue is removed. Remind little ones that it's important to keep water clean so the animals will be healthy and happy.

Did You Know?

Dawn dishwashing liquid is regularly used to remove crude oil from marine wildlife after an oil spill! Its ability to remove most oils and nonirritating ingredients make it effective yet gentle.

Science Explorations

Pretty in Pink

Youngsters explore a unique vegetable with this low-prep investigation!

idea contributed by Svetlana Borukhova
Herbert G. Birch Western Queens Early Childhood Center
Long Island City, NY

Materials:
beet
knife (for teacher use only)
container of water

STEP 1

Show students the beet and ask them what the object reminds them of and what they think it is. Prompt several youngsters to share and then lead them to conclude that the object is the root of a plant, it's a vegetable, and it's called a beet.

STEP 2

Allow each child to touch and describe the beet. Ask him what color the beet is. Next, cut the beet in half and prompt students to observe and describe the interior. Once again, ask youngsters to describe the color of the beet. Students may change their minds once they see its vibrant interior!

STEP 3

Ask students to predict what will happen when the colorful beet is placed in the water. After several students share, have a child place the beet halves in the water. Then encourage students to observe. Little ones will notice that the water begins to turn pink! Encourage students to explain why they think the water is changing color.

What Next?

It's time for some beet painting! Boil cut beets in water until the water is quite colorful. Then, when the water is cool, allow students to use it to paint on sturdy paper. (For a simpler version, use the juice from canned beets as paint.)

SONGS & SUCH

Songs & Such

Good Morning!

This wonderful morning song will get everyone moving! Be sure to prompt youngsters to wiggle during the third and fourth lines of the song.

(sung to the tune of "If You're Happy and You Know It")

Good morning, [student name], how are you? (Student: Fine, fine!)
Good morning, [student name], how are you? (Student: Fine, fine!)
With a wiggle, wiggle, wiggle,
And a jiggle, jiggle, jiggle!
Good morning, [student name], how are you? (Student: Fine, fine!)

Angela Myers
Corner Campus
Salisbury, MD

Special Day

Make your students' birthdays even more special with this adorable song! Simply lead little ones in serenading the birthday child, changing "girl" to "boy" if needed.

(sung to the tune of the chorus of "Jingle Bells")

Birthday girl, birthday girl,
It's your special day!
We can't wait to celebrate in a very special way.
Birthday girl, birthday girl,
It's your special day!
We can't wait to celebrate in a very special way!

Randy McGovern
Twin Oaks Country Day School
Freeport, NY

See pages 194–196 for more birthday-themed fun!

Hallway Walking

Here's a little chant that will help little ones remember to walk quietly in the hallway. It's extra effective if you have youngsters recite the chant with quiet voices!

When we're walking in the hall
We mustn't talk—no, not at all.
Only feet move when we walk.
Because it is not time to talk.

Kenda Armstrong
Imogene Glenn Elementary
Yantis, TX

Apple Farmer

Write the letters *A, P, P, L,* and *E* on separate apple cutouts and place them in your pocket chart. Sing the song shown five times, flipping over an apple each time and replacing the letter with a clap like the traditional "Bingo" song.

(sung to the tune of "Bingo")

There was a farmer had some trees.
His apples were so tasty!
A-P-P-L-E!
A-P-P-L-E!
A-P-P-L-E!
His apples were so tasty!

Linda Gill
St. Joseph Catholic School
Chicago, IL

Songs & Such

What Is the Weather?

After your weather boy (or girl) identifies the weather for the day, lead students in singing this catchy song!

(sung to the tune of "Short'nin' Bread")

What is the weather, weather, weather?
What did the weather boy say today?
He said it's [sunny, sunny, sunny]!
He said it's [sunny] outside today!

Krystal St. Louis
Children's Development Center
New Bedford, MA

Getting Settled

This fun action chant is sure to settle little ones for circle time. Begin by wiggling your hands to get youngsters' attention. Then lead them in performing the chant!

I wiggle them to the left.	*Wiggle hands to the left.*
I wiggle them to the right.	*Wiggle hands to the right.*
I wiggle them in the air	*Wiggle hands up in the air.*
And fold them up tight.	*Fold hands beneath your chin.*
I wiggle them on my nose.	*Wiggle hands on top of nose.*
I wiggle them on my chin.	*Wiggle hands on chin.*
I snap and clap.	*Snap and then clap.*
I snap and clap.	*Snap and then clap.*
And then I give a grin!	*Point to smile with both hands.*

China Sheffield
Stoughton Extended Day Preschool
Stoughton, MA

Active Autumn!

This engaging action song will be a fall favorite! Lead students in performing the song, adding the suggested actions.

(sung to the tune of "London Bridge")

Autumn leaves are falling down,   *Wiggle fingers to the floor.*
Falling down, falling down.
Autumn leaves are falling down.
Autumn leaves!

Continue with the following: Rake them up into a pile *(pretend to rake)*; Jump on them and crunch, crunch, crunch *(jump up and down)*; Toss them up into the air *(pretend to toss leaves)*

Kelli Wack, YMCA, Fort Wayne, IN

Boo!

Here's a silly Halloween song that has adorable visuals! Cut out a copy of the patterns on page 156 and attach a piece of tape to the back of each cutout. Lead students in singing the song, attaching the spider to your board when indicated. Repeat the song three more times, attaching a new pattern and changing the word appropriately each time.

(sung to the tune of "Five Little Ducks")

Five little pumpkins I once knew—
Scary ones, happy ones, sad ones too.
But the one in the front with a [spider] on its shoe,
It led the others with a boo, boo, boo!
Boo, boo, boo, boo, boo, boo!
It led the others with a boo, boo, boo!

Jenna Smith, Children's Elite Preschool, Macclenny, FL

For extra fun, give each child a set of cutouts and have him place the appropriate cutout on his own shoe for each verse!

Songs & Such

All Through the Night

What makes noise on a fall night? Youngsters find out with this song! Lead students in singing the song shown. Then continue with other suggested verses.

(sung to the tune of "The Wheels on the Bus")

The wings on the bat go flap, flap, flap,   *Flap arms.*
Flap, flap, flap, flap flap, flap!
The wings on the bat go flap, flap, flap—
All through the night!

Suggested verses: The legs on the spider go skitter, skitter, skitter *(wiggle fingers over arm)*; The beak on the owl goes click, click, click *(move hand like a beak)*; The wind through the trees goes groan, groan, groan *(move arms like branches)*; The moon in the sky shines bright, bright, bright *(hold arms to make a circle)*

Annette Payne
Lawrence County Early Childhood Center
South Point, OH

Hungry Pilgrims!

These little Pilgrims are ready for a Thanksgiving Day meal!

Five little Pilgrims were in a grumpy mood.
The first one said, "I'm ready for some food!"
The second one said, "Some turkey would be nice."
The third one said, "Or a pumpkin pie slice!"
The fourth one said, "Mashed potatoes, please."
The fifth one said, "And some nice green peas!"
With a chew and a gulp and a munch, munch, munch,
The five little Pilgrims were a happy bunch!

Kristen Hill
Sea Island Presbyterian Day School
Lady's Island, SC

Chilly Winter!

Give each child a piece of rope tinsel. Then encourage students to swirl their tinsel through the air as you lead them in singing this song.

(sung to the tune of "Twinkle, Twinkle, Little Star")

Wintertime brings lots of snow.
Chilly winds just blow and blow.
Snowflakes swirling through the air,
Twirling, whirling here and there.
Wintertime brings lots of snow.
Chilly winds just blow and blow.

Deborah Garmon
Groton, CT

Happy Hanukkah!

Here's a catchy song that helps little ones learn the signs and symbols of Hanukkah!

(sung to the tune of "This Old Man")

Candles shine,
Dreidels spin,
Crafts to make,
And coins to win.
There are tasty latkes,
Gifts and songs and plays!
Hanukkah lasts eight great days!

Jacqueline Schiff
Moline, IL

Songs & Such

Assemble a Tree

To make props for this interactive rhyme, cut the following from felt: three green triangles in different sizes (evergreen branches); a brown rectangle (trunk); red, yellow, and blue circles (ornaments); colorful squares (presents); and a yellow star (tree topper). Give each felt shape to a child. Then lead students in reciting the rhyme and placing the pieces on a felt board when indicated.

Every year at Christmas,	*Place largest triangle.*
We have a Christmas tree.	*Place medium triangle.*
It looks so good; it glistens.	*Place smallest triangle.*
It's as pretty as can be!	*Place trunk.*
And on it we hang ornaments,	*Place ornaments.*
Some red, some yellow, some blue.	
And underneath are presents,	*Place presents.*
Some for me and some for you!	
Way up at the top,	*Place star.*
Put up high and oh so far,	
Is my favorite decoration—	
It's a sparkly Christmas star!	

Robin Johnson
Cromwell, MN

Disappearing Candy Canes!

Lead students in performing this adorable action chant five times, reducing the number by one each time. Finally, perform the final verse. Then ask little ones to share who they think ate the candy canes.

Five little candy canes hanging on the tree.	*Hold up five fingers.*
Somebody ate one, but it wasn't me!	*Hold up one finger; point to self.*
Momma told grandma, and grandma said,	*Move hands so they resemble mouths.*
"No more candy canes. Now get to bed!"	*Shake index finger.*

Final verse:

Zero little candy canes hanging on the tree.	*Make a zero with fingers.*
They disappeared—what a mystery!	*Throw arms out to side.*
We've searched everywhere high and low.	*Look high and low*
Who could have eaten them? I'd like to know!	*Shake index finger.*

Adapted from an idea by Arlene McLean, Calvary Christian Preschool, Concord, CA

Happy New Year!

Chinese New Year begins on February 10, 2013. Spotlight this holiday with a joyful song!

(sung to the tune of "Ten Little Indians")

[Happy, happy Chinese New Year]!
[Happy, happy Chinese New Year]!
[Happy, happy Chinese New Year]!
Good luck all year long!

Continue with the following:
Let's say hello by saying, "*Ni hao.*"
Let's have fish and tasty dumplings.
Let's give packets filled with money.
Let's hear lots of firecrackers.

adapted from an idea by Betty Cheng
Ocean View Preschool
San Pedro, CA

Ni hao.

The Traffic Light Song

Youngsters are sure to ask for repeats of this active song. Get red, green, and yellow circle cutouts. Then lead youngsters in singing the song as you hold up each circle when indicated. Prompt youngsters to march quickly when you're holding the green circle and slowly when you're holding the yellow circle.

(sung to the tune of "This Old Man")

Red means *stop*.
Green means *go*.
Yellow light means *please, go slow*.
When you're out, watch the lights,
And then you will know
When to stop and when to go!

Debbie Love, BUF Preschool, Plainfield, NJ

Songs &Such

Valentine Time!

To prepare for this song and activity, write each child's name on a separate heart cutout (valentine) and place it in a tote bag. Give the bag to a child (mail carrier) and seat the remaining students in a circle. Have the mail carrier walk around the circle while leading students in singing the song. Then have the mail carrier draw a valentine and help him sing the second verse of the song. Have him identify the name and then give the valentine to the appropriate child. Continue with a different mail carrier.

(sung to the tune of "The Muffin Man")

Do you have a valentine,
A valentine, a valentine?
Do you have a valentine,
A valentine for me?

Yes, I have a valentine,
A valentine, a valentine.
Yes, I have a valentine.
Who is it for? Let's see!

I'm an Artist!

Grab little ones' attention with this song before engaging them in an art project!

(sung to the tune of "Clementine")

I am drawing with my markers.
I am shaping with my clay.
I am painting with my brushes.
I am making art today!

I am gluing colored paper,
Fingerpainting in a tray.
I am shaking sparkly glitter.
I am making art today!

Jacqueline Schiff
Moline, IL

Colorful Clothing

This active song makes a terrific time filler! Lead students in performing the song. Repeat the song several times, changing the underlined color each time.

(sung to the tune of "If You're Happy and You Know It")

If you're wearing [green], then jump up and down!
If you're wearing [green], then jump up and down!
If you're jumping up and down,
Clap your hands and turn around.
If you're wearing [green], then jump up and down!
Ka-boom! (spoken)

Children wearing green jump up and down.

Children wearing green clap their hands and turn around.

Children wearing green jump up and down.
Children sit down.

Susan Truss, Giant Steps, Hartford, CT

Circus Clown Countdown

Little ones will enjoy clowning around with this simple chant!

The circus clown knocked on the door.
One, two, three, four.   *Pretend to knock.*

The circus clown slapped his knees.
One, two, three.   *Slap your knees.*

The circus clown touched his shoes.
One, two.   *Touch your shoes.*

The circus clown looked at the sun
And counted only one.   *Shade eyes and then point.*

The circus clown sat on the ground.   *Sit down.*
And now we are done!

Marie E. Cecchini, West Dundee, IL

Songs & Such

Spring Is Here!

Lead students in singing this splendid song about spring! For extra performance pizzazz, give each child a length of curling ribbon in a pastel color. While students sing, encourage them to move the curling ribbon through the air as desired.

(sung to the tune of "Are You Sleeping?")

Spring is here!
Spring is here!
Flowers bloom
Here and there.
Rain is drippy droppy.
Mud is slippy sloppy.
I smell spring
In the air.

Turtle Time

Little ones pretend to be turtles with this action rhyme!

Here is a turtle curled up in its shell,
Hiding away so we can't tell.
Soon it will creep out of its shell—
Head, front legs, back legs, and tail!

Curl up in a ball with head sticking out.
Tuck head in.

Push out body parts and wiggle hips for the tail.

Janet Boyce, Cokato, MN

I Am a Kite!

Guide youngsters in swooping around the room as they sing this windy-day song!

(sung to the tune of "Five Little Ducks")

I am a kite. I love to play
Up in the sky on a windy day!
You can watch me dance and watch me sail.
Up in the sky, I flick my long kite tail,
Long kite tail, long kite tail.
Up in the sky, I flick my long kite tail.

I am a kite. I love to play
Up in the sky on a windy day!
You can watch me swoop. It's so much fun!
But when there is no wind, my time is done,
Time is done, time is done.
But when there is no wind, my time is done.

Suzanne Moore
Tucson, AZ

Bird Calls

Here's a toe-tapping song that's sure to be popular with your youngsters! To add an instrumental element to the song, give each of three children a different instrument, such as a triangle, a tambourine, and a maraca. Assign a different bird to each child. Then lead students in singing the song, prompting each child to play his instrument during his bird call.

(sung to the tune of "The Muffin Man")

Do you hear the [robins] sing?
"[Cheer-up, cheer-up]," their voices ring.
Do you hear the [robins] sing
On this fine day in spring?

Continue with the following: *bluebirds, Chur-lee, chur-lee; sparrows, Teedle-eet, Teedle-eet*

Jacqueline Schiff
Moline, IL

Songs & Such

Happy Mother's Day!

Have little ones sing this song for a Mother's Day celebration!

(sung to the tune of "This Old Man")

Hugs for you,
Kisses too!
Thank you, Mom, for all you do!
So sit back and relax—it's a special day!
Have a happy Mother's Day!

Suzanne Moore
Tucson, AZ

Five Pretty Flowers

Have five students (flowers) stand in a row facing the class. Then lead students in singing the first verse of the song, encouraging one flower to wilt to the ground when appropriate. Continue for three more rounds. Then sing the final verse. Finally, pretend to water the flowers and encourage them to all spring back up!

(sung to the tune of "Five Little Speckled Frogs")

[Five] pretty purple flowers
Stand in the sun for hours,
Waiting for all the bees to come. (Buzz! Buzz!)
One wilted to the ground.
No water could be found.
Now there [are] just [four] purple [flowers]. (Buzz! Buzz!)

Final Verse:
One pretty purple flower
Stands in the sun for hours,
Waiting for all the bees to come. (Buzz! Buzz!)
It wilted to the ground.
No water could be found.
Now there are no more purple flowers. (Buzz! Buzz!)

Pamela Cloyd, Kids R Kids, Hixson, TN

Daddy Sea Horse

This sweet song about a daddy sea horse is sure to be requested again and again! For extra fun, encourage your little ones to slowly "swim" around the room as they sing!

(sung to the tune of "Clementine")

Daddy sea horse, daddy sea horse,
Swimming in the deep blue sea,
Holding tightly to his babies
In his pouch so snuggly!

Babies hatching, babies hatching,
Hatching in the deep blue sea.
Thank you, daddy, daddy sea horse.
You have taken care of me!

Robyn Fox, Kiddie Kampus Preschool, Upland, IN

The Four Seasons

Here's an action song that's perfect throughout the year! Lead students in singing the song and pantomiming each verse.

(sung to the tune of "London Bridge")

In the fall, the leaves fall down,
Leaves fall down, leaves fall down.
In the fall, the leaves fall down.
I love seasons!

In the winter, brrrr, its cold!
Brrrr, it's cold! Brrrr, it's cold!
In the winter, brrrr, it's cold!
I love seasons!

In the spring, the flowers bloom,
Flowers bloom, flowers bloom!
In the spring, the flowers bloom.
I love seasons.

In the summer, it is hot!
/h/, /h/, hot! /h/, /h/, hot!
In the summer, it is hot!
I love seasons!

Alexandra Chrysosferidis
Mansell Child Development Center
Roswell, GA

Songs & Such

Five Little Bumblebees

You'll certainly hear a buzz of excitement about this adorable song! If desired, attach five bee cutouts to a flannelboard and remove one for each verse! Hint: Tweak the final verse slightly to work with just one bumblebee.

(sung to the tune of "Five Green and Speckled Frogs")

[Five] little bumblebees
Buzz round the flowers and trees,
Doing a happy honey dance. (Buzz, buzz!)
One went into a dive
And flew into the hive.
Now there are just [four] bumblebees. (Buzz, buzz!)

Sarah Booth
Messiah Nursery School
South Williamsport, PA

Beach Ball Bounce

Little ones will have a ball with this rhyme! Encourage students to pretend to bounce the ball as they count for each verse.

I found a ball upon the beach
[With stripes of red and blue].
I tossed the ball
And watched it fall.
[Then bounced it—one, two!]

Continue with the following:
As round as round can be/Then bounced it—one, two, three!
Where waves all splash and roar/Then bounced it—one, two, three, four!
Where seagulls fly and dive/Then bounced it—one, two, three, four, five!

Marie E. Cecchini
West Dundee, IL

Picnic Time!

Here's a catchy picnic-themed song that's just perfect for summer! For fun instrumental accompaniment, give each child two plastic utensils. Then lead children in singing several rounds of the song as they tap the utensils together. For additional instruments, have students tap heavy-duty disposable plates or plastic cups.

(sung to the tune of "Twinkle, Twinkle, Little Star")

Picnic, picnic—oh what fun!
Chips and hot dogs in a bun.
Ants are marching in a row,
Stopping by to say hello!
Picnic, picnic—oh what fun!
Chips and hot dogs in a bun.

adapted from an idea by Jana Sanderson
Rainbow School
Stockton, CA

Let's Go!

It's time for a vacation at the beach! Lead youngsters in performing this action song.

(sung to the tune of "The Farmer in the Dell")

We're going to the beach.	*March.*
We're going to the beach.	*March.*
[Let's put our swimsuits on!]	*Pretend to put on a swimsuit.*
We're going to the beach!	*March.*

Continue with the following:

Let's put our sunscreen on!	*Pretend to rub in sunscreen.*
Let's get our sand toys out!	*Pretend to shovel sand.*
Let's get our sunglasses!	*Make circles with fingers and place in front of your eyes.*
Let's pack a picnic lunch!	*Rub tummy.*

Cherie Durbin
Hickory, NC

TEC41063

TEC41063

TEC41063

TEC41063

STORYTIME

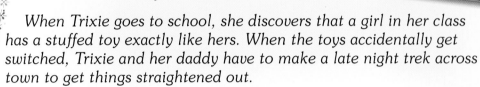

Knuffle Bunny Too: A Case of Mistaken Identity

By Mo Willems

When Trixie goes to school, she discovers that a girl in her class has a stuffed toy exactly like hers. When the toys accidentally get switched, Trixie and her daddy have to make a late night trek across town to get things straightened out.

ideas contributed by Margaret Aumen, Emory United Methodist Nursery School
New Oxford, PA

Before You Read

Display the cover of the book and read the title aloud. Explain that the story is about a little girl named Trixie and her stuffed bunny. Invite little ones to share how they think Trixie feels about her bunny and why they think this. Then ask them to talk about favorite stuffed toys they might have. Finally, ask little ones how they would feel if their toys were misplaced or lost. After youngsters share their thoughts, have them settle in for a read-aloud of the story.

I think she loves her bunny!

After You Read

Trixie and Sonja easily mix up their two bunnies because they look so similar! Cut out a copy of the cards on page 160 and put them in a bag. To begin, ask little ones to study the bunnies in the story and name differences between the two. They will be sure to notice that Sonja's bunny has a bow between its ears and Trixie's does not. Next, tell students that you have some other bunnies you would like them to look at. Have a child choose two cards from the bag. Encourage her to study the bunnies and name a difference. Then have her place the cards back in the bag. Continue in the same way with other volunteers.

Who Ate All the Cookie Dough?

Written by Karen Beaumont
Illustrated by Eugene Yelchin

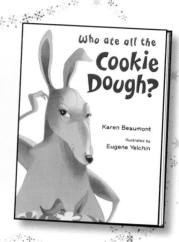

Kanga is all set to make some cookies, but where has the cookie dough gone? She checks with other animal friends to see if they ate her cookie dough and then discovers that the culprit is her own little joey!

Maybe a dog ate the cookie dough!

Before You Read

In advance, write an ingredients list for chocolate chip cookies on chart paper. Read the list aloud and prompt little ones to guess what could be made with the ingredients. When students have guessed correctly, explain that you have a mystery for them to solve. Hold up the book and read the title aloud. Ask, "Who do you think ate the cookie dough?" Have little ones make predictions. Then have youngsters listen to this attention-grabbing story!

After You Read

Create an adaptation of this adorable story! Place an empty bowl and spoon in your classroom before youngsters arrive. Also ask an adult helper or fellow teacher to write a brief note confessing that she ate the cookie dough. Place the note in your room. To begin, look in the bowl and say, "Oh my goodness! My cookie dough is gone!" Then recite the first part of the chant shown, inserting a child's name. Encourage the child to reply as directed. Continue until each child has had a turn. Then notice the note revealing the guilty culprit!

Teacher:
(Child's name), (child's name),
Do you know
Who ate all the cookie dough?

Child:
I don't know.
It wasn't me!
Maybe (classmate's name),
Let's go see!

Bunny Cards
Use with "After You Read" on page 158.

TEC41062

TEC41062

TEC41062

TEC41062

TEC41062

TEC41062

Halloween Mice!
Written by Bethany Roberts
Illustrated by Doug Cushman

When mice dress up for Halloween, what do they do? Why, they skitter through the cornfield, scamper through the pumpkin patch, have a party, and scare a cat, of course!

ideas contributed by Tricia Kylene Brown
Bowling Green, KY

Mice might trick-or-treat for cheese!

Before You Read
Ask youngsters what people do to celebrate Halloween. After students share their thoughts, hold up the book and ask them what they think mice would do to celebrate Halloween. Finally, have little ones settle in for this read-aloud filled with action words and sounds!

After You Read
Encourage youngsters to act out the story with mouse puppets! Cut out five copies of the mouse pattern on page 163 and transform each cutout into a stick puppet. Place the puppets and the book near a pumpkin and a stuffed toy cat. Then encourage students to use the props to act out the story.

This Is the Turkey

Written by Abby Levine
Illustrated by Paige Billin-Frye

Thanksgiving Day dinner is almost ready. Aunts, uncles, cousins, and neighbors have all gathered. Mom is walking out with the turkey when she trips, and the turkey lands in the fish tank! Will Thanksgiving Day be ruined?

It could be ruined if there wasn't any food!

Before You Read

Hold up the book and read the title aloud. Then explain that this is a story about a Thanksgiving Day that is almost ruined! Ask youngsters to predict how a Thanksgiving Day might be ruined. After students share several thoughts, have them listen to this engaging read-aloud modeled in the pattern of This Is the House That Jack Built.

After You Read

Your youngsters will get a terrific gross-motor workout attempting to land a turkey in a fish tank like Max's mom did! Cut out several card stock copies of the turkey pattern on page 163 and attach each one to a beanbag (or a paper plate). Place a tape line on the floor and put the turkeys next to the line. Then place a tub (fish tank) several feet away. Encourage a child to toss the turkeys, attempting to get them in the fish tank!

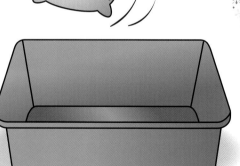

Mouse Pattern
Use with "After You Read" on page 161.

Turkey Pattern
Use with "After You Read" on page 162.

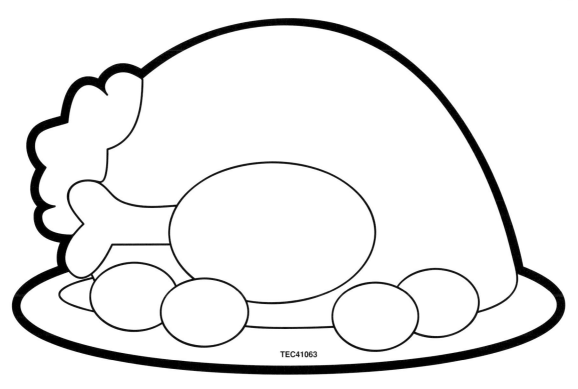

Storytime

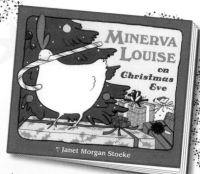

Minerva Louise on Christmas Eve

By Janet Morgan Stoeke

Minerva Louise sees colorful fireflies sparkling in a tree, fancy-horned goats on a snow-laden roof, a farmer in a red hat who slides down a well, and a tree decorated with eggs! Is it possible that this lovable hen is confused about her Christmas Eve assumptions?

ideas contributed by Tricia Kylene Brown, Bowling Green, KY

One time I was confused when I thought we were going to the grocery store but we weren't!

Before You Read

Show students the cover of the book and explain that the book is about a very confused hen named Minerva Louise. Ask, "What do you think *confused* means?" Help students understand that when a person (or hen!) is confused, she doesn't understand what is going on. Sometimes being confused can be upsetting until things are explained. Encourage students to discuss times when they've been confused. Then read aloud this entertaining story about a hopelessly muddled hen!

Minerva Louise is funny. I like the story. She did not know who Santa was! —Carli

After You Read

Have each student make her own crafty Minerva with this activity! Give each child a white construction paper shape similar to the one shown. Have her attach a yellow beak cutout and red crest to the shape. Finally, have her use a marker to make dot eyes. Ask each youngster to give her opinion of the story; then write her thoughts on her craft.

All You Need for a Snowman

Written by Alice Schertle
Illustrated by Barbara Lavallee

Could it be possible that one small snowflake is all you need for a snowman? The colorful illustrations and simple rhyming text in this story show that there's much more to building a snowman than one tiny snowflake!

I could go sledding on lots of snowflakes!

Before You Read

Engage little ones in a wintry brainstorming activity! Put a class supply of craft foam snowflakes in a bucket. Just prior to reading the story, toss the snowflakes in the air, creating an indoor snowstorm. Have each child pick up one snowflake. Then ask, "What could you do with one real snowflake?" After students respond, ask, "What could you do with a billion real snowflakes?" After each child has the opportunity to share her thoughts, read the story aloud to show what a group of children do when billions of snowflakes fall to the ground!

See page 166 for snowman sequencing cards! Encourage youngsters to put them in order to show the progression from snowballs to a decorated snowman.

After You Read

Have youngsters study the watercolor illustrations, encouraging them to notice the unique texture of the snow. Then explain that sprinkling salt on watercolor paint can give the picture that fun texture! Next, have each student use blue watercolors to paint a sheet of paper. Then immediately sprinkle table salt on the wet paint. When the paint is dry, have students brush off the salt to reveal the unique texture. If desired, prompt students to add snowflake stickers to the painting!

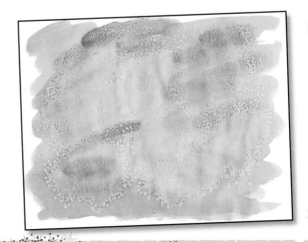

Snowman Sequencing Cards

Use with "*All You Need for a Snowman*" on page 165.

TEC41064

TEC41064

TEC41064

TEC41064

Storytime

One Fish, Two Fish, Red Fish, Blue Fish
By Dr. Seuss

This zany adventure starts out with a few simple fish and then becomes filled with silly creatures, rhyming words, and opposites!

ideas contributed by Margaret Aumen
Emory United Methodist Nursery School, New Oxford, PA

Green fish!

Orange fish!

Before You Read

Have children sit in a circle. Display the cover of the book and read its title aloud. Then lead youngsters in saying the title, placing emphasis on the number and color words. Next, pass out a class supply of fish cutouts in several different colors. Say, "One fish, two fish" and have a pair of students hold up their fish and say, "[color] fish, [color] fish," prompting each child to insert the color word for her fish. Repeat the process with the remaining students. Then have little ones settle in for this wonderfully wacky read-aloud! **Identifying colors**

My name is Micah.
I saw a spicah!

After You Read

Encourage each student to create a rhyming couplet that features him and a zany creature of his own! Give each child a paper programmed as shown and help him write his name in the appropriate space. Read the text aloud, prompting him to think of a silly word for a creature that rhymes with his name. Write the word in the space provided and have him illustrate the creature. If desired, bind the pages together to make a class book titled "From Here to There—Silly Creatures Are Everywhere!" **Rhyming, dictating information**

Roadwork

Written by Sally Sutton
Illustrated by Brian Lovelock

This rhythmic read-aloud takes the reader on a noise making, eye-opening, road-building journey from groundbreaking plans to a brand-new road!

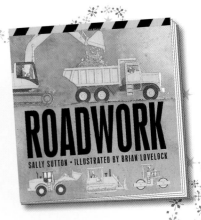

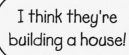

I think they're building a house!

Before You Read

To prepare, cover the front of the book. Tell youngsters that today's story is about a construction project, but before reading the story, you want them to try and guess the project. Keeping the pages concealed, read just the noise words from the story, stopping every few pages to let the children guess what the project is. Continue until the project is guessed. Then reveal the book and read it in its entirety. ***Predicting story events***

After You Read

Invite each child to create a road construction scene just like in the story! Set out construction paper, construction vehicle cutouts (patterns on page 169), gray paint, grated crayons, and a small foam paint roller. Encourage each youngster to make a road by rolling gray paint across a sheet of paper and sprinkling the wet paint with grated crayons. Then have her use the remaining materials to add desired details. ***Responding to a story through art***

TEC41065

TEC41065

TEC41065

TEC41065

Storytime

Bunny Party

Written and illustrated by Rosemary Wells

Max and Ruby are throwing a birthday party for Grandma. Ruby thinks her guest list of seven stuffed-toy friends is complete. But her brother, Max, has other plans, creating a counting catastrophe for Ruby!

ideas contributed by Heather A. Eades, Golden, CO

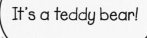

It's a teddy bear!

Before You Read

This prereading activity is a fun way to challenge youngsters' visual memory and practice counting! Gather five stuffed toys. Display three of the toys and keep two hidden from view. To begin, have students identify each toy and then count them aloud. Then have little ones close their eyes as you add one of the hidden toys to the ones on display. Prompt students to open their eyes; then lead them in recounting the toys to discover that there's one more! Have youngsters guess which is the new toy. Then have them close their eyes again and repeat the process. Finally, explain that today's story is about a birthday party with uninvited guests that mysteriously appear!

After You Read

Youngsters learn different ways to make ten with this Jellyball Shooter Spider reminiscent of Max's toy! Attach eight pipe cleaner legs to a bowl and then add ten pom-poms (jellyballs) for each student. For each child, use a permanent marker to divide a resealable plastic bag as shown. Invite each child, in turn, to sit near the spider as you gently toss him ten jellyballs to seal inside his bag. Then, to use the bags, ask youngsters to slide a specific number of jellyballs to each half of his bag. Lead students in counting each set and then in counting the total number of jellyballs to confirm that there are ten. Repeat the process to help youngsters make other combinations of ten.

Whopper Cake

Written by Karma Wilson
Illustrated by Will Hillenbrand

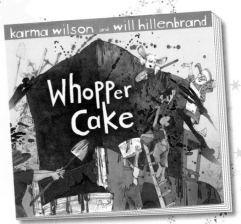

Today is Grandma's birthday, but she tells Granddad not to make a fuss. His cakes (and messes) are getting bigger every year!

They're painting a house!

Before You Read

To prepare, conceal the title of the book with a piece of paper. Then display the partially concealed book cover and ask students to study the picture. Have them describe what they see happening and name tools that are being used. Then invite little ones to guess what the characters in the illustration might be doing. After students share their thoughts, remove the paper, read the title, and have students settle in for this entertaining read-aloud with an over-the-top story plot!

After You Read

Invite your little ones to create their own whopper cake recipe with this class book! Give each child a copy of page 172 and ask her to dictate a number and ingredient for a whopper cake. Then encourage her to illustrate the ingredient and decorate the cake. Bind the pages together and title the book "Specialty Cake!"

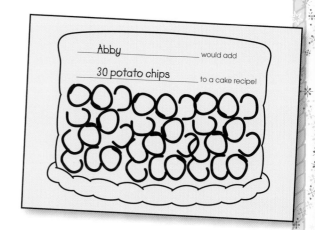

_____ would add

_____ to a cake recipe!

Note to the teacher: Use with "After You Read" on page 171.

Storytime

The Pout-Pout Fish

Written by Deborah Diesen
Illustrated by Dan Hanna

Mr. Fish is sure it is his destiny to be a gloomy guy until an unexpected friend shows him how to turn his pout into a smile.

ideas contributed by Heather A. Eades
Sunnycrest Christian Academy, Golden, CO

Before You Read

Have children sit in a circle. Display the cover of the book and ask students to name words to describe Mr. Fish. Then read the title aloud and discuss with youngsters what it means to pout. Pass an unbreakable mirror to the child beside you and invite him to make his best pouting face. Then have him show his pouting face to his classmates and complete the sentence starter "I put on my pout-pout face when..." Repeat the process with the remaining students. Then have youngsters settle in for a read-aloud of this delightful tale. **Oral language**

I put on my pout-pout face when we have broccoli for dinner.

My sister does funny things to turn my frown upside down.

After You Read

Encourage youngsters to write about a time someone made them smile just like the silver fish made Mr. Fish smile. Explain what it means to turn a frown upside down. Give each child a simple mouth cutout and a sheet of white paper labeled with a circle. Have the child draw her face without a mouth. Then help her use a brad to attach the mouth to her face. Below the face have her dictate to tell about someone making her frown turn upside down. Bind the pages together to make a class book. Read the book aloud and invite each child to turn her mouth from a frown to a smile as you read her page. **Making connections, dictating information**

Beetle Bop
By Denise Fleming

Beetles of all shapes, colors, patterns, and sizes dance across the pages of this thoroughly buggy book!

Before You Read

Show little ones the cover of the book and read the title aloud. Explain to students that a beetle is a type of bug. Invite a few volunteers to describe beetles that they have seen before. Then discuss with youngsters that sometimes people use the word *bop* to describe an energetic dance. Play a recording of lively music and invite youngsters to bop to the music. At the end of the dance, have students sit. Display the cover again. Encourage students to discuss what they think the book might be about. Then have students settle in for this engaging read-aloud. ***Developing vocabulary***

After You Read

Invite each child to make his own colorful bopping beetle scene. Set out white construction paper, ink pads with washable ink, fine-tip markers, glue, and glitter. Have each youngster make several colorful fingerprints on his paper. Then direct him to use markers to add details to the fingerprints so they resemble beetles. Next, invite him to add dots and swirls of glue to the page and then sprinkle glitter on the glue. ***Responding to a story through art***

BOOK UNITS

A Visitor for Bear

Written by Bonny Becker
Illustrated by Kady MacDonald Denton

Bear does not like visitors. When a very proper little mouse pops up repeatedly in Bear's house asking for tea and cheese, Bear promptly ushers him to the door. But this tenacious mouse gets his teatime eventually, and Bear finds that he rather likes having a visitor.

ideas contributed by Ada Goren, Winston-Salem, NC

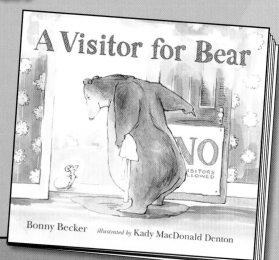

What Happens?
Making predictions

Before sharing the story, show youngsters the cover of the book and read the title aloud. Then ask, "Who do you think the visitor will be?" After little ones identify the visitor, reveal a mouse stick puppet (pattern on page 178). Ask little ones how many times they think the mouse visits the bear and allow each child to hold the mouse when he answers. Continue, asking youngsters how many times they think the mouse visits. Then have students settle in for a read-aloud to find out what really happens.

Welcome!
Responding to a story through art

The sign on Bear's door is not very welcoming! Encourage youngsters to create signs that will encourage visitors! Review the words on Bear's sign with your little ones. Then ask them to describe a sign that would be friendlier. Next, give each child a sheet of construction paper labeled "Welcome." Have each child decorate his sign and "write" friendly messages on it to encourage visitors. Attach the signs to your classroom door to welcome visitors and any friendly mice that happen to wander by.

For a neat follow-up to this activity, attach cutout copies of the mouse pattern on page 178 around your classroom door and on the finished signs before youngsters arrive for the day. Then have little ones notice that many mice have come to visit. The friendly signs must have made them feel welcome!

Good Manners, Bad Manners
Dictating information

Bear displays both bad manners and good manners in the story. Make a simple chart similar to the one shown. Then attach a different bear head cutout to each column. (See the patterns on page 178.) Flip through the book and have students notice examples of bad manners and good manners; write each example in the appropriate column. Finally, have youngsters tell about times when they have used both bad manners and good manners, just like Bear!

Bad Manners	Good Manners
uses mean words holds Mouse by the tail tells mouse to go away	shares his tea and cheese offers mouse more tea

There Is the Mouse!
Positional words

Mouse shows up in a bowl, in the bread drawer, in the refrigerator, and in the teapot! Where will Mouse show up in your classroom? Cut out a copy of the mouse pattern on page 178 (or get a stuffed mouse). Hide Mouse in your classroom before youngsters arrive. Then, while students are gathered for circle time, pretend to accidentally stumble upon the mouse, exclaiming "There is the mouse!" with great dramatic flair. Help youngsters use positional words to identify where the mouse is hiding. Then, when youngsters aren't looking, hide the mouse in a different location and play the game again!

Who Is the Visitor?
Contributing to a class book

To make this class book based on the story, have each child glue a photo of himself on a preprogrammed page. Then help him glue a doorway flap to the page as shown. Write his name on the interior of the flap. Bind the pages together with a cover titled "Who Is Visiting Bear?" Then read the book aloud to small groups of youngsters.

Who is visiting Bear?

Evan!

Mouse Pattern

Use with "What Happens?" and "Welcome!" on page 176 and "There Is the Mouse!" on page 177.

Bear Patterns

Use with "Good Manners, Bad Manners" on page 177.

Fabulous Felines

A Trio of Cat Books

Katie Loves the Kittens
by John Himmelman

When Sara Ann brings home three little kittens, Katie the dog gets so excited she scares them with her howling. With a lot of self-discipline, Katie learns to control herself around her new playmates.

ideas contributed by Ada Goren
Winston-Salem, NC

 So Excited!

Making a personal connection

Katie just can't contain herself around the sweet little kittens! After a read-aloud of the story, ask youngsters to share a time when they were so excited they could hardly contain themselves. After each child shares her thoughts, have her classmates howl an enthusiastic "Aroooo!" just like Katie does!

 What's Happening?

Describing a relationship between illustrations and text

Get a cat toy (or other cat-related item, such as a food bowl). Give the toy to a child and then open the book to one of the illustrations. Help the child recall what is happening at that time in the story. Then encourage her to pass the cat toy to another child and continue with a different illustration. Continue for several rounds.

 Kittens on Cards

Recognizing beginning sound /k/

With this activity, youngsters fine-tune their phonological awareness skills by listening for the sound of the letter *K* and hard *C*. Cut out a copy of the cards from page 182. Also copy and cut out the kitten patterns from page 183 so you have ten kittens. Place the cards faceup on the floor. Have students listen carefully to the words *Katie* and *kittens*, noticing that they both begin with /k/. Next, have a child point to a card on the floor and name the picture. If the picture name begins with /k/, have her put one of the kittens on the card. If not, have her flip the card over. Continue with each remaining card.

 See page 180 for more practice with /k/!

If You Give a Cat a Cupcake

Written by Laura Numeroff
Illustrated by Felicia Bond

If you give a cat a cupcake, he's going to want sprinkles on it. And that's going to lead to a beach trip, a gym workout, and other outings until this inexhaustible cat ends up wanting a cupcake all over again!

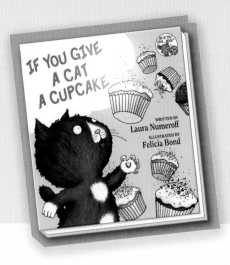

🐾 On the Move 🐾

Developing gross-motor skills

The cat is on the move throughout the story, and your youngsters will be as well! Do a picture walk through the story and have youngsters pantomime the cat's movements, such as adding sprinkles to the cupcake, building a sand castle, lifting weights in a gym, and running on a treadmill.

If you give Sarah a cupcake, she will want to eat it all up and then have a big glass of milk.

🐾 What Would You Do? 🐾

Creating a story innovation

Give each child a simple construction paper cupcake shape. Then encourage her to "frost" the top of the cupcake with a mixture of white glue and nonmentholated shaving cream. Have her sprinkle confetti on the mixture. Lead her to discuss what she would do if you gave her a cupcake. Then write her words on the project in the format shown.

🐾 Flip a Card 🐾

Recognizing beginning sound /k/

Your little ones listen for beginning sound /k/ with this cute idea! Cut out a copy of the cards from page 182 and place them facedown in a stack. Provide cupcake liners and a 12-cup cupcake pan. To begin, reinforce that *cat* and *cupcake* begin with the /k/ sound. A child flips a card and names the picture. If the picture name begins with /k/, he places a liner in the cupcake tin. He continues with each card. At the end of the activity, there are two empty spaces in the pan. Help the child name two more words that begin with /k/ and then place liners in those sections.

Cookie's Week

Written by Cindy Ward
Illustrated by Tomie dePaola
Cookie the cat gets into a different kind of mischief six out of the seven days of the week! What will Cookie do on that final day?

More Adventures?

Dictating information to write a letter

Have little ones write a letter to the author to suggest further adventures for Cookie! Guide them to write the beginning of the letter, explaining how they enjoy the book. Then prompt them to name other adventures Cookie might have, such as Cookie knocking over a mixing bowl, getting into a bag of cat food, or knocking over a television.

> Dear Ms. Ward,
>
> We love your book, Cookie's Week. It makes us laugh. Could you write another book? We would like you to have Cookie knock over a mixing bowl in the kitchen. There would be flour and eggs everywhere!

What About Sunday?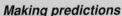

Making predictions

What mischief will Cookie get into on Sunday? Lead students in singing the quick song shown. Then have a child say what he thinks Cookie will do next. Lead youngsters in another round of the song and then call on a different youngster. Continue for several rounds.

(sung to the tune of "The Farmer in the Dell")

Oh, Saturday is through.
Now what will Cookie do?
Will Cookie rest or be a pest?
Oh, how I wish we knew!

 Beautiful Artwork

Expressing oneself through art

Have youngsters study Tomie dePaola's watercolor illustrations, particularly paying attention to the colorful splotchy background colors. Give each child a chunky paintbrush and encourage her to use watercolors to paint a background on a sheet of paper. Then encourage her to color and glue a cutout copy of a cat (patterns on page 183) on the paper. There's Cookie!

Picture Cards

Use with "Kittens on Cards" on page 179 and "Flip a Card" on page 180.

TEC41063

TEC41063

TEC41063

TEC41063

TEC41063

TEC41063

TEC41063

TEC41063

TEC41063

TEC41063

TEC41063

TEC41063

TEC41063

TEC41063

Never Tease a Weasel

Written by Jean Conder Soule
Illustrated by George Booth

You could give a fox some socks or you could give a goat a coat, but never tease a weasel! Rollicking, rhyming story text accompanied by comical illustrations humorously portray an important message—teasing isn't nice!

ideas contributed by Roxanne LaBell Dearman
Early Intervention for Children Who Are Deaf or Hard of Hearing, Charlotte, NC

Bug Gets a Mug
Rhyming

Youngsters will enjoy this rhyme that's reminiscent of the message in the story! Cut out a copy of the picture cards on page 186. Write the rhyme on individual sentence strips, leaving space for placing cards as shown. Arrange the strips in a pocket chart and display the object cards in the bottom row. To begin, present a critter card and have students identify the animal. Then ask students to name the rhyming object card. When a rhyming pair is confirmed, place the two cards in the chart, as shown, and lead the group in saying the rhyme. Remove the two cards and set them aside; then repeat the process with the remaining cards.

Please Don't Tease
Connecting to prior experience

Review the story pages that show the weasel being teased. Briefly discuss what's happening and how the weasel might feel. Then ask youngsters to share experiences where they were teased and tell how it made them feel. After each child has the opportunity to share, ask, "Have any of you ever teased someone?" Invite little ones to share those experiences as well. To conclude the activity, remind youngsters that teasing isn't nice because it's hurtful to others.

/w/, /w/, Weasel!
Beginning sound /w/

Print out a picture of a weasel (an Internet image search turns up many options) and place it on the floor. Provide bubble solution and a bubble wand. Show students the picture in the book where the children are blowing bubbles to tease the weasel. Then help youngsters notice that *weasel* begins with /w/. Call on a child and prompt him to say another word that begins with /w/. Then give him the bubble wand and encourage him to blow bubbles at the weasel. Have the remaining children say, "Never tease a weasel!" Play several rounds of this giggly activity!

You Gave It a What?
Dictating information

Except for the weasel, the animals in the story were treated kindly in a silly sort of way. For example, the kittens got mittens, the fox got socks, and the spider got cider! Invite your little ones to be silly in the same sort of way. Have a child draw an animal on a sheet of paper (or provide animal tracers and have him trace an animal). Encourage him to cut out a magazine picture of something unusual to give the animal and glue the picture to the page. Then invite him to dictate a sentence about the animal and its silly gift.

I gave the giraffe a scarf to keep its neck warm!

Be Kind, Please!
Speaking

Arrange youngsters in a seated circle and hand a child a stuffed toy animal, such as a dog or a cat. Lead students in chanting, "It's not nice to tease, so be kind, please!" At the end of the chant, prompt the child holding the toy to tell how he would be kind to the animal if it were real. Repeat the activity several times.

Rhyming Picture Cards
Use with "Bug Gets a Mug" on page 184.

TEC41064

TEC41064

TEC41064

TEC41064

TEC41064

TEC41064

TEC41064

TEC41064

Llama Llama Mad at Mama

Written and illustrated by Anna Dewdney

It's shopping day for Mama Llama, but Llama Llama wants to play. He can't stay home alone, of course, so off they go to Shop-O-Rama. Not long after the shopping begins, so does Llama Llama's drama!

ideas contributed by Ada Goren, Winston-Salem, NC

Play or Shop?
Making text-to-self connections

Llama Llama would rather stay home and play than go shopping with Mama Llama. Find out which one your preschoolers would rather do with this paper bag graph. Label a grocery bag as shown and place a name card for each child in the bag. To begin, take a card from the bag and ask that child if she would rather stay home and play or go shopping. After she responds, help her attach the card to the appropriate column on the bag. Continue until each child has a turn. Then discuss the graph's results and invite youngsters to explain their responses.

Shopping for Sounds
Beginning sounds

Gather several items whose names begin with the same sound (see suggestions), along with a few distracter items. Set out a toy shopping cart or basket. Lead students in practicing the beginning sound you wish to reinforce. Then pretend to be Mama Llama and have youngsters pretend to be Llama Llamas. Display an item and have your little llamas say its name and beginning sound. If the name begins with the practiced sound, children say, "Llama Llama shops with Mama!" and you put the item in the shopping cart. If not, they pretend to have a tiny tantrum. To "calm them down" say, "Llamas, llamas, that's enough!" and set the item aside. Continue with each remaining item.

Suggested items:
- carrot, corn, toy car, cup, cupcake cutout
- doll, dish, dice, domino, toy dinosaur, toy dog
- feather, toy fish, fork, football, toy fire truck
- map, macaroni, mug, mitten, mushroom
- pen, pencil, pear, pillow, popcorn, paint, pot, penny

Shopping Cart Art
Responding to a story through art

Set out copies of page 189, a store circular, light-color construction paper, unwrapped crayons, and glue. Attach plastic canvas to a tabletop; then lightly tape a copy of page 189 atop the canvas. To give the shopping cart an authentic look, invite a child to rub the side of a crayon across the paper. Then have him trim around the cart and glue it to construction paper. Encourage him to cut from the store circular items he would buy at Shop-O-Rama and glue them above the cart.

Sam

Mama, Llama, Shop-O-Rama!
Rhyming

During a second reading of the book, have students notice the words that rhyme with *llama,* such as *Shop-O-Rama, drama,* and *Mama.* Get a toy shopping cart and have youngsters sit in a circle. Walk around the circle pushing the cart, chanting, "Mama, llama, Shop-O-Rama!" Stop the cart. Then encourage the child nearest you to say a nonsense word that rhymes with *llama.* Encourage him to take your place and walk around the circle with the cart. Continue for several rounds.

tip → No toy shopping cart? Here's a simple solution! Use a paper grocery bag and set it in front of the child.

One time, I got mad when...
my brother took the last banana!

Touchy Tempers
Dictating information

In advance, snap a photo of each student making her best angry face. Trim around the photo and glue it to a sheet of paper programmed with the prompt shown. Revisit the pages in the story that show Llama Llama losing his cool. Then give each child her prepared page and invite her to tell about a time she lost her temper. Record her words on the page and encourage her to illustrate the situation. Bind the pages together with a cover titled "Mad Memories!"

TEC41065

Up, Down, and Around

Written by Katherine Ayres
Illustrated by Nadine Bernard Westcott

From seeds to the table, this story is chock-full of garden veggies that grow up; grow down; and climb, wind, and twine around!

ideas contributed by Roxanne LaBell Dearman
NC Early Intervention Program for Children Who Are Deaf or Hard of Hearing
Charlotte, NC

Munch Your Lunch!

Making text-to-self connections

What garden goodies would your youngsters munch for lunch? Find out with this idea! Get a paper plate. Then review the last page of the book to discuss the garden vegetables and fruits the characters are eating. Discuss other garden produce one might have for lunch. Then say, "Munch, munch. What's for lunch?" and hand the plate to a child. Have her name what garden food she would like for lunch. Then prompt her to pass her plate to another child. Repeat the chant and hear that child's thoughts. Repeat the activity for each remaining child.

I would love to have tomatoes for lunch!

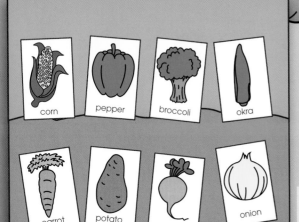

Which Direction?

Investigating living things

Little ones investigate vegetables with this activity! Cut apart a copy of the vegetable cards on page 192 and put them in a bag. Also attach light blue paper to brown paper to represent a garden. Display the garden on a wall. Have a child pull a card from the bag. Help him identify the item and decide whether it grows up or down, using the book's illustrations for help as needed. Then have another child use a glue stick to attach the card to the garden to show how the item grows. Continue with each remaining card.

For a more realistic take on this activity, purchase produce that grows up and grows down. Then have youngsters attach sticky notes labeled "D" or "U" to each item.

Seed Packets
Matching letters, recognizing that words are groups of letters

Attach cutout copies of desired vegetable cards from page 192 to small manila envelopes to make seed packets. For each packet, write the letters of the vegetable name on individual oversize seed cutouts and place them in the packet. Place the packets at a center along with a brown paper strip (soil) for each one. A child chooses a packet and empties out the seeds. Then he refers to the label on the packet to spell the vegetable name atop the soil.

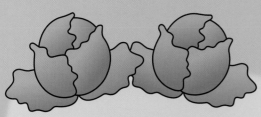

On the Move
Listening with purpose, developing gross-motor skills

This story rereading and activity helps fine-tune students' listening skills and enhance their large-motor development! Have students stand with space between them; then reread the story. Have students stand on their tiptoes and reach for the sky whenever they hear the word *up*, squat down and touch the floor when they hear the word *down*, and spin around once and stop when they hear the word *around*. Now that's an active rereading!

Broccoli Brushes
Expressing oneself through art, developing fine-motor skills

Break a head of broccoli into small clusters and place each cluster near a separate pan of paint. Gather two or three students and give each child a sheet of construction paper. Tape each sheet to the table to prevent it from moving. Then have each child choose a broccoli cluster and dip it in the paint. Chant, "Up, down, and around!" as youngsters move the cluster up, down, and in circles on their papers. After a few rounds, have students choose a different cluster and color of paint. Continue until youngsters' papers are filled with lovely swirls of color.

Looking for some process art?

Vegetable Cards

Use with "Which Direction?" on page 190 and "Seed Packets" on page 191.

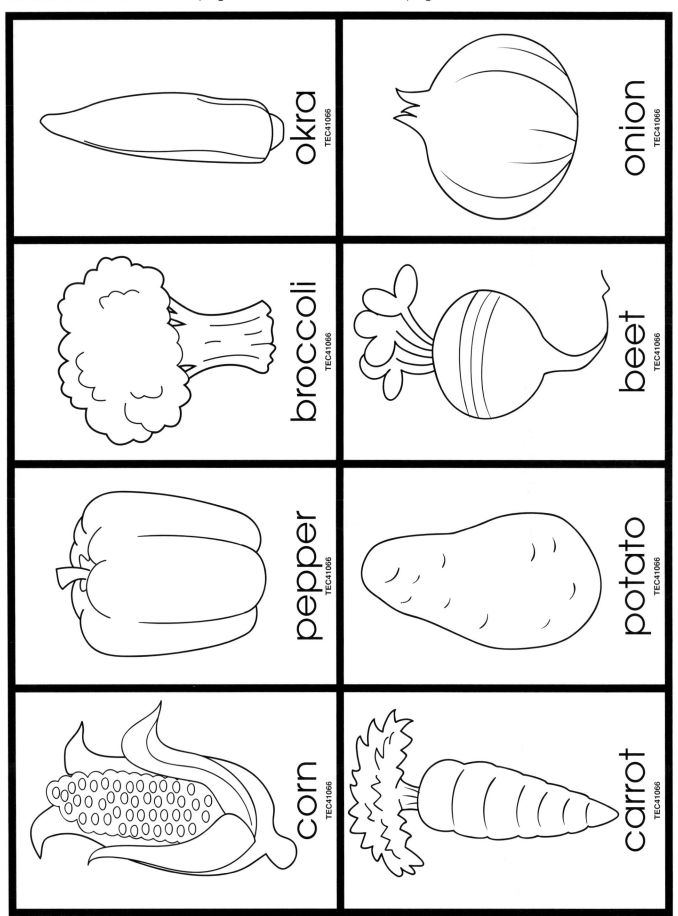

okra
TEC41066

onion
TEC41066

broccoli
TEC41066

beet
TEC41066

pepper
TEC41066

potato
TEC41066

corn
TEC41066

carrot
TEC41066

CENTER UNITS

Birthday Centers!

Spotlight birthdays with these adorable celebratory centers!

Beautiful Balloons

Math Center

Place bingo daubers and copies of page 196 at a center. Have a child color a copy of the page and then count the strings. Then have him use a bingo dauber to make a mark (balloon) at the end of each string. Prompt him to count the number of balloons and encourage him to notice that the number of strings and the number of balloons are the same.

Roxanne LaBell Dearman
NC Early Intervention Program for Children
   Who Are Deaf or Hard of Hearing
Charlotte, NC

Let's Bake a Cake!

Literacy Center

Help little ones understand that people read for many purposes! At a center, place copies of cake recipes, recipe books, and empty cake mix boxes, along with measuring cups and spoons, mixing bowls, mixing spoons, cake pans, and spatulas. Encourage youngsters to pretend to read the recipes and mix directions so they can make pretend birthday cakes with the props.

Birthday Batter

Sensory Center

Youngsters explore cake batter with this easy-to-prepare center! Empty a couple boxes of cake mix into a tub and then add water and vegetable oil until the mix reaches a pleasing consistency. Encourage youngsters to squish, squeeze, and smell this fabulous batter!

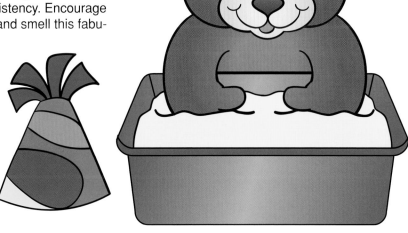

Crafty Candles

Art Center

To make this nifty birthday candle craft, each child paints a small cardboard tube with a mixture of glue and paint. Then he rolls the wet tube in a shallow pan of birthday-themed confetti. Finally, he stuffs yellow tissue paper into the tube so the paper resembles a flame.

Roxanne LaBell Dearman
NC Early Intervention Program for Children Who Are Deaf or Hard of Hearing
Charlotte, NC

Outstanding options for this craft!
- Attach a card to each candle with the student's name and birth date. Then mount the candles on a wall to make a permanent birthday display.
- Set the candles upright on your floor. Have a child roll a die and count the dots. Then encourage her to pretend to blow out that many candles!

Card Creation

Writing Center

Attach birthday cards to a wall near your writing center for inspiration. Then provide folded blank cards (Use copy paper from your recycle bin to save paper), paper scraps, random craft items, glue, and crayons. Encourage youngsters to write and decorate birthday cards!

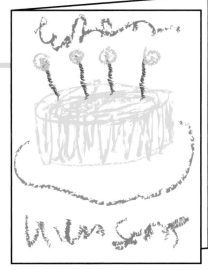

Crust, Sauce, and Toppings!
Playful Pizza Centers

Roll Out the Crust
Fine-Motor Area

Youngsters manipulate a variety of rolling pins to make pretend pizza crust! Provide pizza pans and play dough (pizza dough) along with large and small rolling pins, pieces of dowels, and other cylindrical objects. Youngsters roll pizza dough with a variety of the cylindrical objects, evaluating which one works best. Then they pick up the crust and put it on a pan. Finally, they crimp the edges of the crust with their fingers so it looks like a real pizza crust!

Tricia Kylene Brown, Bowling Green, KY

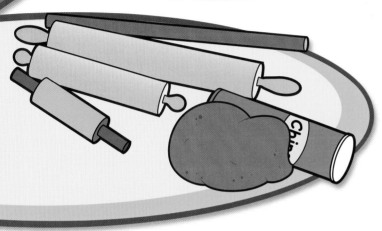

"Sense-ational" Sauce (and More!)
Sensory Center

Place a variety of items at your center for a pleasing pizza-themed sensory experience! To prepare, put sliced onions and green peppers in separate containers and punch small holes in the lids. Put sauce in a resealable plastic bag and then secure the seal with tape. Provide a small container with flour and a ball of pizza dough. Little ones sniff the toppings, manipulate the sauce, run their fingers through the flour, and then squeeze the dough!

Tricia Kylene Brown

To round out this sensory center, consider playing some Italian music and providing samples of cheese and pepperoni for a taste test!

Let's Compare
Math Center

Little ones explore weight with traditional toppings! Provide a balance scale and a variety of items used to top pizza, such as a tomato, a green pepper, an onion, a mushroom, and a sealed package of pepperoni (the variety that does not need refrigeration). A youngster chooses two items and guesses which one is heavier. Then he puts the items on the scale to determine whether his guess was correct. He continues with two different items.

Clap a Topping
Literacy Center

Cut out a copy of the cards on page 199 and place them at a center along with a pizza crust cutout. Station an adult helper at the center and have her arrange the cards facedown. To begin, the helper tells a child that he is a pizza chef and he's gotten an order for a pizza with everything on it! She prompts him to flip a card and name the topping. Then she helps him clap the name and identify the number of claps. Finally, he puts the topping on the pizza. He continues with each remaining card. **For a group option,** a child flips a card, all the youngsters clap the name, and then the child puts the card on the pizza.

Kathryn Davenport, Partin Elementary, Oviedo, FL

Pep-pers!

ham
pepperoni
peppers
mushrooms
olives
cheese
onions

P Is for Pizza
Art Center

This crafty project transforms the letter *P* into a pizza! Make a *P* cutout for each child. A youngster visits the center and spreads red paint (sauce) on her letter. Then she cuts scraps of construction paper to make toppings and presses them in the wet paint. If desired, she dictates for you to write on a card what toppings she has put on her *P* pizza and attaches the card to the project.

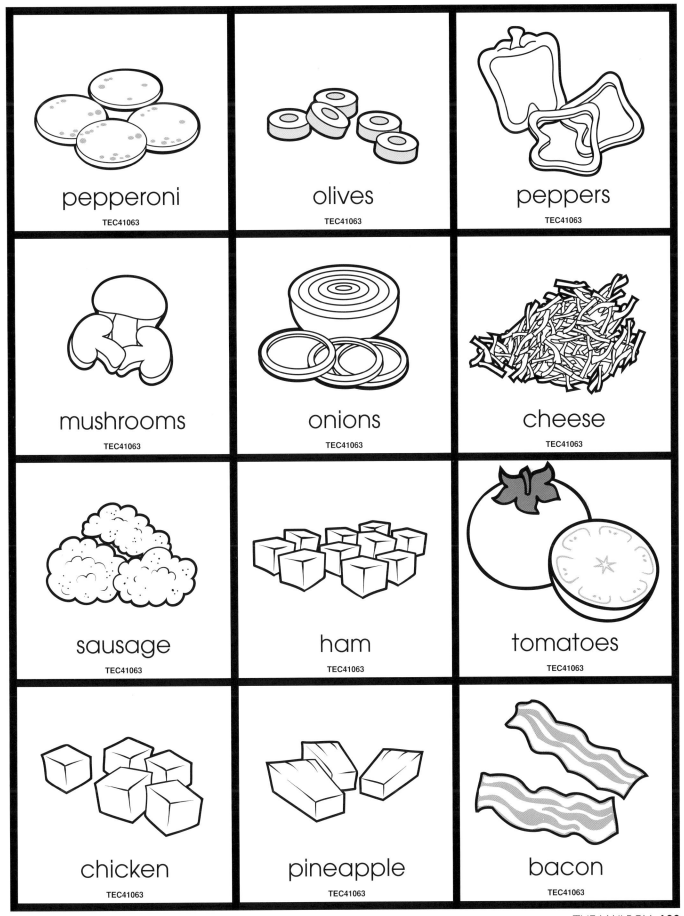

pepperoni

TEC41063

olives

TEC41063

peppers

TEC41063

mushrooms

TEC41063

onions

TEC41063

cheese

TEC41063

sausage

TEC41063

ham

TEC41063

tomatoes

TEC41063

chicken

TEC41063

pineapple

TEC41063

bacon

TEC41063

It's Center Time:

Let's Add Some Literacy!

Your centers will be chock-full of literacy development with this selection of fun options!

ideas contributed by Ada Goren, Winston-Salem, NC

Block Center

- Attach a set of alphabet stickers (or labeled cards) to individual blocks. Post an alphabet strip in the area and provide toy vehicles. Encourage youngsters to build a road by placing the blocks in alphabetical order, using the strip as a guide.

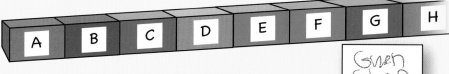

- Provide craft sticks, index cards, and tape. Encourage students to use the items to make a variety of street signs to add to their block creations. (To make the signs self-standing, a child simply tapes them to separate blocks.)

- Add a few picture books that depict different types of structures—such as *The Three Little Pigs, Jack and the Beanstalk,* and *Goldilocks and the Three Bears*—to the center. Provide additional building materials as needed. Encourage students to use the books as building inspiration.

Sensory Center

- Bury magnetic letters in a tub of rice. Have students search for the letters using a magnetic wand. If desired, have students match the letters to a letter strip.

- Draw letters on sandpaper, Bubble Wrap cushioning material, wallpaper, and other textured materials. Have youngsters trace the letters with their fingers, experiencing the texture.

- Place classroom items with distinctive beginning sounds in separate socks (or Christmas stockings). Provide a letter card for each beginning sound. A child feels the item through the sock and tries to identify it. Then he removes it and matches its beginning sound to a letter card.

Art Center

- Have students write on paper with white crayon. Then have them paint their papers with watercolors to reveal the writing.

- Provide die-cut letters for youngsters to use for collages.

- Encourage youngsters to paint papers as desired and then write in the wet paint with craft sticks.

- Place large sheets labeled with bubble letters at the center. A child transforms a letter sheet into a masterpiece as desired.

Fine-Motor Area

- Attach letter stickers (found at craft stores) to a sheet of paper and tape the paper to a tabletop. Provide copy paper and unwrapped crayons. A child places paper over the stickers and makes letter rubbings.

- Provide letter punches and stencils for students to explore.

- Label clothespins with letters. A child chooses a clothespin and clips it to a sign or poster in the room that has a matching letter.

A is for apple.

Gross-Motor Area

- Gather picture books with hopping characters, such as *Jump, Frog, Jump!* by Robert Kalan, *Marsupial Sue* by John Lithgow, and *My Friend Rabbit* by Eric Rohmann. Encourage students to look at the books and then practice their favorite hopping moves as well as other actions in the stories.

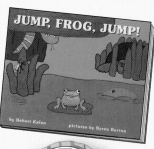

JUMP, FROG, JUMP!

by Robert Kalan   pictures by Byron Barton

- Label beanbags with letters and place them at the center. Students use the beanbags for tossing and balance practice, identifying letters as they play.

- Use wide masking tape to make a long zigzag line on the floor. Write the letters from *A* to *Z* in order along the tape. Invite a child to move along the line in a variety of ways, singing the alphabet song as he goes.

"Paws-itively" Precious!

Pet Centers

ideas contributed by Tricia Kylene Brown
Bowling Green, KY

Feed the Pup

Literacy Center

Place at a center a stuffed toy dog and a plastic bowl (dog bowl). Put a cutout copy of the cards from page 204 in an empty dog treat box. Tell youngsters that Boris the dog is finicky and only eats treats with pictures that begin with /b/, like his name. Then have each child, in turn, take a "treat" from the box and name the picture. If it begins with /b/, the child pretends to feed Boris and then puts the card in the bowl. When it shows a different letter, he sets the card aside. He continues with each card. *Beginning sounds*

Hamster Habitat

Art Center

Collect enough small boxes (such as those from shoes, gifts, and bakery items) so there's one for each child. To create a habitat, a child glues light brown crinkle shreds to the inside bottom of a box. Then he glues a plastic lid or condiment cup (feeding dish) to the shreds and a cardboard tube (for climbing and chewing) inside the box. To make a hamster, he glues a yarn tail and eye cutouts to a large brown pom-pom. When the glue is dry, he maneuvers his tiny pet around in its habitat! *Fine-motor skills*

Stock the Aquarium
Math Center

For this partner activity, set out a copy of the aquarium on page 205 and stack number cards facedown. Give youngsters a cup of fish-shaped crackers. A student flips a card and identifies the number. She counts out the corresponding number of fish and places them on one half of the aquarium. Her partner repeats the process, placing the fish on the remaining half. Then the partners count the total fish. They remove their fish from the aquarium, set the cards aside, and repeat the process with the remaining cards. Afterward, they nibble on a fresh cup of fish crackers! *Counting, making and combining sets*

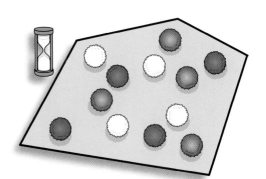

A Houseful of Mice!
Games Center

Put a house cutout on the floor and place gray, white, and brown pom-poms (mice) on the house. Get a minute sand timer. Have two students pretend to be cats. A child flips over the timer. Then the cats remove the mice from the house as quickly as possible and sort them into piles by color. **For a challenging option,** provide mice in the colors mentioned and in two different sizes. Little ones can sort the mice by color and then re-sort them by size! *Sorting by color and size*

Pet Care Clinic
Dramatic-Play Area

Turn your dramatic-play area into a mock pet clinic and help promote compassion and caring for animals! Stock the area with a variety of stuffed toy pets, a pet carrier (or box), a desk or small table (an examination table), a toy first aid kit, white dress shirts (lab coats), a clipboard with a sign-in sheet, a phone, and a notepad for writing prescriptions. Youngsters use the props to engage in pretend pet care. *Role-playing*

FIRST AID KIT

Dog Bone Cards

Use with "Feed the Pup" on page 202.

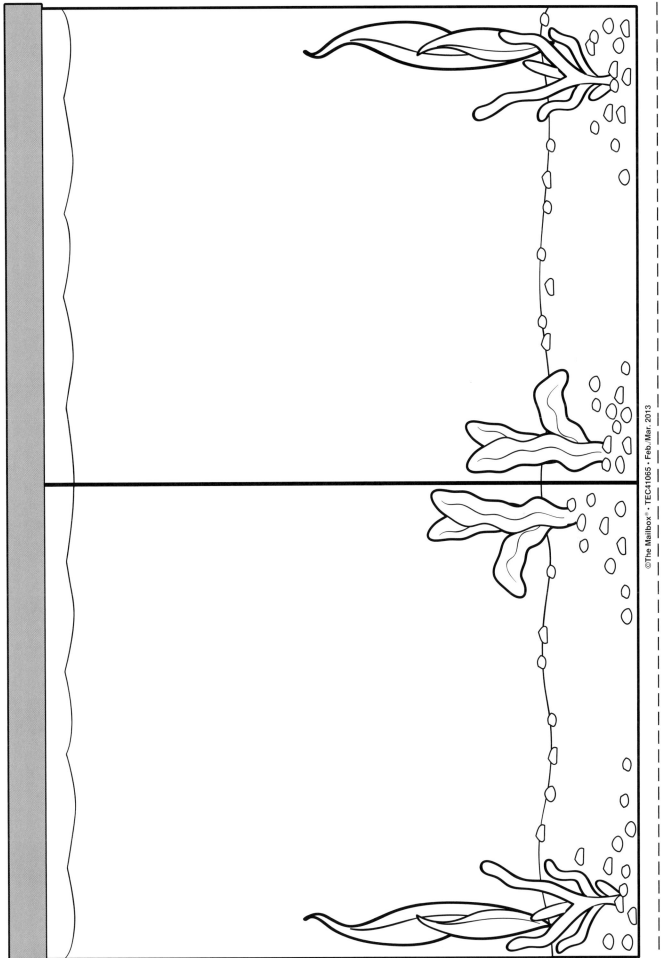

Note to the teacher: Use with "Stock the Aquarium" on page 203.

Tweet, Tweet, Tweet!

Fine-Feathered Bird Centers

▶▶ /f/, /f/, Feather!

Literacy Center

Station an adult helper at this center. Provide an enlarged copy of the bird pattern on page 208, craft feathers, and the list of words shown. Two or three youngsters visit the center. The helper names one of the words. If the word begins with /f/, like *feather*, then the child says, "/f/, /f/, feather" and glues a feather onto the bird. She repeats the process with different words until all the youngsters have had a chance to add at least one feather. Then she calls a new group to the center. After each child has a turn, the bird will be covered with feathers! *Beginning sounds*

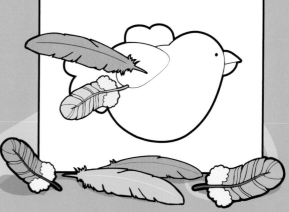

Word List			
fan	fish	road	fork
feet	saw	fight	for
fence	fern	finger	door
five	fox	cake	fall
fire	ball	fin	fun

Feed the Baby ◀◀

Math Center

Cut out a copy of the baby bird pattern on page 208 and attach it to a container. Provide a supply of plastic bugs (or worms), a pair of dice, and tweezers. A child rolls a die and counts the dots. Then she pretends the tweezers are the momma bird's beak, and she "feeds" the baby bird the appropriate number of bugs. She continues for several rounds. *Counting, fine-motor skills*

P. Gail Farmer
Kiddie Kampus of Medford
Medford, NY

▶▶ In the Birdhouse

Art Center

For each child, cut out a very simple birdhouse shape. Cut a hole in the middle of the birdhouse. Have each child cut out a copy of the bird pattern on page 208 and attach it to a sheet of construction paper along with some raffia and yarn. Help each youngster attach the birdhouse to the paper to make a flap. Youngsters can open the flap and see the bird building a nest!
Expressing oneself through art, developing fine-motor skills

Adapted from an idea by Sandy Prosen
Early Childhood Family Education—South Washington
    County
Cottage Grove, MN

Fly–Away Wings ◀◀

Gross-Motor Area

Youngsters will get plenty of exercise flapping these wings. Provide scarves, paper plates, and pieces of crepe paper streamers. Play a musical recording and encourage youngsters to hold an item in each hand and then flap around the area. Prompt children to try all the different options and decide which types of wings are their favorites.
Developing gross-motor skills

Roxanne LaBell Dearman
NC Early Intervention Program for Children Who Are Deaf or Hard of Hearing
Charlotte, NC

▶▶ Bird Watchers

Science Center

Place bird books, drawing paper, and play binoculars (or pretend binoculars made from cardboard tubes) at a center. Youngsters draw pictures of birds and label them as desired. Then they attach them around the room. Classmates can use the binoculars to search for birds.
Investigating living things

P. Gail Farmer, Kiddie Kampus of Medford
Medford, NY

Bird Pattern

Use with "/f/, /f/, Feather!" on page 206 and "In the Birdhouse" on page 207.

TEC41066

Baby Bird Pattern

Use with "Feed the Baby" on page 206.

TEC41066

LITERACY UNITS

It's Rhyme Time!

Get ready for phonological awareness fun with these fabulous rhyming activities!

Let's Sing

This fun and simple idea requires no preparation! Get a ball. Then lead students in singing the song shown. At the end of the song, roll the ball to a child. Help her name a real or nonsense word that rhymes with *whale.* Then have her roll the ball back to you. Sing another round of the song, rolling the ball to another child. If desired, after several rounds, change *whale* to a different word.

(sung to the tune of "The Farmer in the Dell")

What rhymes with [whale]?
What rhymes with [whale]?
It's time to make a rhyme.
What rhymes with [whale]?

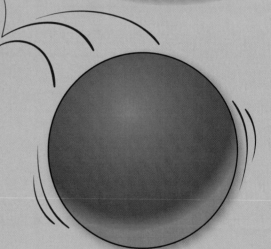

Picture Search

To prepare for this activity, cut out a copy of the rhyming cards on page 212. Choose two rhyming trios of cards and attach them to various locations around the classroom. Encourage a child to find a card, remove it, and then name the picture. After the remaining youngsters repeat the name, have the child put the card in a pocket chart. Have a child find another card and follow the same steps, pausing before she places it in the chart. Help little ones decide if the picture name rhymes with the first picture name. If it does, have her place it next to the first card. If not, have her place it in the next row. Continue with each remaining picture card to create two sets of three rhyming cards.

We Have Pie!

Little ones will love to participate in this rhyming call-and-response chant. Have youngsters repeat each line after you recite it. For extra fun, once students are comfortable with the chant, have them clap a steady beat or play a rhythm instrument as they recite the chant.

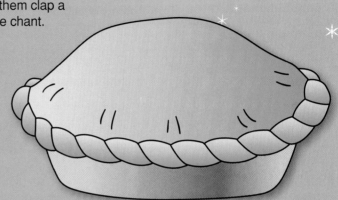

Oh my!
We have pie.
The pie's too sweet.
I'll eat some meat.
The meat's too red.
I'll eat some bread.
The bread's too brown.
I'll go to town.
It's quite a hike!
I'll use my bike.
It has a flat.
So that is that!

Amy Pylant, Rosemont Elementary, Orlando, FL

I See Someone!

Seat youngsters in a circle. Then walk around the outside of the circle, lightly tapping each child's head as you recite the chant shown. At the end of the chant, name the child who is tapped last, using a rhyming version of her name, such as *Bannah* for *Hannah*. Then say, "Wait, that's not right! This is Hannah, not Bannah!" Repeat the game several times.

I see someone, yes sirree!
I see someone. Who could it be?

adapted from an idea by Anita McManus, Christ Church Preschool and Kindergarten, Charlotte, NC

Riddle, Riddle Me

You'll see plenty of smiles with this fun group game! Cut out a copy of the cards on page 212 and place one card from each rhyming trio on the floor faceup. (Set the other cards aside for use with another activity.) Recite the chant shown, naming words that rhyme with one of the cards on the floor. Then prompt a child to identify the correct card and flip it over. Continue with each remaining card.

Riddle, riddle me. I see something you might see.
It rhymes with [frog]. It rhymes with [log].
Riddle, riddle me.

Tonya Bays, Kinder Kampus, Corydon, IN

Picture Cards

Use with "Picture Search" on page 210 and "Riddle, Riddle Me" on page 211.

TEC41062

TEC41062

TEC41062

TEC41062

TEC41062

TEC41062

TEC41062

TEC41062

TEC41062

Icky or Not?

Little ones develop speaking and data-organization skills when they give opinions about these interesting and potentially icky items!

Make a Face!

Some youngsters may find the texture of pumpkin innards fascinating, while others may find them just plain icky! Have youngsters observe when you cut open a pumpkin. Then encourage each child to touch the innards of the pumpkin. Next, take a photo of each child expressing his opinion about the texture of the innards, either by making an icky face if he dislikes the texture or by smiling if he enjoys it. Display the photos with the title and headings shown. Then discuss the results with youngsters.

Preschool Opinion Poll: Pumpkin Goop

Icky	Not Icky

Leggy Little Critters

Label a sheet of construction paper as shown. Provide colorful bingo daubers. Ask a youngster whether she thinks spiders are icky or not and encourage her to make a bingo dauber mark on the appropriate side of the paper. Have her use a fine-tip marker to make legs and eyes on the dauber mark. When each youngster has had an opportunity to add her opinion, prompt little ones to discuss the results.

Feelings About Fingerpainting

Some youngsters dive into fingerpainting with both hands, while others find the texture to be rather icky! Place a length of bulletin board paper on a tabletop. Provide pans of paint and encourage each child to fingerpaint a small portion of the paper. Next, ask, "Do you think fingerpaint feels nice or icky?" Write her words on a card and then attach it to her painting. Continue with each remaining child. Then title the paper "Feelings About Fingerpainting" and display it in your room.

> I think fingerpainting feels icky because it's slimy and makes your hands look funny.
> —Eva

Nuts About Writing!

These fabulous writing activities are all about the fall season!

ideas contributed by Ada Goren
Winston-Salem, NC

Squirrels
are

_____ brown
and
_____ furry

Squirrels Are...

Youngsters ponder squirrels with this descriptive word activity! Make a copy of page 216 for each child. Have students look at photos of squirrels (an Internet search turns up many options) or encourage them to observe squirrels through a classroom window. Help each child come up with two words that describe squirrels and then have the child write the words in the blanks on a squirrel. (Rewrite the words below the child's writing if necessary.) Then mount the resulting squirrels on a fall-themed display.

A Fall Scene

Display a fall-themed magazine page. Then use it for these excellent writing options!

- Ask a student to name something he sees on the page. Encourage him to write the name of the object on a sticky note. (If desired, rewrite his words below his writing.) Then have him stick the note to the page.
- Ask students, "What do you see happening in this picture?" Write students' dictation on a sheet of chart paper.
- Have each child "write" a story about what she sees in the picture. (Rewrite the story beneath her writing as needed.)

My, Oh My—Pie!

Forget traditional apple and pumpkin pies. These pies are as unique as your little ones! Give each child a tan circle cutout programmed as shown. Have each child write what she would put in a pie. (Rewrite her words below her writing if needed.) These pies look adorable displayed with the title "My Oh, My—Pie!"

My, oh my!
Let's have some pie!
If you don't mind,
Here's a new kind!

This pie has spaghetti and cookies in it. It is yummy! My mom would like it.
—Samantha

To add more writing to center time or free play, try this tip from Susan Browder of Northwest Michigan Community Action Agency Head Start in Houghton Lake, Michigan. Place sticky notepads around the room. When a child needs to wash her hands, go to the bathroom, or talk to a teacher, she can write her name on a sticky note and place it on the toy she's playing with to save it. Classmates won't necessarily be able to read the note, but they'll know that a sticky note means the toy is saved!

All About Pumpkins

Have youngsters fingerpaint an oversize pumpkin cut from bulletin board paper. When the paint is dry, attach the pumpkin to a wall and add yarn vines. Give each child a green leaf cutout and have him write something he knows about pumpkins. (Rewrite his words as needed.) Then attach the leaves to the vine.

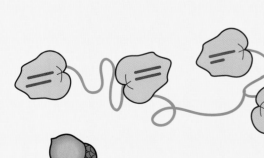

Squirrel Pattern

Use with "Squirrels Are..." on page 214.

Squirrels
are

_____

and

_____.

TEC41063

Up and Down, Big and Small... Opposites!

It's This, Not That

This whole-group activity is perfect for reinforcing familiar opposites! To prepare, gather a cup (empty), a cotton ball (soft), a rock (heavy), sandpaper (rough), and a moist sponge (wet). To begin, slowly tip the cup and say, "This [cup] is [empty], so it is not…" pausing and prompting youngsters to say the opposite of empty, *full*. Continue with the remaining items, replacing the underlined words with an object's name and the adjective shown in the parentheses.

Suzanne Moore
Tucson, AZ

Dandy Ditty

Engaging in this kinesthetic activity is a sure-fire way to help little ones remember opposite pairs! Arrange youngsters in an open area with plenty of space between them. Then lead students in performing this fun action song.

(sung to the tune of "This Old Man")

> Jump up high,
> Squat down low,
> Clap really fast, and
> Now clap slow.
> Take a big step and then
> Take a small step too.
> I love opposites.
> Don't you?

Suzanne Moore

Action!

Invite little ones to dramatize opposites! To prepare, cut out a copy of the cards on pages 220 and 221. Have two children stand facing the group. Give each child one card from a pair of opposites, keeping the illustrations hidden from their classmates. Prompt each student to act out the opposite featured on her card. (You will need props for certain pairs.) Then encourage the class to guess the opposites. Repeat the activity with different children and other opposite pairs.

Marianne Cerra
Riverside Elementary
Reading, PA

Fast and Slow

Gather a plastic toy turtle and rabbit (or two other animals known for being slow and speedy). Have each child use a small foam paint roller to roll desired colors of paint on a piece of paper. Then encourage him to move the turtle slowly across the paper, making marks in the paint. Next, give him the rabbit and encourage him to move the rabbit quickly. Lead the child to conclude that the turtle is slow and the rabbit is fast, emphasizing that slow and fast are opposites.

Musical Opposites

Use music and movement to help youngsters learn a variety of opposites! Write "fast" on the board. Play a recording of music with a fast tempo and encourage students to dance. Then help students determine that slow is the opposite of fast. Write "slow" on the board and have little ones dance to music with a slow tempo. Next, write "loud" on the board. Turn the music up and have students clap loudly to the beat. Then repeat the process with "quiet," encouraging them to clap quietly. Continue in the same way, having youngsters dance while they make big and small movements and happy and sad movements.

Tracy Henderson, Brook Hollow Weekday Program
Nashville, TN

Land Rover

Try this fun twist on the game Red Rover! Make copies of pages 220 and 221 to make a class supply of cutout cards. For extra fun, attach each card to a paper plate steering wheel. Group the wheels into two sets, with one of each opposite pair in each set. Arrange the class in two even teams and have them stand on opposite sides of the room. Give one set of wheels to one team and the remaining set to the other. To play, have one team say, "Land rover, land rover, drive [long] right over!" Prompt the child with the "long" card to "drive" to the opposite team. Then have his old team determine the opposite of *long* and repeat the chant, substituting *short* and encouraging the child with the appropriate card to "drive" to that team. Collect the two cards. By the end of the game, all team members will have switched sides.

Brooke Beverly
Dudley Elementary
Dudley, MA

Flip and Find

Cut out a copy of the cards on pages 220 and 221. Place one of each pair facedown in a pocket chart and put the remaining cards faceup in the bottom row. Invite a child to stand near the chart as you lead the group in singing the song shown. Then have him flip a card and say the picture word. Encourage him to find the corresponding opposite card in the bottom row and place it with its matching half. Lead the group in saying the opposite pair; then repeat with other students until all the cards are paired.

(sung to the tune of "The Muffin Man")

Oh, can you find the opposite,
The opposite, the opposite?
Oh, can you find the opposite
Of this picture word?

Opposites Picture Cards

Use with "Action!" on page 218 and "Land Rover" and "Flip and Find" on page 219.

long

TEC41064

short

TEC41064

in

TEC41064

out

TEC41064

asleep

TEC41064

awake

TEC41064

sit

TEC41064

stand

TEC41064

heavy

TEC41064

light

TEC41064

open

TEC41064

closed

TEC41064

slow

TEC41064

fast

TEC41064

loud

TEC41064

quiet

TEC41064

My Tongue Is Tangled!

4 Phonological Awareness Activities With Tongue Twisters

ideas contributed by Ada Goren, Winston-Salem, NC

1 My Own Tongue Twister

Youngsters will adore having their own personal tongue twisters! Help each child create a tongue twister based on the first letter in her name. Write her tongue twister on a sheet of paper and encourage her to say it several times, leading her to notice that most of the words begin with the same sound her name begins with. Finally, encourage her to illustrate her tongue twister. These personalized projects look extra special displayed in the classroom.

Cara collects cuddly cats.

2 Popcorn Jump!

Cut a class supply of popcorn shapes from construction paper and label each one with a consonant. Attach the popcorn to the floor. Lead students in reciting the tongue twister shown as they hop and jump around the popcorn. When you say, "Freeze," have students stop on a piece of popcorn. Encourage each child to say, "Pop, pop, popcorn!" substituting the initial sound in each word with the sound of the letter on her popcorn piece. Continue with several other youngsters. Repeat the game several times until all youngsters have had an opportunity to recite the phrase. Lop, lop, "lop-corn"!

Pop, pop, popcorn,
Hop, hop, "hop-corn"!
Pick a popcorn, please.
Pop, pop, popcorn,
Stop, stop, "stop-corn"!
Pick a popcorn—freeze!

3 Betty's Batter

Little ones are sure to get the giggles when they add their own unique words to this tongue twister! Write the tongue twister shown on your board. Lead students in reciting the rhyme several times. Then guide students to name a different word that begins with /b/. Write the word on the board. Then encourage students to recite the rhyme, replacing the word *batter* with the suggested word. How silly! Repeat the activity with different words.

Betty bought a big bottle of buttery batter.
But, Betty, Betty—what's the matter?
"This big bottle of batter won't do!"
Back at the store, Betty bought two!

bears
boxes
buses
balloons

For extra fun, gather two large plastic bottles to represent Betty's batter bottles. Then have a child pretend to be Betty. Encourage the remaining students to recite the first, second, and last lines of the tongue twister. Betty acts out the twister and recites the third line. Repeat with different volunteers, changing "Betty" to "Bob" when needed.

4 Waffles for Winnie

Cut out a copy of the cards on page 224 and place them in a bag. Put brown construction paper squares (waffles) on a plate. (If desired, make the waffles look more realistic by making a rubbing over textured material.) To begin, teach little ones the tongue twister "Winnie wants warm waffles." Encourage youngsters to say the tongue twister slowly, listening for the /w/ sound. Have a child choose a card from the bag and say the name of the picture. If the name begins with /w/, have him place the card on the plate with Winnie's waffles. If it doesn't, have him set the card aside.

Picture Cards

Use with "Waffles for Winnie" on page 223.

Rise and Shine With Literacy!

Little ones will be bright eyed and wide awake with these fabulous morning-themed literacy activities!

ideas contributed by Roxanne LaBell Dearman
NC Early Intervention Program for Children Who Are Deaf or Hard of Hearing
Charlotte, NC

Toast!

Recognizing /p/

Little ones pretend to be toast popping out of a toaster with this active idea! Cut out a copy of the cards on page 227 and place them facedown on the floor. Have youngsters crouch down around the cards. Then have a child turn over a card and say its name. If the word begins with /t/, like *toast*, prompt students to pop up as if they were toast popping up from a toaster. Continue until all the cards are turned over.

Good morning, teddy bear!

Good Morning, Sun!

Writing, dictating information

This project is inspired by the classic story *Goodnight Moon*! Read aloud *Goodnight Moon* by Margaret Wise Brown. Then give each child an enlarged yellow construction paper copy of the pattern on page 226. Have each child write (or dictate) the name of something in his room that he would say "good morning" to. Then encourage him to tear strips of yellow and orange construction paper (sun rays) and glue them around the sun. If desired, display these sunny projects!

The Wake-Up Song

Tracking print from left to right and top to bottom

In advance, write the words to the song on sentence strips and place them in your pocket chart. Attach a sun cutout (or sticker) to a jumbo craft stick to make a pointer. (For extra zip, add gold glitter to the sun!) Use the pointer to follow the words as you teach youngsters the song. Then have volunteers take over tracking the print.

(sung to the tune of "Good Night, Ladies")

Wake up, sunshine!
Wake up, two legs!
Wake up, ten toes!
It's time to start the day.

Wake up, two arms!
Wake up, both eyes!
Wake up, whole head!
It's time to start the day.

Sun Pattern
Use with "Good Morning, Sun!" on page 225.

Good morning,

_____!

TEC41065

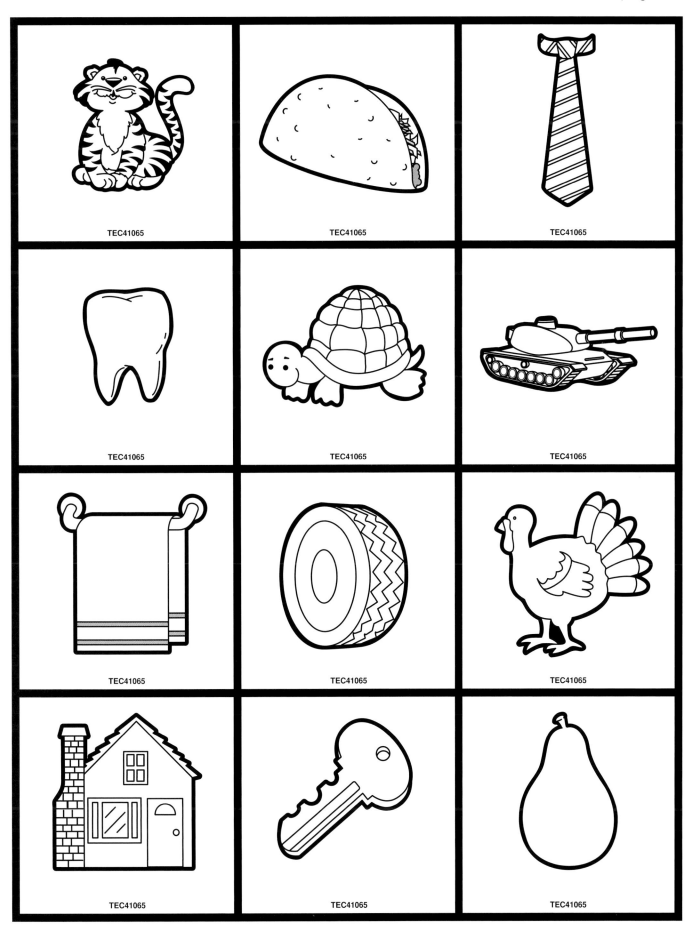

TEC41065

TEC41065

TEC41065

TEC41065

TEC41065

TEC41065

TEC41065

TEC41065

TEC41065

TEC41065

TEC41065

TEC41065

The Buzz on Letters and Sounds

What's all the buzz about? "Bee" sure to check out this engaging collection of literacy activities to find out!

ideas contributed by Ada Goren, Winston-Salem, NC

Sounds and Stripes

Identifying matching beginning sounds

Give each child a yellow construction paper bee cutout (patterns on page 230) along with a black crayon. Focus youngsters' attention on the fact that these bees have no stripes. Then say, "We're going to play a fun listening game that will help add stripes to your bees." Demonstrate by saying two words with the same beginning sound, such as *bee* and *ball.* After confirming that the words have the same beginning sound, invite each child to draw a stripe on her bee. Repeat with words that do not begin with the same sound, resulting in no additional stripe. Then continue the activity until all the bees have several stripes.

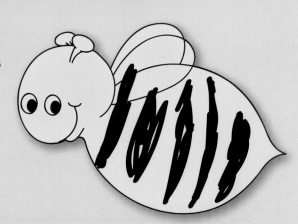

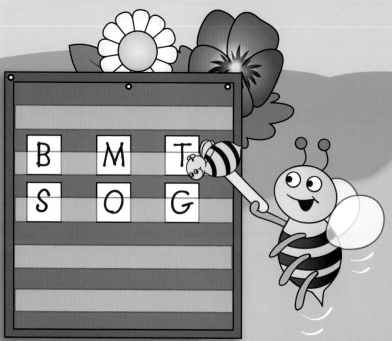

Buzzzz...

Recognizing letters

For this large-group activity, make a bee pointer (patterns on page 230) like the one shown and display assorted letter cards in a pocket chart. To begin, give each child in the group a yellow pom-pom (bee); then invite a volunteer to take the pointer. Recite the rhyme shown, inserting a desired letter; then prompt the volunteer to touch the bee to the designated letter. If he's correct, his classmates buzz their bees through the air and then land them in their laps. If he's incorrect, they do nothing. Continue in the same way with other volunteers and letters.

Buzz, buzz, goes the bee.
Can you find a(n) [letter] for me?

Buzzing Around
Identifying letters

Label a class supply (minus one) of die-cut flowers with assorted letters. Invite one child to be the "bee" and have the remaining students sit in a circle (flower garden). Give each seated student a flower. Play a musical recording (Rimsky-Korsakov's "Flight of the Bumblebee" would be perfect!) and have the bee buzz around the outside of the garden. After a few moments, stop the music and prompt the classmate nearest the bee to hold her flower in the air. Have the bee identify the letter (with help as needed) and then switch places with the classmate. Continue for several rounds.

Honeycomb Letters
Letter formation

Forming letters is the focus of this edible activity! Give each child a beehive mat (see page 231) and a cup of honeycomb-shaped cereal. Also set out several letter cards. A youngster chooses a card and places it near his mat. Then he uses the cereal to form the letter atop the beehive. After forming the letter, he scrambles the cereal and repeats the process with a different card. Then, when he's finished with the activity, he eats the cereal!

Could It "Bee" That Letter?
Letter-sound association

To prepare, draw two or more flowers on a dry-erase board and label each one with a different letter. Attach Sticky-Tac to a bee cutout (patterns on page 230). To begin, lead students in naming each letter and practicing its sound. Next, announce a word and place the bee above one of the flowers. Then have youngsters say the word and the chosen letter sound. If the beginning sound of the word and the letter sound match, little ones buzz around like bees. If not, continue moving the bee until the correct flower is found. Continue in the same way for several rounds.

Bee Patterns

Use with "Sounds and Stripes" and "Buzzzz…" on page 228 and "Could It 'Bee' That Letter?" on page 229.

TEC41066

TEC41066

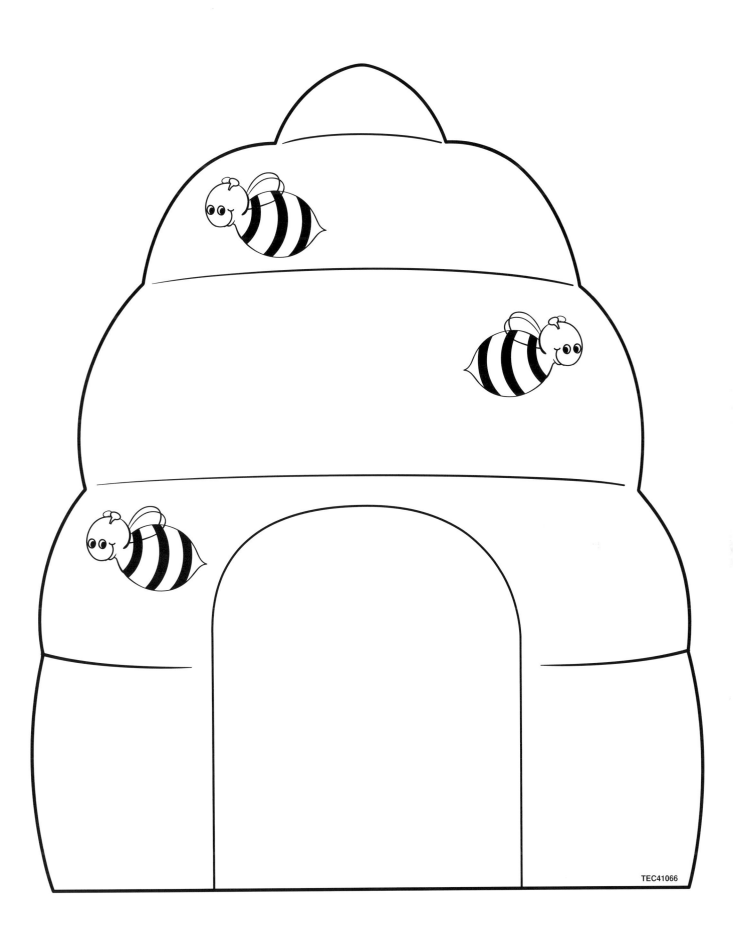

TEC41066

So Many Words!
Building Vocabulary

Basketful of Words

Looking for a way to build your students' vocabulary? Then make a vocabulary basket! Write words on plain index cards and add a corresponding sticker, stamp, or clip art picture to each one. Be sure to use simple, less familiar words as well. Put the cards in a basket and then use the basket for the following activities:

- Place it at your writing center or reading area. When youngsters visit the area, encourage them to use the cards to dictate or tell a story.

- Display a card and ask the group to identify the word. Then help a child use the word in a sentence.

- Have each child identify a word as she transitions to a new activity.

Ruth Zabelin, Kleberg Elementary, Kingsville, TX

What Did Granny Buy?

Here's a fun whole-group activity that builds vocabulary using synonyms! Cut out a copy of the cards on page 234. Program sentence strips as shown, leaving space where indicated to insert a card. Display the strips in a pocket chart. To begin, show a card and identify the picture according to its label. Then slide the card into the space on the strip and lead youngsters in chanting the rhyme. At the end of the rhyme, ask students to name another word that can be used for the featured item, leading them to name the synonym shown in the list. Repeat the rhyme using the synonym; then remove the card and repeat the process with a different card.

Synonym suggestions: *dish, plate; bunny, rabbit; present, gift; pail, bucket; couch, sofa; rug, carpet; rock, stone; jet, airplane*

Donna Butler, Nicholson, GA

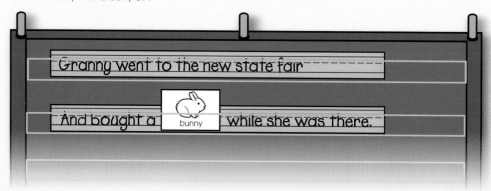

60-Second Stories

This fast-paced, giggle-inducing activity keeps everyone on their toes! Attach six cards from page 234 to a cube-shaped box. Also obtain a timer. Tell students they're going to play a game that allows them to tell a story that is either *fact* or *fiction.* After defining the two words, invite a child to roll the cube and identify the picture. Then set the timer for one minute and prompt her to tell a real or make-believe story involving the featured object. When the timer goes off, lead her classmates in a round of applause and invite another youngster to roll the cube.

Marcell Gibison, Stevens, PA

New-Word Box

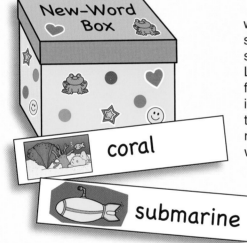

Introduce new themes and theme-related vocabulary with this clever idea! Write several theme-related words on separate paper strips. Add a corresponding picture to each strip, if possible, and then put the strips in a decorated box. Lead students in singing the song shown; then take a strip from the box and show it to the group. Help youngsters identify the word and talk about its meaning. Then display the strip in a pocket chart or on a wall. Repeat with each remaining strip, prompting youngsters to guess the theme with each new word.

(sung to the tune of "Goodnight, Ladies")

Let's learn new words.
Let's learn new words.
Let's learn new words.
I wonder what they'll be!

Shelley Hoster, Jack & Jill Early Learning Center, Norcross, GA

What in the World Is That?

Little ones definitely need their thinking caps for this vocabulary-building activity! Conceal in a bag a few familiar items along with a few not-so-familiar items, such as a melon baller, a money clip, a garlic press, a shower cap, and a shoehorn. Invite a child to take an item from the bag and identify it. If she doesn't know what the item is, prompt her to say, "What in the world is that?" Then provide several clues, eventually revealing the item's name and discussing how it's used. Repeat the process with each remaining item.

adapted from an idea by Roxane Fox, East Preschool, Eaton, OH

Picture Cards

Use with "What Did Granny Buy?" on page 232 and "60-Second Stories" on page 233.

dish
TEC41067

bunny
TEC41067

present
TEC41067

pail
TEC41067

couch
TEC41067

rug
TEC41067

rock
TEC41067

jet
TEC41067

MATH UNITS

Circles, Squares, Triangles, Rectangles!
A Shapely Collection of Ideas

Hide-and-Seek

While youngsters are out of the room, place paper shapes around the classroom and put an empty container nearby. To begin, look in the container and feign surprise that it is empty. Tell youngsters that the shapes have escaped, and they want to play hide-and-seek. Invite a few volunteers to be the seekers. Lead the class in saying the rhyme shown as the seekers look for the designated shape. After checking for accuracy, have each seeker put his shape in the container. Repeat the rhyme using a different shape each time.

We're going on a shape hunt.
We're going to find some [square] ones.
What's that you see?
Bring it to me!

Cari Charron
Red Bluff Strong Start
Quesnel, British Columbia, Canada

In the Hoop

Youngsters exercise their gross-motor skills along with math skills during this engaging activity. In an open area, place a plastic hoop on the floor and set a container of plastic lids nearby. A child chooses a lid and traces it with his finger, identifying the shape. Then he tosses it, attempting to get it in the hoop. He continues with each remaining lid. To incorporate number skills into the activity, have youngsters count and compare to determine if more lids landed inside or outside the hoop.

Kim Criswell
Wilson Elementary
Wilson, KS

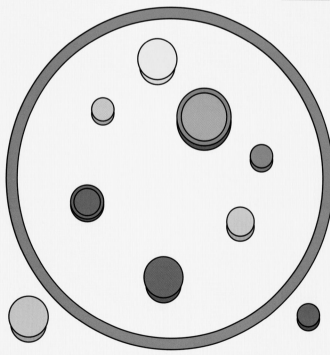

A Shapely Symphony!

In advance, gather rhythm instruments that show various shapes, such as triangles, tambourines, cymbals, and sand blocks. Distribute the instruments. Then name a shape. Lead youngsters in singing the song while students with the corresponding instruments play. Repeat the activity using a different shape each time. Then sing a final verse of the song, replacing the underlined word with the word *shapes* while all the youngsters play and sing!

(sung to the tune of "Are You Sleeping?")

Play little [triangles].
Play little [triangles].
What a sound,
All around!
Let's hear all the [triangles].
Let's hear all the [triangles].
What a sound,
All around!

Janet Boyce, Cokato, MN

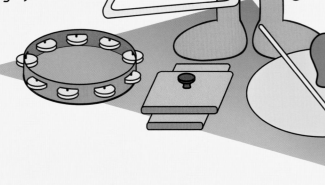

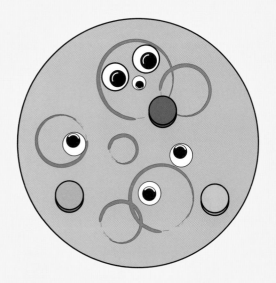

Circle Monsters

A variety of circles are used for this adorable art project! To prepare, gather shallow containers of paint; craft foam circles; jumbo and mini wiggle eyes (or eye stickers); and objects that make circle prints, such as cardboard tubes or bottle caps. Have each child make circle prints on a large paper circle. Then direct him to glue foam shapes and wiggle eyes to the circle. Set the projects aside to dry.

Trisha Cooper
Little Learner's Preschool
Spanish Fork, UT

Look and See

Cut a triangle from a manila folder and place colored sheets of paper in the folder. Hold up the folder and say, "[Color] triangle, [color] triangle, what do you see?" Remove the first sheet of paper to reveal a different color and guide youngsters to reply, "I see a [new color] triangle looking at me." Continue with the remaining colors of paper. After youngsters are comfortable with the activity, place the folder at a center for independent practice. Consider making folders for other shapes!

Beth Lemke, Highland Family Center Head Start
Columbia Heights, MN

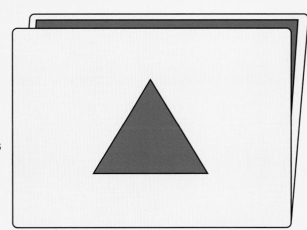

Shapes on the Go!

Place shape cutouts in the top row of your pocket chart. Then put a class supply of matching shape cutouts in a tub and place the tub on the other side of the classroom. Choose a child and have him run to the tub, choose a shape, and run back to the pocket chart. Help him identify the shape and place it beneath the matching shape. Then have him sit down. Repeat the process with each remaining student.

Carol Warren, Valley View Baptist Church School
Tuscaloosa, AL

Betty Silkunas of Lower Gwynedd Elementary in Ambler, Pennsylvania, suggests this entertaining way to practice drawing shapes! Distribute small flashlights to youngsters. Dim the lights. Then name a shape and have each child use her flashlight beam to "draw" the shape on the ceiling or a wall.

Shapes, Shapes Everywhere!

This shapely lift-the-flap booklet will be popular with your little ones! For each child, prepare a blank four-page booklet with a cover titled "Shapes, Shapes Everywhere!" Also, cut out a copy of page 239 for each child. Help each youngster glue the text strips and matching object cards to each booklet page. Then encourage her to glue (or tape) a small card over each picture to make a flap. (If desired, draw the corresponding shape on each flap for extra reinforcement.) Help the child read his booklet, lifting each flap and identifying the object.

Ada Goren
Winston Salem, NC

Shapes, Shapes Everywhere!

by Janie

Circles, circles everywhere!
Lift the flap to see what is there.

Circles, circles everywhere!
Lift the flap to see what is there.

TEC41062

Squares, squares everywhere!
Lift the flap to see what is there.

Triangles, triangles everywhere!
Lift the flap to see what is there.

Rectangles, rectangles everywhere!
Lift the flap to see what is there.

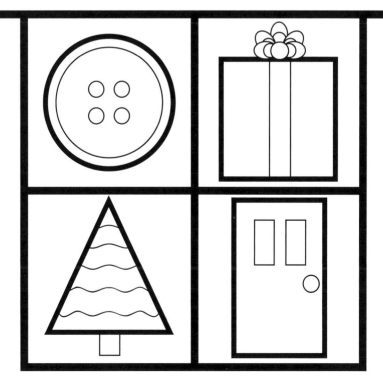

Math With Little Boy Blue

Recite the traditional rhyme "Little Boy Blue" with your youngsters. Then guide them through this collection of math activities!

ideas contributed by Roxanne LaBell Dearman
NC Early Intervention for
Children Who Are Deaf or Hard of Hearing
Charlotte, NC

Livestock on the Loose

Sorting, counting, one-to-one correspondence

Little Boy Blue could sure use some help gathering all those sheep and cows! Scatter a class supply of large white and brown pom-poms (sheep and cows) on the floor. Invite each youngster to "catch" a sheep or a cow and then help students sort them into two groups. Prompt students to count and compare the number of sheep and cows. Then encourage youngsters to line them up one to one.

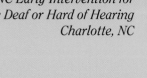

Where Is That Boy?

Positional words

For each child, cut apart copies of the booklet pages on pages 241–243 and then staple them between two construction paper covers labeled as shown. Also give each child a copy of the Little Boy Blue pattern on page 243. Then guide her through the directions below.

Directions:

1. Color the pages.
2. Color the Little Boy Blue pattern and transform it into a stick puppet.
3. Attach a pocket to the first page to store Little Boy Blue.
4. Listen to the story and manipulate the puppet to match the text.

Meadow Shopping

Estimation, nonstandard measurement

The sheep are looking for a new meadow that is just the right size! Make several copies of the sheep cards on page 243 and cut them apart. Then prepare three green paper meadows being sure that only one is sized so all the sheep cards will fit. Have students predict which meadow they think will be the right size for all the sheep. Then direct students to place the sheep cards on each meadow to determine if their guesses are correct.

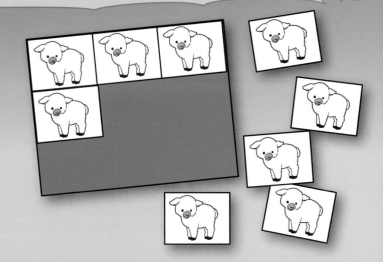

2

He's under the haystack, fast asleep!

1

Little Boy Blue

Little Boy Blue,
Come blow your horn.
The sheep's in the meadow.
The cow's in the corn.
Where is the boy
Who looks after the sheep?

Glue pocket here.

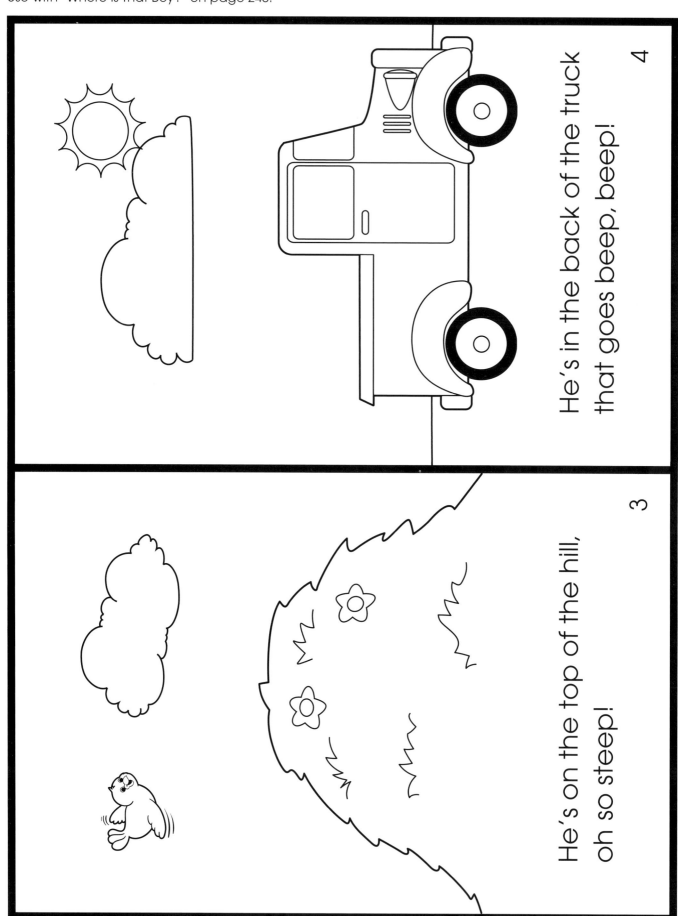

4

He's in the back of the truck
that goes beep, beep!

3

He's on the top of the hill,
oh so steep!

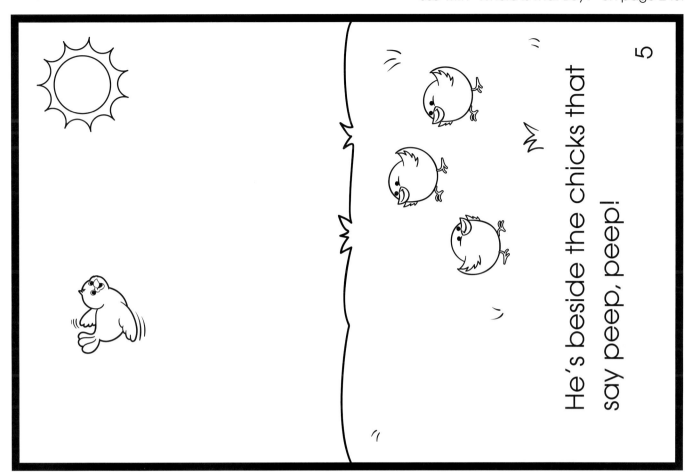

He's beside the chicks that say peep, peep!

5

TEC41063

TEC41063

TEC41063

A Blizzard of Measurement Ideas

This storm of measurement practice is just perfect for the winter season!

ideas contributed by Tricia Kylene Brown, Bowling Green, KY

Shoveling Snow
Exploring capacity

Place a supply of cotton balls (snow) in a sensory table (or tub). Set a few different-size containers and a plastic shovel nearby. Display two containers and encourage students to discuss which container they think will hold more snow. Invite a volunteer to shovel scoops of snow into one of the containers as the group counts the scoops. Then repeat the process with the other container. Guide youngsters to compare the amounts to their original predictions. Repeat with other pairs of containers.

Splendid Scarves
Comparing lengths

Scarves are not only fashionable winter wear but are also great tools for measurement practice. Place scarves of different lengths at a center. Encourage each center visitor to choose a scarf and then find objects in the classroom that are shorter than her scarf. After each child has had an opportunity to do some scarf measuring, change the goal of the center and ask youngsters to find objects that are longer than the scarves.

Gingerbread Man Measurement
Measuring height using nonstandard measurement

This is some tasty measurement! Cut apart several copies of the gingerbread man cards on page 246. Invite a pair of students to join you in an open area and have one child lie on the floor. Direct another student to measure her by placing gingerbread man cards end to end. Have him count to determine his partner's height. Then have the youngsters switch roles. Finally, guide the twosome in comparing their heights.

April Thompson, Mansfield, OH

The block is eight snowballs long.

Snowball Rulers

Measuring length using nonstandard measurement

Give each child a tagboard strip and ten cotton balls (snowballs). Direct him to glue the snowballs side by side on the strip. Trim the strip if necessary. Then invite him to use his snowball ruler to measure objects around the classroom. To conclude the activity, have each youngster choose an object and measure it for the group.

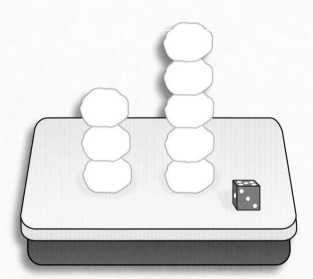

Building Snowmen

Comparing heights

Tall and small and everything between! These snowmen come in a variety of heights! Make several balls from white play dough so they resemble snowballs and place them at a table. Have two youngsters visit the table. One child rolls a die and counts the dots. Then she builds a snowman with that number of snowballs. Her partner repeats the process. Then students compare the heights of their snowmen, using words such as *shorter*, *taller*, and *equal*.

Shiny Icicles

Ordering by length

Reinforce measurement skills with this cool art activity. Place at the art center sheets of blue construction paper, strips of aluminum foil in a variety of lengths, glue, a paintbrush, and iridescent glitter. A center visitor chooses five strips of different lengths and then tears along the sides of each strip so it resembles an icicle. She glues the icicles along the top of her paper from shortest to longest. To add extra sparkle to her project, she brushes glue on each icicle and then sprinkles glitter on the glue.

Gingerbread Man Cards

Use with "Gingerbread Man Measurement" on page 244.

TEC41064

TEC41064

TEC41064

TEC41064

Math
for Little Leprechauns

This collection of St. Patrick's Day math activities is marvelous for March!

Catch a Color
Recognizing colors

To play this colorful game, have two students hold hands and raise their arms to make a rainbow. Encourage the remaining youngsters to line up behind the rainbow. Then lead students in saying the rhyme shown as they walk under the rainbow. After a color is named, the youngsters making the rainbow lower their arms to catch a child wearing that color. The child steps aside. After the students catch a second child, they return to the line. The students who were caught make a rainbow, and play continues.

Red and orange, yellow and green,
Blue and purple are the colors we've seen.
[Red] is the color we're looking for.
We'll catch a friend and then one more.

Donna Olp, St. Gregory the Great Preschool, South Euclid, OH

Follow the Trail
Nonstandard measurement

Reinforce measurement skills with the help of a mischievous little visitor. A few days prior to St. Patrick's Day, post a leprechaun cutout (pattern on page 249). Introduce youngsters to the leprechaun and explain that he promises to stay right there and behave if they will allow him to watch their class. After youngsters leave for the day, move the leprechaun to a different location and place a line of yellow circles (gold coins) between the two locations. Feign surprise when little ones notice the coin trail and the leprechaun's new location. Guide the group in counting the coins to find out the distance between the two locations. Repeat the activity each day until St. Patrick's Day.

Cynthia Billings, Kay's ABC's of Child Care, Belton, MO

Leprechaun Ladders

Patterning

Place tagboard strips and light green and dark green shamrock cutouts at a center. A child glues shamrocks to a strip to make a pattern. Then two youngsters place their strips parallel to each other and glue short strips between them to make a leprechaun ladder. Help each twosome attach its ladder somewhere in the classroom so the little leprechauns can climb and play at night. After students leave, sprinkle a little gold glitter (leprechaun dust) near each ladder and around the room. Youngsters are sure to be excited when they return to find the evidence of leprechaun mischief.

Beth Kossen
Olivia's House Learning Center
Kansas City, MO

Fill the Pot

Counting

Oh no! The leprechaun's pot is empty. Enlist the help of a small group of youngsters to fill it with gold. Set out a plastic pot, a small cup of popped corn cereal (gold) for each child, and a large foam die. In turn, each child rolls the die, counts the dots, and puts that number of gold pieces in the pot. Play continues until one player's cup is empty.

Suzanne Moore, Tucson, AZ

Clovers Collected

3 leaves	4 leaves

Are We Lucky?

Graphing

Cut out several copies of the clover cards on page 250 and place them on a length of green bulletin board paper (clover field). Post a graph like the one shown. Invite each youngster to visit the clover field, find a clover, and place it in the correct column of the graph. Continue until all the clovers have been "picked." Then lead youngsters in counting each column and comparing the amounts. Exclaim with delight that they found more four-leaf clovers, which means they are very lucky preschoolers!

Roxanne LaBell Dearman
North Carolina Early Intervention Program for Children Who Are
    Deaf or Hard of Hearing
Charlotte, NC

 tip
To celebrate youngsters' good luck, have a lucky snack like the simple and tasty option on pages 86 and 87!

TEC41065

Clover Cards
Use with "Are We Lucky?" on page 248.

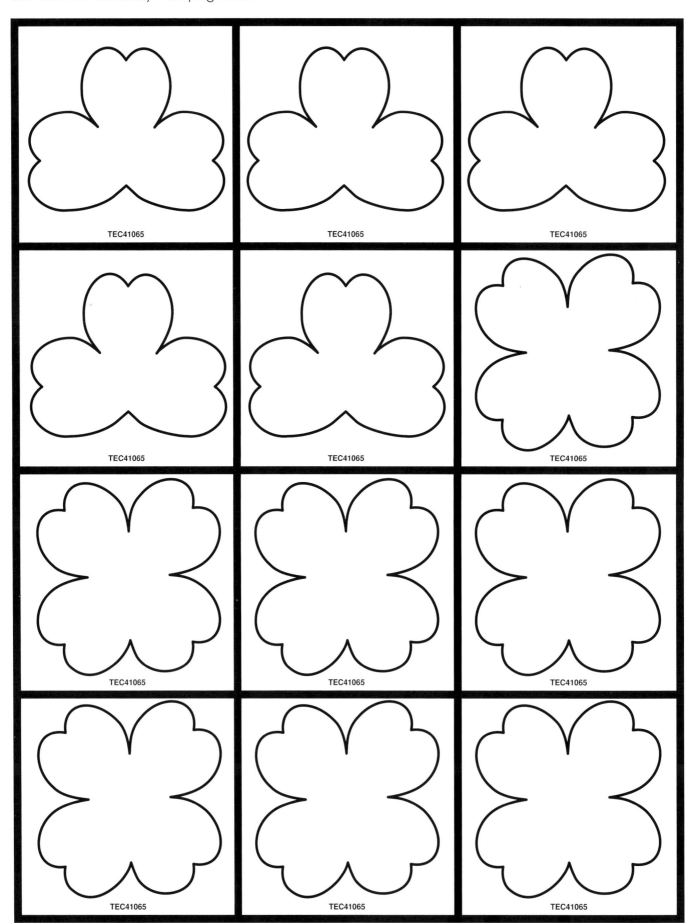

TEC41065

TEC41065

TEC41065

TEC41065

TEC41065

TEC41065

TEC41065

TEC41065

TEC41065

TEC41065

TEC41065

TEC41065

Peas, Carrots, Potatoes, and Beans
Veggie Math

Lima Count
Identifying numbers, counting
Nurture number skills with that much-maligned veggie—the lima bean! Make simple green pod cutouts, as shown, and get a supply of dried lima beans. Give a child a small cup of beans and several pods. Have each child count a set of ten beans and then place it on a pod. Have him continue with sets of ten and different pods until he runs out of beans. Encourage him to count how many sets of ten he made. Then, if desired, have him decide how many beans he would need to add to his remaining beans to make a final set of ten. When the activity is finished, store the beans for safekeeping.

Tricia Kylene Brown
Bowling Green, KY

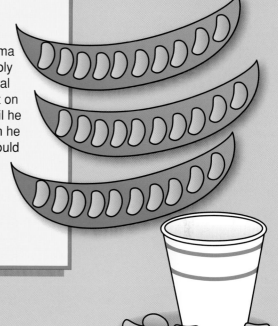

Taters!
Comparing weights, predicting
To prepare for this center, gather several different types of potatoes—such as Idaho, red, and sweet—and provide a balance scale. A child visits the center and explores the differences between the potatoes. Then he chooses two potatoes and predicts which one is heavier. Next, he places a different potato in each side of the balance scale to confirm his prediction. He continues with different pairs of potatoes.

Suzanne Moore, Tucson, AZ

Peas and Carrots

Sorting, patterning

Cut orange craft foam into small squares and then place the squares in a bowl along with small green pom-poms so the mixture resembles peas and carrots. Gather a small group of youngsters. Have each child take a scoop of the peas and carrots and then sort them into two piles. Next, give each child a strip of paper and encourage her to arrange her peas and carrots on the strip to make a pattern. Have her read her pattern and then glue the peas and carrots into place.

Suzanne Moore
Tucson, AZ

A Real-Life Dilemma

Estimating

Present a bag of fresh green beans to your youngsters and explain that you have a problem. You want to know if you have enough green beans to feed three people. Explain that for three people, you want to have a total of 30 beans. Help each child write the word "yes" or "no" on a sticky note to show whether he believes you have 30. Stick the notes to a wall in two groups according to youngsters' answers. Then count and compare the sets of notes. Finally, have students help you count the beans aloud to determine whether you have 30.

Ruth Zabelin, Kleberg Elementary, Kingsville, TX

Complete the Carrots

Matching sets and numbers

Cut out several copies of the cards on page 253. Label the carrot tops with numbers and the bottoms with matching dot sets. Sort the cards by type and then turn over each set. Encourage a youngster to flip over a top and a bottom. If they match, have her place them together and set them aside. If they do not, instruct her to flip them back over. Have youngsters continue until all the tops and bottoms are matched.

Tricia Kylene Brown
Bowling Green, KY

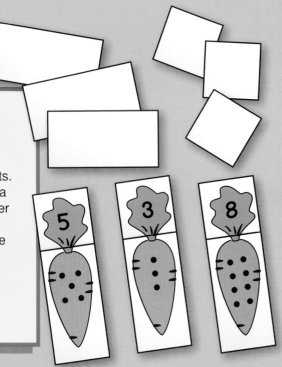

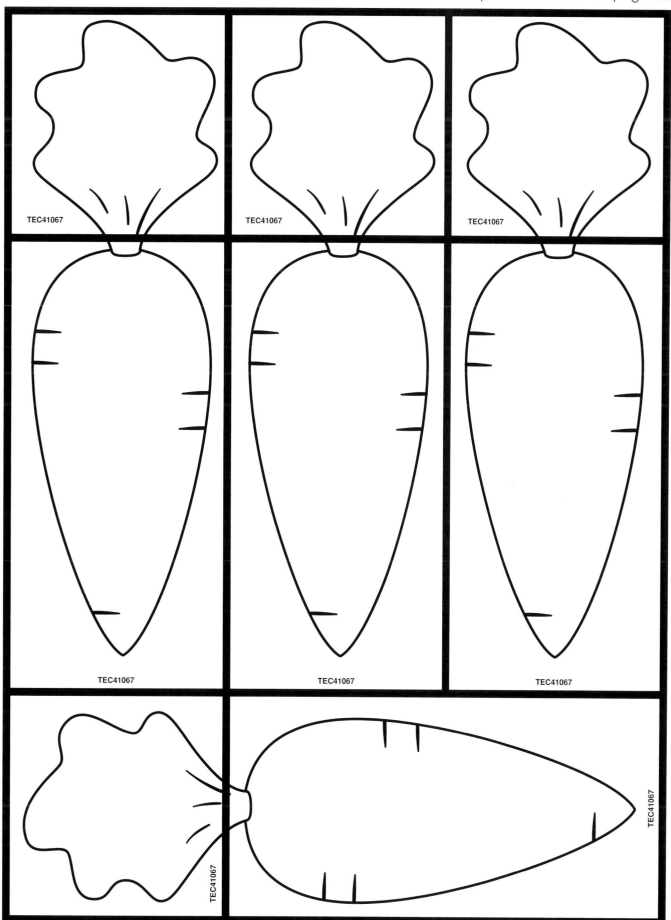

TEC41067

TEC41067

TEC41067

TEC41067

TEC41067

TEC41067

TEC41067

TEC41067

Perfectly Preschool Math

These simple and engaging math activities are perfect for any time throughout the year!

Build a Wall

Identifying numbers, counting

Youngsters build a wall for Humpty Dumpty with this easy-to-prepare center! Make a copy of the spinner pattern on page 256, cut it out, and attach a brad and paper clip to the cutout. Provide a weighted plastic egg programmed with a face (Humpty Dumpty) and blocks. Two students visit the center. One child spins the spinner, identifies the number, and stacks or removes the corresponding number of blocks as directed. A second child repeats the process with her own stack of blocks. Students continue taking turns until one child makes a stack of ten blocks. Then she places Humpty Dumpty on top of her finished wall. The students tear down the walls and repeat the game.

MaDonna Reiter, Beloit Elementary Preschool
Beloit, KS

How Many in All?

Combining sets, making a set of ten, counting

In advance, trace your hands on a sheet of paper and obtain a container of small blocks (or another type of small manipulative). Gather a small group of youngsters. Have a child count out five blocks and place them on one hand tracing. Then have a second child place five blocks on the other hand tracing. Have the remaining youngsters help count all the blocks on both hands. Then lead little ones in singing the song shown as you gesture to each appropriate hand. Repeat the activity with different set combinations that make ten, guiding students to notice that each combination they have made results in ten. **For an extra challenge**, have students write the different number combinations that make ten.

(sung to the tune of "Skip to My Lou")

[Five] blocks on this hand.
[Five] blocks on that hand.
Ten blocks altogether.
[Five] and [five] make ten.

Jamie Madorma Hartless
Chapel Hill, NC

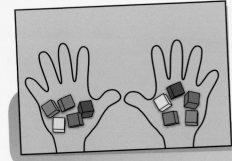

Cube Cover

Spatial skills, manipulating geometric shapes

Trace one-inch cube blocks to make a one-inch, two-inch, three-inch, and four-inch square on a sheet of construction paper. Place the sheet at a center along with one-inch blocks. A child uses blocks to cover each shape. Then he counts the number of blocks in each shape and notices that each one is a square!

Janet Boyce
Cokato, MN

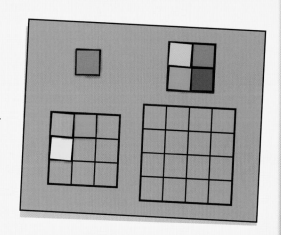

Shake Those Beans!

Counting, making sets

Gather a small group of students and give each child a small disposable cup. Provide a container of beans and a pair of dice. Have a child roll the dice and count the dots. Then prompt each child to count out a matching number of beans and place them in her cup. Guide each student in placing one hand over the top of her cup and the remaining hand beneath her cup as she recites the chant shown, shaking the cup when indicated as she counts the number of beans. Next, have each youngster spill her beans back in the container. Repeat the activity several times.

Three beans in my cup—
I count them out and shake them up!
[One, two, three]!

Laura Chapman, Chapel Glen Elementary
Indianapolis, IN

Color Concentration

Identifying colors, matching colors

Gather a few pairs of paint color strips from a local home-improvement store. Then cut the strips into separate colors. Place the pieces at a center and prompt students to explore them as desired, matching them, playing a concentration-style game, organizing them by color family, and identifying the colors.

Jennifer Cochran, Morgan County Primary
Madison, GA

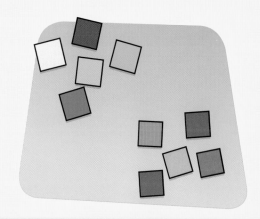

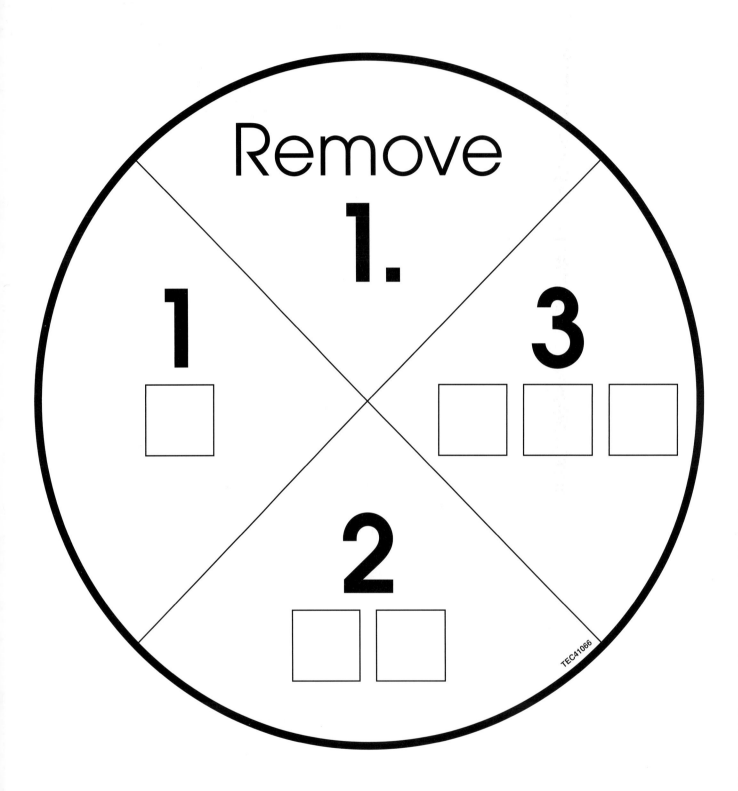

TEACHER RESOURCE UNITS

7 Engaging Discovery Centers

1 That's the Tops!

Place a variety of tops in the discovery center. Encourage youngsters to visit the center to explore how the tops can move. After youngsters have had a chance to explore, place other manipulatives in the center and prompt little ones to discover which items spin and which ones do not. *Kelly Tincher, Saint Edmond School, Fort Dodge, IA*

2 Wet It Down

Put items such as a rain boot, cotton batting, wooden and plastic blocks, yarn, and plastic containers in an empty water table. Also provide a small spray bottle of water. Encourage youngsters to spray the items to see how rain would affect each one.
Janet Boyce, Cokato, MN

3 Totally Texture

Provide a tub full of textured items. For example, place seashells, tinsel, Velcro fasteners, scrub brushes, feathers, sandpaper, cotton balls, bath poufs, and makeup brushes in a tub. Youngsters touch, dig through, and explore the soft, scratchy, rough, and smooth items.
Sarah Berkey, Growing Tree Preschool, Chambersburg, PA

Seasonal Selections

Need discovery center items to go with each season? Look no further! Here are splendid options your little ones will love to investigate!

4 Fall: brown pom-poms (acorns) hidden in a tub of twigs, pinecones, fall leaves, and cedar shavings (small-animal bedding) *Janet Boyce*

5 Winter: salt and glitter mixture (snow), small toy cars, plastic ice scraper (snowplow) *Janet Boyce*

6 Spring: real and artificial flower petals and leaves, plastic magnifying glasses

7 Summer: sand pails and shovels, bottles, funnels, dry oatmeal

Many centers involve sand or rice. Why not use dry oatmeal for variety! The texture is unique and appealing.

Think Outside the Box!

Creative Ideas for Using Boxes

Pretty Prints

Save small sturdy gift boxes or ask parents to donate them. For a fun activity that reviews shapes, set out the boxes, shallow containers of paint, and blank paper. A child makes a variety of prints on her paper using the tops and bottoms of the boxes.

Donna Green
Walnut Grove Children's Learning Center
Mechanicsville, VA

Cruising Critters

Youngsters use lidless boxes as transportation for toy critters! Stock your block center with lidless boxes and stuffed toy animals. (Tissue boxes are perfect for this idea!) Youngsters build roads, train tracks, and buildings with the blocks. Then they put toy animals in the boxes and have the toys "drive" around the city!

Suzanne Moore, Tucson, AZ

Sculpture Time!

In advance, ask parents to send in small and medium-size boxes. Invite each youngster to choose several boxes and arrange them to create a sculpture. When children are out of the room, hot-glue the boxes together. The following day, set out paints, paper scraps, and other craft materials. Encourage the child to paint and decorate his sculpture as desired.

Naomi McCall, Virginia Beach, VA

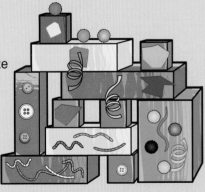

A Crafty Collection

Add the sign shown to a large box and then decorate it as desired. Ask parents and coworkers to donate materials that can be used for art projects, such as cardboard tubes, material scraps, scrapbooking paper, yarn, spools, and tissue boxes. Store the donations in the box and put the box in your art area. When a center visitor is feeling especially creative, invite him to rummage through the box and choose a few items to use to create a unique piece of art.

Bonnie C. Krum, St. Matthews Early Education Center, Bowie, MD

Artwork in Pairs

Partners, pairs, duos, and chums! Budding artists are sure to enjoy this cozy collection of cooperative art activities!

ideas contributed by Janet Boyce, Cokato, MN

Duo Designs

Put a sheet of large white construction paper in a plastic tub or box lid. Invite two students to each squeeze white glue designs on the paper; then have them sprinkle salt on the wet glue. When they're finished, gently shake off the excess salt and place the paper on a table. Have each child dip a small paintbrush in watercolors and then gently dab the brush on the salted designs, repeating with other colors as desired. The resulting artwork is gorgeous!

Chalk Chums

Set out 12" x 18" light-color construction paper, black electrical (or craft) tape, scissors, and chalk. Instruct a pair of youngsters to cut tape strips and attach them to a sheet of paper so the strips create open spaces as shown. Then have little ones color the spaces using the chalk.

 tip → When the artwork is complete, mist the paper with hair spray to set the chalk.

Straw Snippets

Place two sheets of construction paper side by side in a shallow container. Provide bowls of tinted glue, a spoon for each bowl, colorful drinking straws, and scissors. Have two children drizzle glue over the surface of each paper. Next, encourage each child to snip the straws above the container so the pieces fall onto the papers. Then have the pair drizzle additional glue over the straw snippets.

Partner Printing

Invite each of two children to dip a sponge in paint and dab it on a 12" x 18" sheet of bubble wrap. (If desired, use a permanent marker to divide the wrap in half.) Have them continue with different colors of paint as desired. Then have the pair place a sheet of construction paper atop the wrap and gently rub their hands across the paper. Help them remove the paper to reveal the transferred print; then set the paper aside to dry.

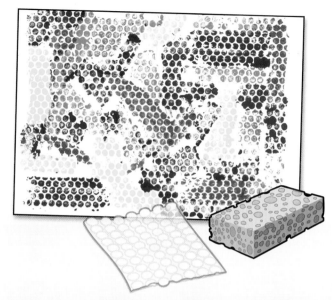

Paired Puff Painting

Set out two or more colors of puff paint (mix equal parts of tinted glue and nonmentholated shaving cream), a spoon for each paint color, and a file folder. Have each of two youngsters spoon dollops of puff paint on opposite sides of the open file folder; then encourage each child to swirl, blend, and sculpt the paint. Have students gently close the folder, pat it with their hands, and then reopen it. Allow several days for the artwork to dry. Then separate it at the fold so each child can take home half of the project.

Shake, Rattle, and Roll

Tape sheets of construction paper to the inside bottom and top of a lidded container. Gather several objects, such as a small ball, a jingle bell, a linking cube, and a milk cap. Have one child use a spoon to dip an object in paint and transfer it to the container. Have him close the lid and vigorously manipulate the container, saying, "Shake, rattle, and roll!" as he works. Have him remove his item. Then repeat the process with a second child. Invite youngsters to continue for several turns; then remove the artwork.

Simply Spanish!

Looking for ways to incorporate simple Spanish vocabulary into your curriculum? Then try these fun activities that focus on colors, counting, sizes, objects, and more!

Word of the Week

Little ones will be eager to speak Spanish with the help of a Spanish-speaking puppet! Obtain a puppet. Post a paper labeled with a Spanish word, the English translation, and a picture of the word. Help the puppet greet youngsters with a Spanish greeting like "¡Hola!" Next, have the puppet introduce the Spanish word of the week and explain what it means in English. Then have the puppet lead students in practicing the Spanish word and telling its English translation. Post a new word each week and bind the used pages with metal rings to make a class book titled "Simply Spanish."

Melanie Whitmire, Fulton, MO

libro
(book)

Name That Color

Youngsters learn and reinforce English and Spanish color words with this fun song! Gather construction paper in several different colors. Label each sheet with its color name in both languages. Display a sheet and have youngsters identify its color in English. Next, have students say the color word in Spanish. Then lead little ones in singing several verses of the song shown, inserting a new color word and examples each time. (Color suggestions are blue/*azul*, green/*verde*, yellow/*amarillo*, orange/*anaranjado*, brown/*marrón*, black/*negro*, and white/*blanco.*)

red
rojo

(sung to the tune of "Where Is Thumbkin?")

What is [*rojo*]?
What is [*rojo*]?
[Apples] are [*rojo*].
[Cherries] are [*rojo*].
[*Rojo*] is a color.
[*Rojo*] is a color.
[*Rojo*] is [red].
[*Rojo*] is [red].

Ruth Zabelin, Kleberg Elementary, Kingsville, TX

Seasonal Sizes

Make small, medium, and large die-cut flowers (or other seasonal shapes). Label a three-column graph with the words *pequeño* (small), *mediano* (medium), and *grande* (large) and appropriate die-cuts. Place the remaining die-cuts in a bag. After teaching youngsters the size words, have a child choose a flower from the bag, say its size in English and Spanish, and then place it in the correct column. Continue for each child.

Joanna Lewis
Mooresville, NC

To incorporate more Spanish vocabulary into this activity, use the words *más* (more), *menos* (less), and *igual* (equal) when interpreting the graph.

| pequeño | mediano | grande |

I spy *un gato.*

Spanish I Spy

Spice up this popular preschool game with Spanish vocabulary words! Post pictures of familiar objects such as a cat (*un gato*), a dog (*un perro*), a car (*un coche*), a horse (*un caballo*), a shoe (*un zapato*), and a book (*un libro*). Also add several die-cut numbers to the display. Review the Spanish words for each picture word and number. Then say, "I spy [picture word or number]," saying the word in Spanish. A child goes to the display and points to the picture or number. Continue for several rounds.

Kate Hogenson, Preschool of St. Andrews
Mahtomedi, MN

Roll, Count, and Jump!

Counting in Spanish will be a breeze after several rounds of this gross-motor activity! Invite a volunteer to roll a jumbo die and count the dots aloud in Spanish, providing help as needed. After confirming the number of dots is correct, prompt the group to jump that many times while counting aloud in Spanish. When youngsters are proficient at counting from one to six in Spanish, add a second die and count to twelve.

Franklin Mays, Averill Elementary, Lansing, MI

Uno, dos, tres, cuatro, cinco.

Parachute Play!

Does enthusiasm for parachute play in your class seem to go up and down? Then try these uplifting ideas!

Youngsters can be any age they want with this parachute game and rhyme! Announce a child's name; then lead the group in chanting, "Birthdays are for you and me! How old would you like to be?" Prompt the child to say a number and then help students count and lift the parachute that many times. *Stephanie Finnell, Honeysuckle Home Daycare, Sedalia, MO*

Spread a colorful parachute on the ground and have students stand around it several feet from the edge. Hand a child a small, stuffed toy and ask him to face away from the parachute. Lead the group in saying, "One, two, three, toss!" prompting him to toss the toy over his shoulder. Then have him turn around and identify the color the toy lands on. *Jennifer Askuecollins, School for Small Scholars, Midlothian, VA*

Toss a handful of pom-poms (magic beans) onto a parachute. Help youngsters vigorously shake the parachute until all the beans fall to the ground. Then ask little ones to tell what might happen if the magic beans begin to grow. *Karen Eiben, LaSalle, IL*

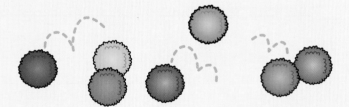

Put items under the parachute to represent treasure and invite two children to be deep-sea divers. On your signal, the group lifts the parachute and walks in a circle singing the song shown. At the same time, each diver "swims" beneath the parachute, takes a piece of treasure, and continues to the other side before the song ends and the parachute is brought down. *Darlene Taig, Willow Creek Co-op Preschool, Westland, MI*

(sung to the tune of "Did You Ever See a Lassie?")

Have you ever found some treasure,
Some treasure, some treasure?
Have you ever found some treasure
Deep under the sea?
Be careful of sharks there!
Go quickly and take care!
Have you ever found some treasure
Deep under the sea?

THEMATIC UNITS

A Rootin'-Tootin' Western Welcome!

Welcome your little buckaroos to preschool with these wonderful western-themed ideas!

Corral the Cattle

Attendance display

This herd of cattle will tell you who is present for the day! Cut out and personalize a copy of the cow pattern on page 269 for each child. **For a tabletop or floor display option**, arrange blocks to make a corral. **For a wall display option**, attach a rope to your wall in an oval. Place the cows nearby. When a youngster arrives, she finds her cow and places (or attaches) it in the enclosure. One look at the cows outside the corral will tell you who is absent.

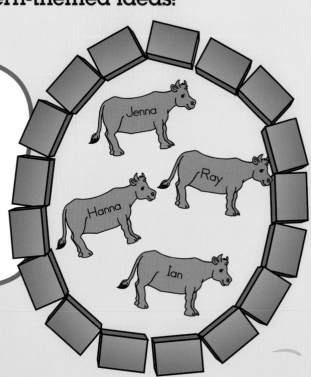

Who's That Cowpoke?

Getting-acquainted activity

If desired, have little ones help you stack real rocks and logs in the center of your circle-time area to make a pretend campfire. Sit with little ones in a circle around the campfire. Then lead students in reciting the chant, inserting the name of the child sitting next to you. Help the student identify her neighbor. Prompt youngsters to say, "Howdy, [student name]!" Next, recite the chant, inserting that child's name. Continue around the circle until everyone has received a "howdy"!

Howdy, [student name]!
How do you do?
Who's that cowpoke next to you?

Mary Boand, Louis B. Russell Jr. Elementary, Indianapolis, IN
Suzanne Moore, Tucson, AZ

Ranch Hands Wanted!
Job chart

Assign jobs to your little ranch hands with this excellent old-west display! Make a copy of the wanted poster on page 270 for each job in your classroom. Then label the pages with the job titles and display them with the title "Wanted: Ranch Hands." Print out a photo of each youngster wearing a bandana or cowboy hat. (If you don't want to use photos, cut out and personalize copies of the cowboy hat pattern on page 269.) To assign jobs, simply attach a photo (or hat) to each poster.

Marie Bortz from The Learning Experience in Nazareth, Pennsylvania, uses wanted posters in a nifty classroom display! She attaches a photo of each child in a cowboy hat to a copy of a wanted poster (see page 270) and then displays the posters with the title "Miss Marie's Most Wanted Preschoolers!"

A "Wheel-y" Fun Project
Literacy center

Write students' first initials on separate sheets of construction paper. Provide wagon wheel (rotelle) pasta. (If desired, dye the pasta first.) A child traces the first letter of his name with his finger. Then he dabs glue on the letter and presses the pasta in the glue. He continues until the entire letter is covered. If desired, encourage him to attach western-themed stickers to the page.

Phyllis Prestridge, West Amory Elementary, Amory, MS

Handy Bandanas
Gross-motor activity

Give each youngster a bandana and then explain that cowboys could use bandanas for many things. Describe each function of a bandana shown below, encouraging little ones to manipulate their bandanas. Finally, play a recording of square dance music and prompt students to move their bandanas through the air.

Dust mask: wrap around the nose and mouth
Protection from sunburn: wrap around neck
Earmuffs: wrap over the head and under the chin
Pot holder: wrap around hand
Bandage: wrap around knee or other body part
Sweatband: wrap around forehead

Suzanne Moore, Tucson, AZ

Lasso Painting
Process art

To make this simple painting project, tie a short piece of rope (or clothesline) so it resembles a lasso. Attach a cow cutout (see page 269) to a colorful sheet of construction paper. Then dip the lasso in a shallow container of paint and move it across the paper, pretending to lasso the cow. Prompt youngsters to randomly yell, "Yee-haw!" as they paint!

I'm a Cowboy!
Song

What do cowboys do? Youngsters find out with this entertaining song!

(sung to the tune of "If You're Happy and You Know It")

I'm a cowboy [riding horses] all day long, (Yee-haw!)	*Pretend to hold reins; bounce up and down.*
Watching cattle, singing lots of cowboy songs. (Yee-haw!)	*Pretend to hold reins; bounce up and down.*
And I'm wearing cowboy jeans;	*Slap thighs.*
And I'm eating cowboy beans.	*Pat tummy.*
I'm a cowboy [riding horses] all day long. (Yee-haw!)	*Pretend to hold reins; bounce up and down.*

Continue with the following: wearing boots, *(stomp feet)*; roping critters, *(pretend to swing lasso)*; in the hot sun, *(wipe forehead)*

Suzanne Moore, Tucson, AZ

A Cowboy Confection
Storytime

Get a copy of *The Gingerbread Cowboy* by Janet Squires. **Before you read,** have youngsters study the cover of the book. Ask them to guess what is beneath the cowboy hat. What do they think this critter will do? After youngsters share their thoughts, read the story aloud. **After the story,** gather a small group of youngsters and tell them that the gingerbread cowboy ran so hard, he left a trail of lovely gingerbread decorations! Have each youngster practice fine-motor control by squeezing a meandering trail of glue on a brown sheet of paper. Then encourage her to sprinkle glitter, sequins, and western-themed metallic confetti on the glue.

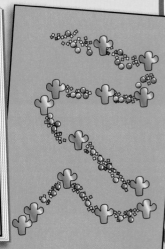

Cow Pattern

Use with "Corral the Cattle" on page 266
and "Lasso Painting" on page 268.

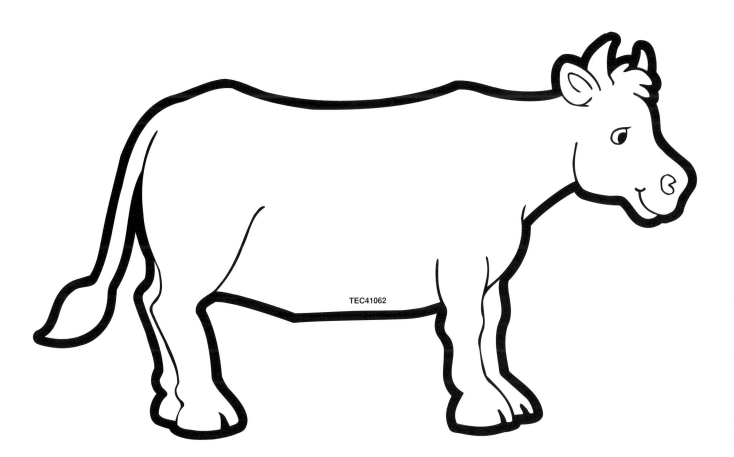

TEC41062

Cowboy Hat Pattern

Use for cubby tags and other classroom
labeling or displays.

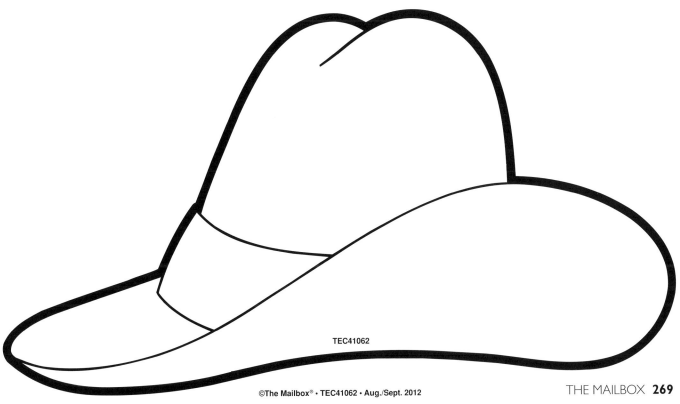

TEC41062

Wanted Poster Pattern

Use with "Ranch Hands Wanted!" on page 267.

TEC41062

What's Inside Us?
Bones!

They're Necessary!

Developing gross-motor skills

Lead students in performing this fun action song emphasizing the importance of bones!

(sung to the tune of "My Bonnie Lies Over the Ocean")

I have lots of bones in my body.	*Hug self.*
They help me to stand straight and tall.	*Stand tall.*
'Cause if there were no bones inside me,	*Throw arms out to sides.*
My body would crumple and fall!	*Crumple gently to floor.*
I need bones!	*Stand and point to self.*
They help me to stand and to move, you see.	*March.*
I need bones!	*Point to self.*
My bones are important to me!	*March.*

Suzanne Moore, Tucson, AZ

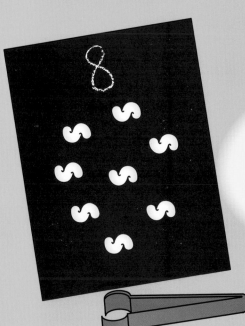

Bone Count

Making sets, counting

Label pieces of black construction paper with numbers and provide a container of white packing peanuts (bones). Have a child use tongs to place the correct number of bones on each paper.

Lori Dworsky, Middletown, DE

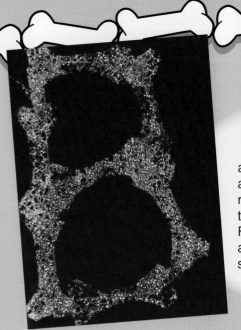

B Is for Bones
Reinforcing letter names, forming letters

These letter *B* projects look spiffy as a Halloween display! In advance, trim a sponge so it resembles a bone. For each child, use a white crayon to write a letter *B* on black construction paper. A child runs his fingers along the letter and says its name. Then he says the word *bone*, noticing that it begins with /b/, the sound of letter *B*. Finally, encourage him to press the sponge bone cutout into paint and then make prints along the letter *B*. For extra pizzazz, have him sprinkle white or green glitter on the wet paint.

Paint a Part
Building vocabulary

Help youngsters learn the names of bones with some mess-free painting! Give each child a clean paintbrush. To begin, tell students to paint their ribs. Encourage each youngster to dip his brush in a pretend pot of paint and then run the brush along his ribs. Next, have each student feel his bottom jaw. Explain that this bone is called the mandible. Then have students "paint" their mandibles. Continue in the same way with other bones such as the clavicle (collarbone), the sternum, the cranium (skull), the humerus (upper arm bone), the scapula (shoulder blade), the patella (kneecap), and the femur (upper leg bone).

Kelly Ash, Waukesha Head Start, Waukesha, WI

Clacking Bones
Identifying beginning sounds

For this small-group activity, cut out a copy of the cards on page 273 and place them facedown. Give each child a pair of rhythm sticks (bones). Turn over a card and have students say the name of the picture. If it begins with /b/ like *bones*, have them clack their bones together. If not, have them stay silent. Continue with each remaining card.

No rhythm sticks? Try unsharpened pencils or dowel pieces!

TEC41063

TEC41063

TEC41063

TEC41063

TEC41063

TEC41063

TEC41063

TEC41063

TEC41063

TEC41063

TEC41063

TEC41063

Fuzzy Funny, and Adorable
MONSTERS!

The Perfect Name!

Recognizing the beginning sound /m/

What shall your little ones name this adorable monster? Anything that begins with /m/! Write silly names on slips of paper, including several names that begin with /m/, such as *Meep, Marvelous, Moop, Merryweather, Mervin, Muddle, Marp, Mip,* and *Meenie.* Place the papers in a bag. Cut out and display a copy of the monster pattern on page 277. Tell students that it's time to name this monster, but its name must begin with /m/, just as *monster* begins with /m/. Have a child draw a slip of paper. Read the name aloud and have students determine whether the monster could have this name. Continue with each slip of paper.

Mervin

Nifty Noses!

Counting, making sets

Adorable little monsters are known for having varying numbers of facial features, so youngsters won't bat an eye at the excessive number of noses on these furry fellows! Draw two simple monsters without noses and gather a supply of pom-poms (noses). Call two youngsters to a table and have one child roll a die and count the dots. Then encourage him to count that number of noses and place them on a monster. Have his classmate repeat the process with the other monster. Then encourage them to compare the sets of noses.

For more facial-feature fun, omit the eyes on your monsters and have students repeat the activity with a supply of eye cutouts!

Monster Design
Writing

With this engaging idea, youngsters help design and label a monster! To begin, call on a student and ask him to tell you if the monster should have a long, skinny body or a wide, fat body. Draw an appropriate body shape on chart paper. Then draw a line from the body and write a description, as shown, along with the child's name. Continue with other limbs, features, and appendages until youngsters are satisfied with their monster.

spiky hair
—Miracle

five eyes
—Anna

big ears
—Aisha

pointed teeth
—Aki

long, skinny body
—John

furry paws
—Evan

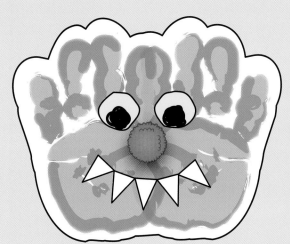

Handy Little Monsters!
Developing fine-motor skills

To make this adorable artwork, help each child paint her palms and fingers, omitting the thumbs. Then encourage her to make side-by-side handprints. Have her add white triangle cutouts for teeth, a pom-pom nose, and eye cutouts. If desired, cut out the projects and attach them to a display titled "A Handful of Little Monsters!"

Tracy Macarages
Richie's Early Learning Academy
Lee, FL

A Not-So-Scary Story
Holding a book correctly, turning pages from right to left

Read aloud the classic and engaging story *The Monster at the End of This Book* by Jon Stone. In this story, Grover—that lovable *Sesame Street* character—warns readers about a monster at the end of the book. He pleads with readers to not turn the page, only to discover that the monster at the end of the book is him! After the read-aloud, place colorful paper, crayons, and markers at a center and encourage students to draw and cut out their own monsters. Once a child has made a monster, prompt her to pick up a book in your reading center, hold it correctly, and turn the pages until she arrives at the end. Then have her slip her monster into the book and close it. Now there's a monster at the end of that book as well!

Cute and Cuddly!

Reciting a rhyming chant, ordinal numbers

Copy and cut out the monster on page 277 to make five. Then place a piece of rolled tape on the back of each one. Lead students in reciting the chant shown, attaching each monster to the board when indicated. After the chant, ask, "Which monster is the first monster?" Prompt a child to point to that monster. Continue with other questions that use ordinal numbers.

Five cuddly monsters, walking down the street.
The first one said, "I have big feet!"
The second one said, "Those feet do smell!"
The third one said, "Yours do as well!"
The fourth one said, "Please do not fight!"
The fifth one said, "Yes, be polite!"
So the first three monsters quarreled no more,
And they all walked away with a great big roar!

adapted from an idea by Doria Owen, William Paca Old Post Road Elementary, Abingdon, MD

Monster Munch

Following directions

Invite your little monsters to prepare and eat these tasty snacks! Encourage each youngster to spread green-tinted cream cheese on a mini bagel half. Have her put carrot strips on the bagel for hair and thin wedges of cucumber for teeth. Then encourage her to add mini chocolate chip eyes to her monstrous creation! Finally, invite her to eat her monster.

Betsey Lepak
Roger Wolcott Early Childhood Center
Windsor, CT

For extra fun, do what Mary Davis of Keokuk Christian Academy in Keokuk, Iowa, does! Add felt eyes, a pom-pom nose, and several felt teeth to socks to make monster sock puppets! Then place them at your centers. Encourage youngsters to visit a center, don a sock monster, and use it to explore the center. What a simple way to expand your cuddly monster unit!

TEC41063

Animals in Winter

Some of them hibernate, some change colors, and some just take a nap! Youngsters will enjoy exploring what animals do during the wintertime.

Zzzz!

Letter-sound association

Which animals hibernate? Your little ones might be surprised! Cut out a copy of the animal cards on page 281. Make seven cards labeled "Zzzz." Place the animal cards facedown on the floor. Have a child flip a card and identify the animal. Then lead students in singing the song. Reveal whether the animal is a hibernator or not. *All these animals are hibernators except for the goose and the deer.* If the animal hibernates, have a child place a "Zzzz" card over the animal. Have students pretend to sleep and say, "Zzzz." Repeat the activity for each remaining card.

(sung to the tune of "London Bridge")

Tell me, do you hibernate,
Hibernate, hibernate?
Tell me, do you hibernate
Through the winter?

When it's cold out, do you sleep
Oh so deep? Not a peep!
If you do, you hibernate
Through the winter!

To introduce the word *hibernation* to your little ones, have them pretend to sleep while breathing slowly. Then explain that many animals do this all winter long and it's called *hibernation*! That's how Marysue Garren from Middleham and St. Peter's Day School in Lusby, Maryland, teaches her students about hibernation!

Where Did It Go?

Developing fine-motor skills

Tell students that the arctic hare does something amazing during the winter—its fur changes color! Explain that the arctic hare is gray in the summertime and white during the winter. Ask, "Why do you think the hare's fur does this?" and lead students to conclude that the hare turns white so it is the same color as the snow and so animals that might eat it can't find it. Next, have students make their very own hidden hares. Have each child fingerpaint a sheet of brown paper white. (For added texture fun, mix flour into the paint!) Then encourage him to glue white ear cutouts, eye cutouts, and a pink nose cutout to the paper. Now where did that hare go?

Margaret Aumen, Emory United Methodist Nursery School, New Oxford, PA

Migrate or Sleep?

Identifying letters

Make several enlarged copies of the goose and frog cards on page 281. Gather a stack of letter cards and tuck the goose and frog cards into the stack. Remind students that frogs hibernate throughout the winter and geese migrate. Then show students each card, in turn, and have them identify the letter. Whenever you hold up a frog, have students curl into a ball and pretend to be asleep. Whenever you hold up a goose, have students "fly" around the room. Continue with each card in the stack.

Adapted from an idea by Margaret Aumen
Emory United Methodist Nursery School
New Oxford, PA

Sleepy Bear

Responding to a story

Read aloud *Bear Snores On* by Karma Wilson. In this story, a bear sleeps during a snowstorm while a variety of forest animals have a get together in his cave! Next, place a box on its side so it resembles a cave. Encourage students to collect natural items—such as leaves, twigs, and pinecones—and place them in the cave. Put a stuffed toy bear in the cave and have students tell it goodnight. Keep this display up throughout the winter and use the interactive ideas below!

"Bear-y" Pleasing Ideas

- Sprinkle cotton balls (snow) outside the bear's cave.
- Help students understand that bears are not true hibernators. Before children arrive, remove the bear and place it somewhere in the classroom. Explain that sometimes bears wake up during the wintertime. When children leave for the day, place the bear back in its cave.
- Place other forest-related stuffed toys near the cave. Discuss whether the animals should risk waking the bear.
- Encourage students to write letters to the bear telling it what it is missing. Youngsters can quietly place the letters in its cave.
- When spring is near, wake up the bear! Then have a spring celebration with bear-appropriate snacks, such as berries, fruit, sunflower seeds, and bear-shaped crackers.

Carol Kulik, Hope Christian School, Levittown, PA

See page 280 for an adorable **bear-themed craft**!

How Many Trees?
Identifying numbers

Explain that deer like to lie among evergreen trees to shelter themselves from the cold and wind. Cut out enlarged copies of the deer card on page 281 and write a different number on each card. Cut a supply of green triangles (evergreen trees) from construction paper. A child chooses a deer card and identifies the number. He says the rhyme shown and then places the appropriate number of trees around the deer. He continues with each remaining deer.

It is winter—let's help the deer.
We'll put [number] evergreens near.

Margaret Aumen
Emory United Methodist Nursery School
New Oxford, PA

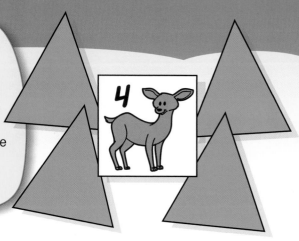

Puffy Cheeks!
Performing a song

This adorable song is sure to get lots of giggles! Explain that chipmunks hold nuts and seeds in their cheeks and take them to their burrows to nibble on throughout the winter. Then lead them in performing this song.

(sung to the tune of "If You're Happy and You Know It")

I'm a chipmunk, and I look for nuts and seeds.   *(Puff out cheeks and poke them twice.)*
I'm a chipmunk, and I look for nuts and seeds.   *(Repeat action.)*
Oh, I bury them so deep
In my home before I sleep.
I'm a chipmunk, and I look for nuts and seeds.   *(Repeat action.)*

adapted from an idea by Danielle Penders, Penders' Home Day Care, Lansdale, PA

A Crafty Bear
Developing fine-motor skills

To make this sweet bear craft, gather a tissue box for each child and trim the hole so it resembles a cave. Then help him follow the steps below.

Steps:
1. Paint the box brown and let it dry. *(This step is optional.)*
2. Color and cut out a copy of the bear and cave patterns on page 282.
3. Glue the bear to a piece of black construction paper.
4. Glue the black paper inside the cave and tape the cave cutout over the opening to make a flap.
5. Add tree cutouts and glue cotton batting (snow) around and inside the cave, if desired.
6. Lift the cave flap and see the sleeping bear!

Suzan Fields, St. Gabriel the Archangel School, Indianapolis, IN

Winter is here—
it's cold and bleak.
What is sleeping?
Take a peek!

Animal Cards

Use with "Zzzz!" on page 278. Use the goose and frog cards with "Migrate or Sleep?" on page 279 and the deer card with "How Many Trees?" on page 280.

Bear and Cave Patterns
Use with "A Crafty Bear" on page 280.

Winter is here—
It's cold and bleak.
What is sleeping?
Take a peek!

TEC41064

TEC41064

Safety at Home

Develop your little ones' safety awareness with this selection of super ideas!

ideas contributed by Roxanne LaBell Dearman
NC Early Intervention Program for Children Who Are Deaf or Hard of Hearing
Charlotte, NC

Is It Safe or Not?

Participating in a game

Youngsters need their safety awareness thinking caps to play this game! Have children stand side by side and position yourself a short distance from them. Then ask at-home safety questions, like "Is it safe to color at a table?" prompting students to respond "No, it's not!" or "Yes, it is!" When the correct answer is "yes," youngsters take a giant step forward. When the correct answer is "no," they stand still. Continue play until everyone reaches you.

Calling 9-1-1

Recognizing emergency situations

Help students recognize emergency situations and understand when it's appropriate to call 9-1-1. To begin, ask, "Does anyone know what the word *emergency* means?" After discussing the concept, explain that 9-1-1 can be called when there is an emergency. Next, lead the group in singing the song shown. Then help a volunteer name a situation in which it's appropriate to call 9-1-1. Repeat the song and then have another child name a situation. Continue for several rounds. Then follow up the activity by having little ones practice dialing 9-1-1 on a play phone.

(sung to the tune of "Three Blind Mice")

9-1-1, 9-1-1,
It's not for fun.
It's not for fun.
It is for an emergency
If something happens to you or me.
Let's discuss it so we agree.
9-1-1.

Which Column?

Identifying items as safe or unsafe

Cut out a copy of the cards on page 285 and program a two-column chart as shown. Display a card and have the group identify the picture. Then ask students to decide whether the featured item is safe or unsafe for a child to use. If they decide the object is safe, they clap their hands to show approval. If they decide it is unsafe, they cross their arms to show disapproval. After determining the correct answer, attach the card to the appropriate column on the chart. When all the cards are in place, review the chart with the group.

Not for Me!

Participating in a song

Youngsters are sure to remember these musical safety tips! Help students brainstorm ways electrical outlets, ladders, and windows are useful and how they can be safety hazards. Then lead the group in singing the song shown.

(sung to the tune of "Shoo Fly")

[Outlets] are not for me,
[Outlets] are not for me,
[Outlets] are not for me,
So I don't play near them, you see!

(Repeat the verse two more times, inserting the words *ladders* and *windows*.)

Outlets are not for me,
Ladders are not for me,
Windows are not for me,
'Cause they're not safe for kids, you see!

Safety Game

Reinforcing unsafe household items

Place a class supply of page 285 at a center. Also provide a circle punch, green construction paper, glue, and fine-tip markers. A child takes a sheet and finds something that isn't safe for him. Then he punches out a green circle, draws a frowning face on the circle, and glues it to the appropriate square. He continues with each remaining item on the page that isn't safe.

TEC41064

TEC41064

TEC41064

TEC41064

TEC41064

TEC41064

TEC41064

TEC41064

Hearts, Chocolates, and Flowers

Happy Valentine's Day!

♥ H-E-A-R-T ♥

Reinforcing letter names

Lead students in a toe-tapping round of this celebratory song! Write the letters H, E, A, R, and T on separate felt heart cutouts and attach them to your flannelboard. Lead students in singing the song, pointing to each letter. Then turn the letter H around so students can't see it. Lead students in singing the song again, replacing H by patting themselves once over their hearts. Continue flipping letters, similar to the traditional song "Bingo", until youngsters are patting themselves five times. What fun!

(sung to the tune of "Bingo")

I have a heart to give to you.
I hope you really like it!
H-E-A-R-T,
H-E-A-R-T,
H-E-A-R-T,
It is a heart from me!

Jennie Jensen
North Cedar Elementary
Lowden, IA

♥ Made With Celery! ♥

Process art

Would you believe it? This super Valentine's Day printmaking project uses celery! Cut the base from two bunches of celery. (Save the stalks for a tasty recipe.) Place each base next to a separate pan of paint. Encourage a child to dip the cut end of the base into paint and then press it onto a sheet of paper. Have her continue making prints as desired. Then have her glue leaf cutouts to the project so it resembles a cluster of roses.

Deborah Schiffler, Trafton Academy, Hammond, LA

♥ A Sweet Shop ♥

Role-playing

For engaging Valentine's Day dramatic play, provide a variety of props such as those shown. Then invite students to put together and "sell" valentine bouquets, candy, cards, and other lovely gifts!

Suggested props:
fake flowers
tissue paper (for wrapping up flower bouquets)
plastic vases
watering can
flower picks
small cards (for messages to go with flowers)
empty candy boxes
brown pom-poms (chocolates)
play money
cards (blank, for designing valentine cards)
paper and crayons (for writing signs and displays)

Heather Goodwin
SpringHouse Learning Station
Eighty-Four, PA

♥ How Many? ♥

Counting, one-to-one correspondence, name identification

Your little sweeties are sure to enjoy this engaging math rhyme and activity! Write each child's name on a separate die-cut heart (valentine) and scatter the hearts on the floor. Place a class supply of envelopes nearby. Lead students in reciting the rhyme, pausing after counting the envelopes. After the envelopes are counted, have youngsters help you match one envelope to each valentine. Then recite the remaining couplet, inserting a child's name. Help her find her valentine and slip it into the envelope. Continue until each valentine is in an envelope. Play several rounds of this game throughout the beginning of February. Then have students take their valentines home.

> Look at all these valentines!
> I made one for each friend.
> I'll put them in some envelopes,
> So each one I can send.
> How many cards do you see?
> Start to count them now with me.
> *(Count the valentines aloud.)*
> How many envelopes do you see?
> Start to count them now with me.
> *(Count the envelopes aloud.)*
>
> [Child's name], can you find your name?
> What a good time valentine game!

Sue Smith
St. Mary's Hospital Early Childhood Center
Green Bay, WI

♥ A Box of Chocolates ♥

Identifying numbers, presubtraction skills

Give each child ten brown pom-poms (chocolates) and a copy of the mat on page 289. Have each child place her chocolates on the heart-shaped box. Then recite the rhyme, prompting students to remove each chocolate and pretend to eat it when appropriate.

I got a box of chocolates from someone very sweet.
I got a box of chocolates that I couldn't wait to eat!
One tastes oh so grand, and two is just divine.
Three is very scrumptious, and four is oh so fine.
Five is full of caramel, and six is oh so sweet.
Seven is like heaven; eight's a lot to eat.
Number nine is hard to chew; after ten, I take a seat.
I have eaten everything; there's nothing left to say.
My tummy is so full on this Valentine's Day.

Billie Kramer
Genesis Christian Preschool
Green Bay, WI

♥ Party Planning ♥

Have a fantastic Valentine's Day classroom party with these simple ideas!

- **Decorations:** Give each child a supersize heart cutout with a piece of tape attached. Prompt the youngster to stick the heart anywhere on a classroom wall for instant and simple decorations youngsters can be proud of.
- **A party twist:** Have a Valentine's Day Tea Party. Each child brings a special stuffed toy. Children sit with their toys to have tea (juice) and heart cookies at tables covered with red paper. Afterward, students and their animal friends pass out valentines! *Jennifer Hamel, Mount Carmel Academy, Springfield, MA*
- **Cardholders:** Send home a personalized brown paper bag and encourage parents to decorate it with their youngsters. Youngsters bring the bag to school and use it to collect their valentines from classmates. *Holly Werkheiser, Volunteers of America Children's Center, Allentown, PA*
- **Passing out valentines:** Play a traditional game of musical chairs. The child who doesn't have a seat goes with a volunteer to deliver his valentines. Then play a couple of rounds where everyone gets a chair before removing one again. This ensures that there is a fair amount of space between youngsters! *Mary Ann Craven, Fallbrook United Methodist Christian School, Fallbrook, CA*

A Box of Chocolates

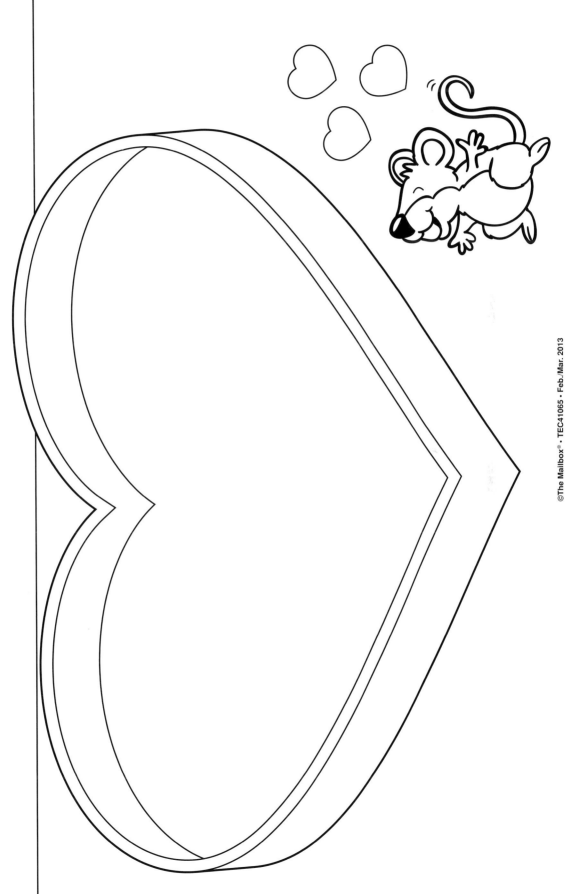

Note to the teacher: Use with "A Box of Chocolates" on page 288. For an **art activity** and a **fine-motor** option, have students color the page and then glue miniature baking liners and brown pom-poms (chocolates) to the heart-shaped box.

Doctors, Dentists, and Nurses:
Health Helpers!

Feeling Sick?

Speaking, participating in a song

Get youngsters talking about their experiences at the doctor's office with this simple silly song! Lead students in singing several rounds of the song. (For extra fun, have little ones tap tongue depressors together as they sing!) Then ask students to discuss times they have had to visit a doctor.

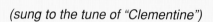

(sung to the tune of "Clementine")

Feeling sickly?
Need help quickly?
Puffy, stuffy,
Oh, achoo!
At the doctor's
They will help you.
They will know just what to do!

Have some spots or
Polka-dots or
Bumpy, lumpy, grumpy flu?
At the doctor's
They will help you.
They will know just what to do!

Doctor or Dentist?

Counting, organizing data

Cut out a copy of the dentist and the doctor patterns on page 292 and place them on the floor. Gather white linking cubes (teeth) and self-adhesive bandages. Then read one of the statements shown. If the statement is talking about a doctor, have a child place a bandage on the corresponding cutout. If it describes a dentist, encourage her to place a tooth on the dentist. If the sentence could apply to both helpers, have her place a manipulative on each one. Continue with the remaining statements. Then have youngsters compare the set of bandages to the set of teeth.

Suggested sentences:
This person uses a stethoscope to listen to your heartbeat.
This person takes your temperature.
This person takes X-rays.
This person wants to keep you healthy.
This person wears a white coat.
This person looks in your ears.
This person looks in your mouth.
This person looks in your nose.
You have to make an appointment to see this person.
This person takes your blood pressure with a cuff that goes around your arm.
This person tells you to brush twice every day.
This person checks for cavities.

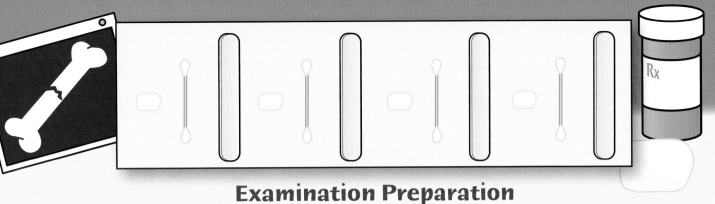

Examination Preparation
Creating patterns
Provide cotton balls, tongue depressors, cotton swabs, and long strips of paper. To begin, explain that nurses and medical assistants help doctors by laying out all the things they may need during an examination. Have a child pretend to lay out the tools a doctor might need, making a pattern with the objects on a strip of paper. When he is satisfied with his work, he glues the items in place.

Tricia Kylene Brown, Bowling Green, KY

Toss the Glove!
Speaking
Get a pair of nonlatex gloves and show them to youngsters. Ask why doctors and dentists wear these gloves, leading students to conclude that the gloves keep any germs the doctor may have from getting on you and any germs you may have from getting on the doctor! Next, blow up a glove and knot it (or use a rubber band to secure it). Then toss it to a child. Have the child name something a doctor or dentist might do during an exam, such as taking your temperature, listening to your heart, or looking in your ears. Encourage him to toss the glove back to you. Play several rounds of this game. Then remove the glove for safekeeping.

Tricia Kylene Brown

Health Helper Art
Developing fine-motor skills, expressing oneself through art
Give each child a selection of items one might find at a doctor or dentist's office, such as self-adhesive bandages, cotton balls, cotton swabs, tongue depressors, and pieces of gauze. Also provide a pair of jumbo wiggle eyes or eye stickers. Encourage a child to attach the items to a sheet of construction paper to make a face. What fun!

Amber Baker, Learn-A-Lot Christian Preschool, Mooresville, IN

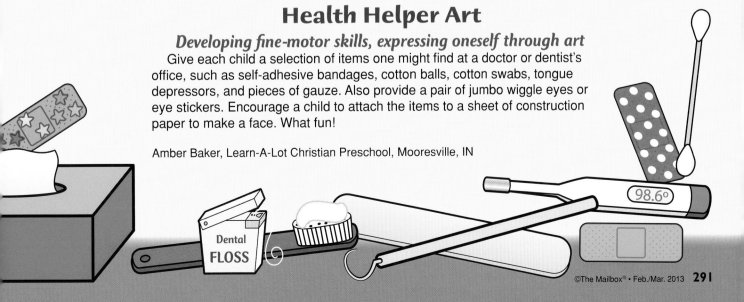

TEC41065

TEC41065

Fabulous Feet!

This collection of foot-themed activities will have your little ones seeing feet in a whole new light!

ideas contributed by Ada Goren, Winston-Salem, NC

Raise Your Feet, Please!
Recognizing rhyming words

To answer a question, students usually raise their hands. But with this activity, they raise their feet! Seat little ones with plenty of space between them; then have them lean back on their elbows. Tell youngsters to listen carefully as you say the word *feet* and one other word. If the second word rhymes with *feet*, youngsters raise their feet in the air. If not, they stay still. Continue for several rounds, making sure to include nonsense words that rhyme with *feet* as well!

Feet, seat!

Toe-Tapping Designs
Expressing oneself through art

Little ones are sure to enjoy this toe-tapping experience! Tape a sheet of paper to a tray. Invite a child to sit on a chair and remove his shoes and socks. Help him prop his feet on an object, such as a crate or another chair; then dab paint on the ball of each toe. Hold the tray in front of his feet and encourage him to repeatedly tap his toes on the paper. Add paint to his toes as needed until he is satisfied with his work. Then help him clean his toes with a wet paper towel or hypoallergenic wipe. For some toe-tapping inspiration, play a recording of lively music while he paints.

Four-Footed Fantasies

Responding to a story, dictating information

Read aloud Laura Hulbert's *Who Has These Feet?* In this nonfiction book, colorful picture clues engage students' critical-thinking skills and preschool-appropriate informative text tells how the feet of each featured animal are perfectly adapted to its habitat. Next, ask youngsters to imagine what it would be like if they had four feet like some of the animals in the book! Give each child a paper programmed with the prompt shown. Read the prompt aloud and have her dictate words to complete the sentence. Then encourage her to illustrate her words.

If I had four feet, I would need special pants!

Who Has These Feet?
Laura Hulbert
illustrated by Erik Brooks

Use your feet to follow this beat!

Keep the Beat With Your Feet!

Patterning

Youngsters exercise their brains and bodies with this kinesthetic patterning activity! Have students stand with space between them. Say, "Use your feet to follow this beat!" Then demonstrate a foot-stomping pattern—such as stomp twice, pause, and stomp twice—and prompt little ones to perform the pattern. Continue in the same way using different foot-stomping patterns.

Fancy Footprints

Beginning sounds

Attach eight footprint cutouts to a large sheet of paper as shown. Cut out a copy of the cards on page 295 and place them face-down near the paper. Each child, in turn, flips a card, names the picture, and then identifies its beginning sound. If the word begins with /f/ like *feet*, he places the card on a footprint. If not, he sets the card aside. Play continues, in turn, with each remaining card.

Fancy Footprints

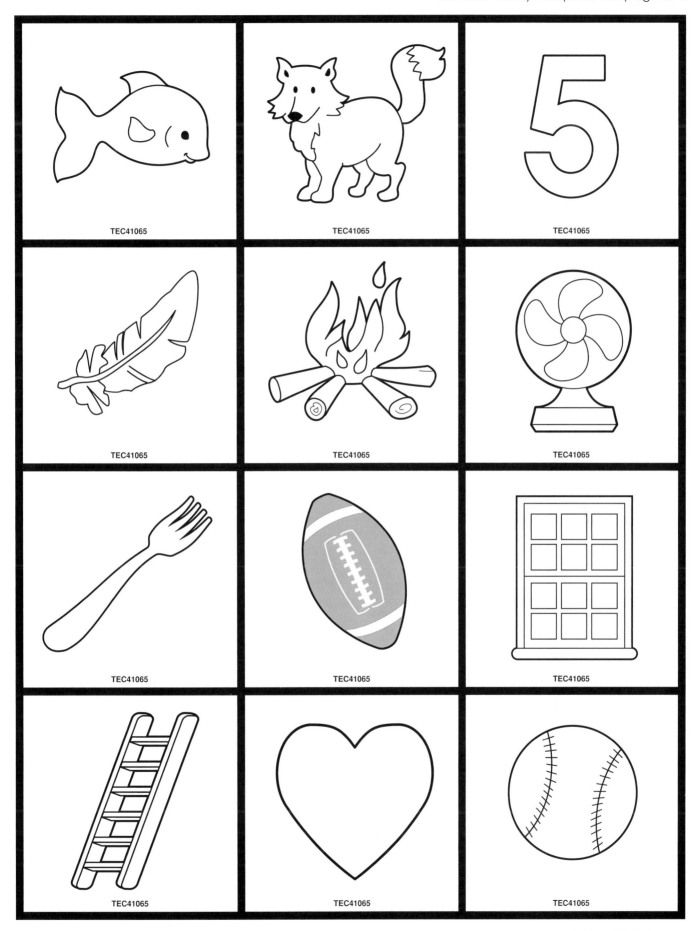

TEC41065

TEC41065

TEC41065

TEC41065

TEC41065

TEC41065

TEC41065

TEC41065

TEC41065

TEC41065

TEC41065

TEC41065

Spring Has Sprung!

Watch little ones bloom with this downpour of spring-related activities!

I Love Spring

Writing, developing fine-motor skills

Youngsters identify common sights and symbols of spring with this three-dimensional craft! Make or gather several spring-related die-cuts, such as those shown. Help each child write "I Love Spring!" on a sheet of construction paper. Then help her accordion-fold a strip of construction paper. Have her choose and identify a die-cut and guide her to understand how the object relates to spring. Then have her glue one end of the strip to the die-cut and the remaining end to the construction paper. Continue with other strips and die-cuts.

Lyn Stevens, A. M. Chaffee Elementary, Oxford, MA

Flower Necessities

Needs of living things, singing a song

Encourage students to think about what a flower needs to live. Guide them to understand that most flowers need water, sunshine, and dirt to live and thrive. Prompt students to pretend to be flowers as you lead them in performing the action song below, encouraging them to perform the motions shown. Then briefly use a spray bottle to spray a mist (water) over their heads, wiggle yellow crepe paper streamers (sunshine) over them, and sprinkle brown paper shreds (dirt) around them. Youngsters will beg for repeats of this activity!

(sung to the tune of "If You're Happy and You Know It")

I need water, I need sunshine, I need dirt. (Yes, dirt!)
I need water, I need sunshine, I need dirt. (Yes, dirt!)
If I want to grow up tall,
If I want to grow at all,
I need water, I need sunshine, I need dirt. (Yes, dirt!)

Ruth Perlstein, Gan Margoliyot, Oak Park, MI

Flying Formations

Forming numbers, identifying numbers

Dye bow-tie pasta (butterflies) different colors and then place the pasta in a container. Put a piece of black felt on a tabletop. (Pasta will not slide around once it is placed on felt.) Provide number cards. A child chooses a card and identifies the number, with help as needed. Then she arranges butterflies on the felt to form the number. **To extend the activity**, have her count out a set of butterflies to match the number.

Amber Dingman
Sterling, MI

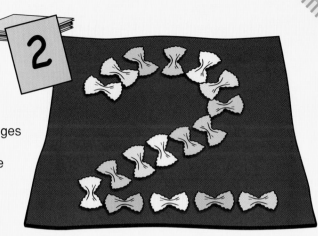

Baby Animal Sing-Along

Phonological awareness: manipulating phonemes, matching letters to sounds

Lead students in several rounds of this song, helping little ones change the first sound in the name "Bingo" to match the first sound in the name of the baby animal.

(sung to the tune of "Bingo")

There was a piglet had a name,
And [Pingo] was its name-o!
[P]-I-N-G-O, [P]-I-N-G-O, [P]-I-N-G-O
And [Pingo] was its name-o.

Continue with the following: *kitten, puppy, duckling, tadpole, gosling, joey*

Dawn Seigel
Evergreen Avenue School
Woodbury, NJ

Rockin' Robins

Gross-motor skills, playing a group game

Gather youngsters in an open area. Have half of the students in the class (baby robins) sit in a random fashion as if each student was in a nest. (If desired, provide plastic hoops to use as nests.) Assign each remaining child (mommy or daddy robin) to a baby. Scatter brown pipe cleaner pieces (worms) around the area. Play upbeat music and encourage the mommy and daddy robins to dance around as they gather as many worms as they can. When the music stops, prompt them to run back to the nest and give the worms to the baby. Play several rounds of this engaging game.

Shelby Witmer, Neffsville Christian Nursery School, Lancaster, PA

Famished Frog!

Making sets, counting

For this engaging center, cut out a copy of the frog pattern on page 299 and attach a red construction paper tongue to the cutout. Provide craft foam bugs (or colorful pom-poms to represent bugs) and dice. A child rolls the dice and counts the dots. Then she places the appropriate number of bugs on the tongue. She removes the bugs and repeats the activity.

Deb Ronga
Sunshine Nursery School
Arlington, MA

Transform this center activity into an individual project! Label a sheet of construction paper with "My frog ate _____ bugs!" Then have each youngster attach frog and tongue cutouts to the page. Prompt her to attach a set of bugs to the tongue and then write the appropriate number in the blank.

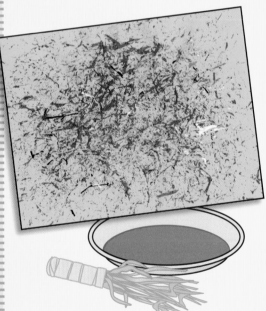

Easter Grass Painting

Expressing oneself through art

Purchase bags of Easter grass when it goes on sale to use for this exceptional process art! Gather a bunch of Easter grass and then wrap masking tape around one end as shown to make a unique brush. A youngster holds the brush by the masking tape and drags it through a shallow container of paint. Then he drags, brushes, and bounces the Easter grass over a sheet of paper. Lovely!

Mary Fowler
North Kids Learning Center
Anderson, IN

How Many Petals?

Counting syllables

Cut out a yellow copy of the flower centers on page 300. Provide a supply of flower petals. (To easily cut out flower petals, simply use a large circle punch!) Scatter the flower centers on the floor and gather youngsters around. Have a child choose a flower center and say the name of the picture. Prompt little ones to repeat the name while they clap the syllables. Then encourage the child to name the number of claps and place that number of petals around the flower center. Continue until all the flowers have petals.

Renée M. Plant
Liberty Elementary
Broken Arrow, OK

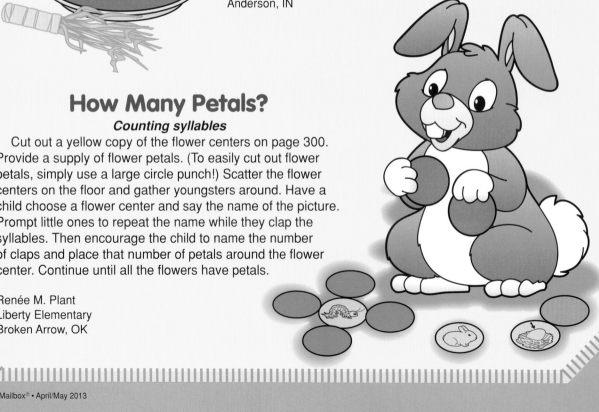

TEC41066

Flower Center Patterns
Use with "How Many Petals?" on page 298.

TEC41066

TEC41066

TEC41066

TEC41066

TEC41066

TEC41066

TEC41066

TEC41066

TEC41066

Splish! Splash!

Water Safety

ideas contributed by Roxanne LaBell Dearman
NC Early Intervention Program for Children Who
Are Deaf or Hard of Hearing
Charlotte, NC

Walk, Don't Run!

Contributing to a class discussion, participating in a song

Get youngsters discussing and practicing an important facet of water safety—walking around a pool! Place a length of blue bulletin board paper (or a blanket) on the floor (pool). Have students sit around the pool; then discuss why it's important to walk, not run, around a pool. Ask youngsters to tell possible consequences of running around a pool. Write each consequence on a sticky note and have students stick them to the pool. Then lead students in singing the song shown several times as they practice walking around the pool. Repeat for several rounds; then invite little ones to "take a swim"!

You could trip.

You could fall down.

You could knock someone in the water.

(sung to the tune of "Row, Row, Row Your Boat")

Walk, walk, walk, don't run,
Near a swimming pool.
Walking feet will keep you safe!
Let's repeat this rule.

Pool Party

Practicing water safety through pretend play

Use your water table and props to help youngsters practice water safety at a pool. Post a list of three or four safety rules near the water table (pool). Attach a ruler (diving board) to one end of the water table and a rectangular plastic lid (slide) to the opposite end. Provide plastic adult and child toy figures, along with other theme-related items that will enhance youngsters' play. Review the pool rules with students and then encourage little ones to incorporate the rules in their play.

Boat Buddies

Participating in a group activity

Make an oversize masking tape boat outline on the floor. Introduce yourself as the boat captain and say, "We're going to take a boat ride. Before we get on board, each person must put on a life jacket." Show a real life jacket (or a picture of one) and discuss why it's important to wear one on a boat; then prompt students to share experiences they've had with life jackets. Next, have each child pretend to put one on. Then invite youngsters aboard the boat and lead them in singing the song shown, encouraging them to sway from side to side as they sing. What a fun way to learn an important safely rule!

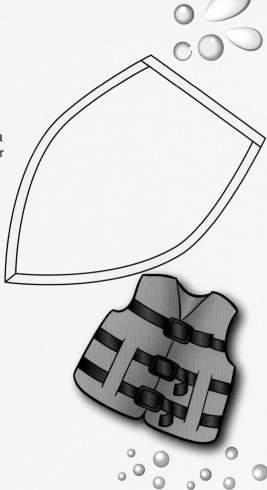

(sung to the tune of "My Bonnie Lies Over the Ocean")

Oh, I always wear a life jacket
When I spend my time in a boat.
It's very important to wear one.
If I'm in the water, I'll float!
Swaying, swaying!
I'm swaying along in a boat—take note!
Swaying, swaying!
I wear a life jacket to float!

Safety First

Fine motor

Place a few life jackets in your fine-motor center and invite little ones to practice putting them on and fastening the closures. Whenever a child is water-ready, have him pretend to take a swim. What a great way to practice and reinforce water safety!

Be Safe and Have Fun!

Dictating information

Give each child a white construction paper copy of page 303. Provide crayons, blue-tinted water, and a paintbrush. Read the text aloud and prompt her to complete the sentence. Record her words on the page; then encourage her to draw an illustration of herself in the pool. When her drawing is complete, have her brush the tinted water on the bottom of the page so the pool water looks blue.

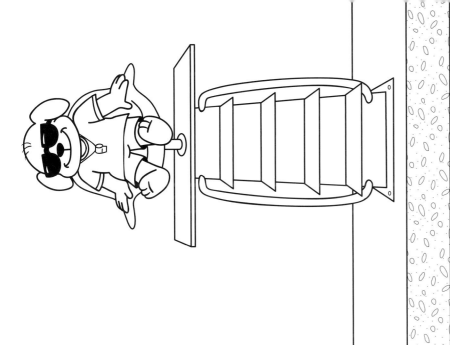

When I go swimming, I stay safe by

©The Mailbox® • TEC41067 • June/July 2013

Note to the teacher: Use with "Be Safe and Have Fun!" on page 302.

Let's Go Camping!

Your little campers will ask for "s'more" when you present this engaging selection of camping-themed activities.

I see a campfire!

What Do You See?

Speaking, building prior knowledge

Youngsters experience the sights of a camping trip with this whole-group activity! Lead students in reciting the rhyme shown. Then call on a child and have her name something she might see on a camping trip. Encourage little ones to pantomime her suggestion. For example, if she says she might see a tent, have students use their arms to make tents over their heads. Then recite the rhyme again and call on a different youngster. Continue for several rounds.

We're going on a camping trip—one, two, three.
Tell me, tell me, what do you see?

Barbara Rackley, Kingdom Academy, Sarasota, FL

Cozy Sleeping Bags

Developing fine-motor skills

To make these adorable projects, take a waist-up photo of each child posing with her hands behind her head. Help each child trim around her photo and glue it to a sheet of black paper. Have her glue a rectangle of fabric (sleeping bag) on the photo as shown. Attach a copy of the poem shown and instruct her to squeeze dots of glue on the page and then sprinkle glitter on the glue (fireflies).

I'm wrapped in my sleeping bag under the trees.
Fireflies blink in the summer breeze.
The campfire fizzles, and the stars shine bright.
I'm camping in the woods on a lovely night!

Bobbie Schwartz
Noah's Ark Preschool
Falconer, NY

Marshmallow Painting

Expressing oneself through art

This process art uses a unique painting tool! Gather pans of paint in campfire-related colors. For each pan, push a large marshmallow onto a stick. A child holds the stick and dips the marshmallow in the paint. Then he drags and bounces the marshmallow over the paper. He repeats the process with other paint colors and tools.

Bears in a Canoe!

Snack, following directions

These camping bears are canoeing along a river! Help each child peel a banana and push a few graham cracker bears into the peeled fruit so it resembles bears in a canoe. Encourage her to place a dollop of blue-tinted yogurt (water) on a disposable plate. Then have her set the canoe in the water. If desired, lead little ones in singing the song shown as they remove and eat each bear. (Tweak the wording as needed when singing the final verse.) Then they can nibble on the rest of the snack.

adapted from an idea by Katie Kirkbride
Riverside County Office of Education
Beaumont, CA

(sung to the tune of "Five Green and Speckled Frogs")

[Four] little camping bears,
Without concerns or cares,
Spend their hot days in a canoe. (Woo-hoo!)
One bear, just on a whim,
Jumps in to take a swim.
Now there are just [three] little bears. ([Three] bears!)

Tent Math

Cut out copies of the tent patterns on page 307 for these fun activities!

- Put a dot set on each tent. Count the appropriate number of toothpicks for each tent and then arrange each set of toothpicks to make mini campfires. **Matching sets**

- Label tents with numbers and provide bear counters. A child places the appropriate number of bears on each tent. **Counting, making sets**

- Label tent cutouts with a series of numbers and encourage youngsters to arrange the tents in numerical order. **Identifying numbers, ordering numbers**

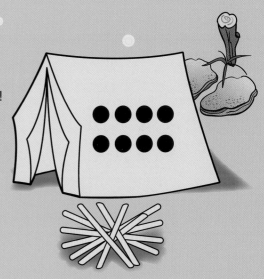

adapted from an idea by Mickey Kendrick, Child's Play, Toledo, OH

Bears, Owls, and Crickets!
Participating in a rhyming song
Guide little ones in singing this engaging song. Once children know the song, have them lie on the floor. Dim the lights in the classroom and have students pretend they are in sleeping bags on a camping trip. Then encourage them to sing several rounds of the song.

(sung to the tune of "My Bonnie Lies Over the Ocean")

We're camping out here in the forest.
Asleep with the bears in the night.
I hear all the owls and crickets.
I'm hoping they stay out of sight!
Camping, camping.
We're sleeping outside with the fireflies!
Camping, camping!
Look up, and you'll see starry skies!

Debra Boudreau
First United Methodist Preschool and Kindergarten
Rocky Mount, NC

A Starry Night
Developing fine-motor skills
What do little ones see from their sleeping bags? Why, a view of the night sky, of course! To prepare for this center, provide small squares of black construction paper and same-size squares of aluminum foil. Place them at a center along with hole punchers. (Hole punchers with an extended reach are helpful for this project.) A student punches holes in a square of paper and then glues it to a square of aluminum foil. The foil shows through the holes and looks like a starry night!

Sarah Berkey
Growing Tree Preschool
Chambersburg, PA

For extra fun, have youngsters make multiple starry sky projects. Attach the projects to a camping-themed display to make one big starry sky!

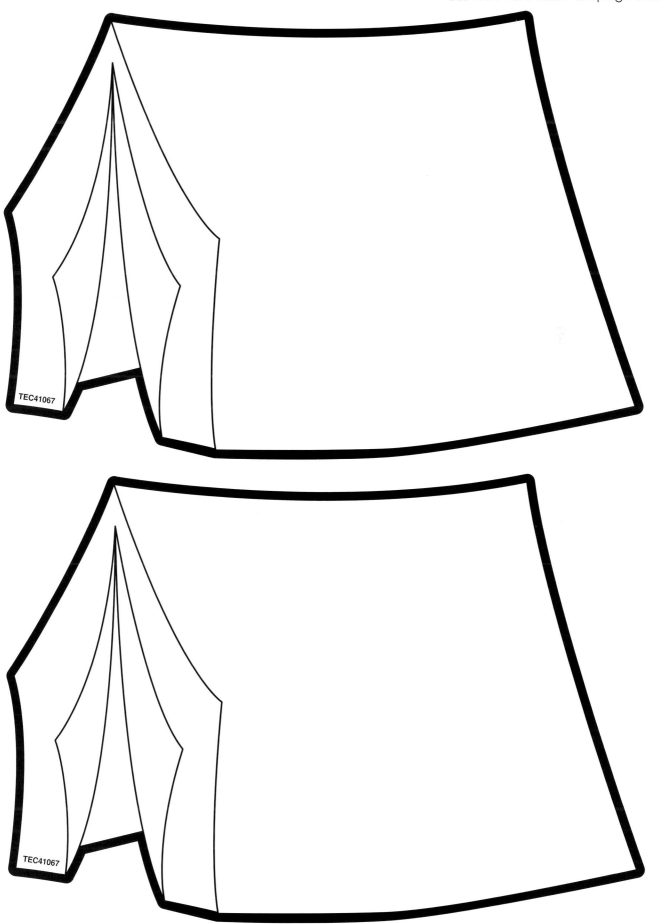

TEC41067

TEC41067

Down in the Swamp

These gooey and glorious alligator-infested ideas are sure to be met with plenty of preschool enthusiasm!

ideas contributed by Roxanne LaBell Dearman
NC Early Intervention for Children Who Are Deaf or Hard of Hearing
Charlotte, NC

Swamp Chomp!

Print awareness, making a booklet

These adorable booklets are simple for little fingers to make! Have each child color a copy of pages 310 and 311 as desired. Then help her follow the steps below to complete the pages. Finally, have her cut apart the pages and staple them in order between construction paper covers.

Steps:

Booklet page 1—Use a brad to fasten a green triangle cutout (tail) to the page.

Booklet page 2—Attach two eye stickers (or mini wiggle eyes) to the page.

Booklet page 3—Make three green fingerprints on the page. Then use a fine-tip marker to draw fins and eyes on the fingerprints so they resemble fish.

Booklet page 4—Draw teeth in the alligator's mouth.

One tail goes swish, swish. 1

Two eyes go blink, blink. 2

Three fish go splish, splash. 3

Many teeth go chomp, chomp! 4

Super Slime

Forming letters, five senses: sense of touch

Spread green fingerpaint (swamp slime) in a tray and provide letter cards. Show a child a card and help her name the letter. Then prompt her to use her finger to draw the letter in the slime. Use a plastic card to smooth out the slime. Then repeat the process with a different letter.

For more swamp-themed fingerpaint fun, have a child wiggle a small plastic snake through the slime and then on a sheet of paper. Have him repeat the process several times to create a piece of unique swamp art!

Water Table Swamp Time!

Exploring through play

A few additions to your water table will provide endless swamp-themed play opportunities! Float thick sticks (logs) and plastic vines and greenery in your water table. Provide plastic alligators, snakes, fish, and turtles. If desired, cut lily pads from craft foam and place them in the water as well. What terrific swampy fun!

Splendid Spanish Moss!

Developing fine-motor skills

Cypress trees covered in Spanish moss are typical sights in a swamp. Youngsters can make their own versions of these trees with this artsy activity! In advance, show youngsters pictures of cypress trees. (An Internet image search for "cypress trees, swamp" turns up many options.) To begin, have each child color a copy of page 312. Next, have her dip her fingers in dark green paint and then lightly tap them on the tree to make leaves. Finally, encourage her to glue Spanish moss (found at craft stores) to the tree.

tip → Do you have gray yarn on hand? Lengths of yarn work well as an alternative to actual Spanish moss in this craft.

Which Plate?

Comparing sets, counting

To prepare for this whole-group activity, draw or stamp different sets of fish on paper plates. Hold up a plate and have students count the number of fish. Then hold up a second plate and encourage students to count those fish as well. Next, place one plate in each hand. Then encourage students to move their arms like chomping alligators and say, "Chomp, chomp, chomp" as they snap at the plate that has more fish. Continue with a different pair of plates.

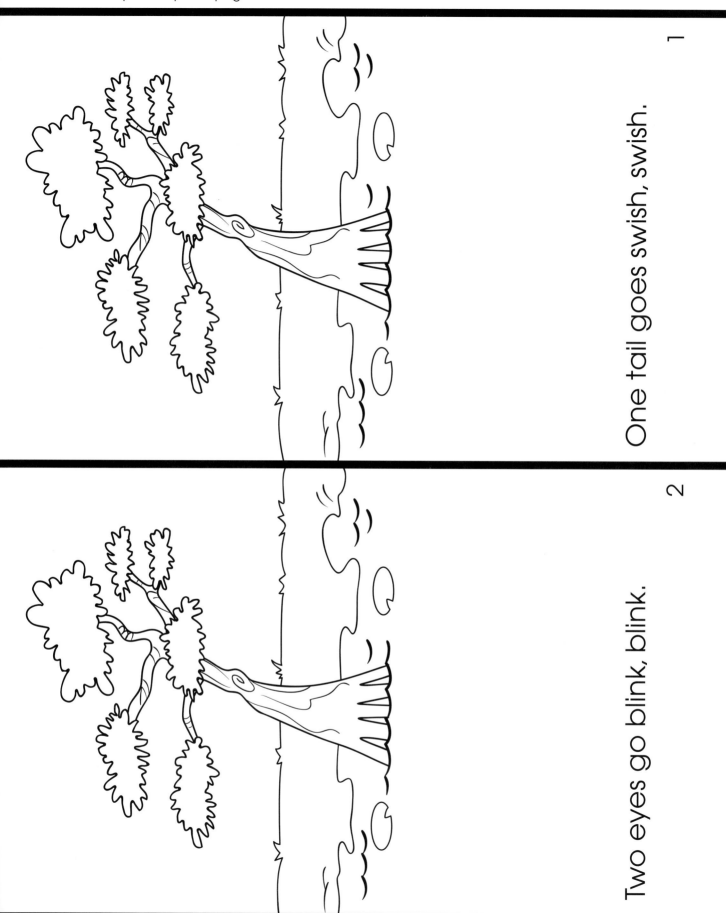

1

One tail goes swish, swish.

2

Two eyes go blink, blink.

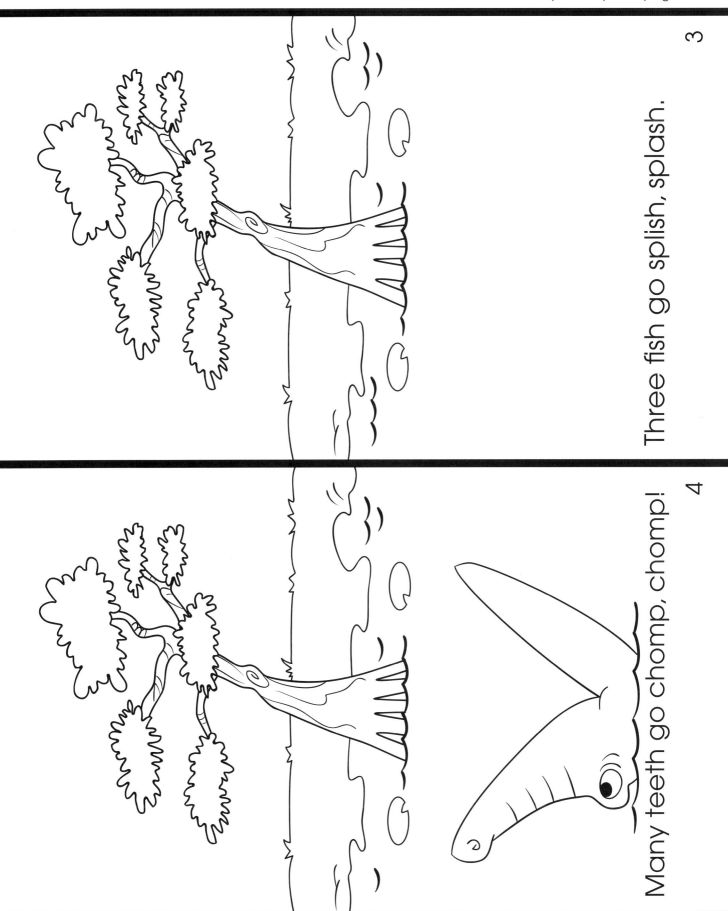

3

Three fish go splish, splash.

4

Many teeth go chomp, chomp!

Note to the teacher: Use with "Splendid Spanish Moss!" on page 309.

INDEX